"*The Oil Curse* is the best and most thorough examination that we have of the causes and consequences of oil wealth for poorly governed states. Oil revenues are massive, opaque, and volatile; they destroy the relationship between a state and its own citizens. Ross substantiates some of the common assertions about oil wealth, finds that others are incorrect, and offers some surprising discoveries. Very worth reading."

—Stephen D. Krasner, Stanford University

"This important book brings new and timely insight into a key global phenomenon. High oil prices have triggered oil strikes concentrated in the poorest countries—the bottom billion. Will this time be different? Will oil drive transformation or cause a repeat of the history of plunder? Ross presents new research in an accessible style. Read it: understanding is the foundation for change."

—Paul Collier, author of *The Bottom Billion*

"This is a masterful book. It provides a balanced and thoughtful overview of the wide variety of issues surrounding the politics of oil while also breaking new ground in research. *The Oil Curse* is essential reading for scholars and those engaged in public debates. An important contribution."

—Robert Bates, Harvard University

"This is the single most important book on the resource curse to date. *The Oil Curse* addresses a timely, policy-relevant issue in a way that nonacademics and academic specialists alike can appreciate. Ross is the preeminent voice on the subject."

—Erik Wibbels, Duke University

"*The Oil Curse* is a great read, one that provides a very accessible but nuanced treatment of an important topic. There is a clear need for a book like this, and Michael Ross is the right person to write it."

—Macartan Humphreys, Columbia University

"Stunning."

—Johnny West, *Huffington Post UK*

"*The Oil Curse* is a landmark book that brings together explanations about the impacts of oil on various key issues from authoritarianism to patriarchy, from conflict to development. It combines qualitative and quantitative methods in a truly interdisciplinary tour de force of political, economic, and social analyses. The book is an excellent source for policy makers as well as scholars of various disciplines, especially Middle East studies."

—Ahmet T. Kuru, *Insight Turkey*

"Ross [is] to be applauded for advancing the conversation beyond reveling in the history of human extraction of resources to expressing sorrow for the negative impacts of mineral rushes, which most social science books in this genre tend to follow. . . . [I]mportant for engineers and chemists to read to further hasten the search for solutions to resource scarcity dilemmas."

—Saleem H. Ali, *Chemical & Engineering News*

"Much has been written about the topic of how oil wealth hampers economic development as well as the building of institutions, but this book will help introduce a much wider audience to this issue. Ross has produced a comprehensive examination of the oil curse, analyzing data from 170 countries. . . . [T]his is a valuable and accessible study of an important topic."

—*Choice*

"Michael Ross is an eminent political scientist, who distinguishes himself even further with this book. . . . Ross's book is readable, and provides substance and nuance to the basic underlying story that resource revenues are hard to manage."

—Mark Henstridge, Business Economist

"His study is nuanced, well documented and precise: he avoids the lure of statistical analysis where a huge database can lead to clichés and easy conclusions. Instead, his statistical analysis is always backed by qualitative comparative analysis. Ross successfully demonstrates what the 'oil curse' means, without falling into the trap of determinism. Instead, he offers alternatives. Oil exporting countries, and mainly oil exporters, should act upon them: with adequate policies, the oil curse can be reversed."

—J.M., *Global Journal*

The Oil Curse

HOW PETROLEUM WEALTH SHAPES THE DEVELOPMENT OF NATIONS

Michael L. Ross

PRINCETON UNIVERSITY PRESS

PRINCETON AND OXFORD

Published by Princeton University Press, 41 William Street, Princeton, New Jersey 08540
In the United Kingdom: Princeton University Press, 6 Oxford Street, Woodstock,
Oxfordshire OX20 1TW
press.princeton.edu

Fourth printing, and first paperback printing, 2013
Paperback ISBN 978-0-691-15963-8

The Library of Congress has cataloged the cloth edition of this book as follows

Ross, Michael, 1961–
    The oil curse : how petroleum wealth shapes the development of nations /
Michael L. Ross.
        p. cm.
    Includes bibliographical references and index.
    ISBN 978-0-691-14545-7 (hardback)
    1. Petroleum industry and trade—Government policy—Developing countries.
2. Revenue—Developing countries. 3. Petroleum products—Prices. 4. Developing
countries—Economic policy. 5. Women—Developing countries—Social conditions.
6. Natural resources—Developing countries. 7. Civil war—Developing countries.
I. Title.
    HD9578.D44R67 2012
    338.9009172'4—dc23

                                                                        2011021743

British Library Cataloging-in-Publication Data is available

This book has been composed in Palatino LT Std by Achorn International, Inc.
Printed on acid-free paper. ∞

Printed in the United States of America

10 9 8 7

For Tina

Contents

Illustrations

Tables

Preface

ANYONE who has dreamed of winning the lottery or finding buried treasure assumes that a large cash windfall will make them better off. But for many developing countries, finding valuable natural resources can have strange and sometimes politically harmful consequences. This book explains the origins and nature of this "curse," and how it might be remedied.

Since I began to research this issue in the late 1990s, a lot has changed. Earlier studies of the resource curse focused on the puzzling commodity booms of the 1970s, which produced mountains of cash but little sustained growth in most resource-rich countries. Since 2000 there has been a new boom in commodity prices, generating a new flood of revenues for mineral-producing countries, and a new interest in the perverse effects of resource wealth. It has also given scholars a wealth of new data on the links between natural resources, economics, and politics.

The political landscape has also shifted. Many petroleum-exporting countries have adopted new institutions to manage their windfalls. Thanks to pressures from nongovernmental organizations (NGOs), new international agreements have been launched to choke off the trade in conflict diamonds, and promote revenue transparency in the oil, gas, and minerals sectors. The World Bank and the International Monetary Fund (IMF)—which I criticized in a 2001 Oxfam report for funding mining projects that did little to help the poor—have embraced the cause of extractive-sector reforms.

When I began to write this book in 2005, I reexamined my own previously published studies suggesting that resource wealth made countries less democratic and more prone to civil war. To my embarrassment, I found more than a few errors, omissions, and hard-to-defend assumptions. Prompted by some smart skeptics—notably Michael Herb, Stephen Haber, Victor Menaldo, Gavin Wright, Robert Conrad, Michael Alexeev, Erwin Bulte, and Christina Brunnschweiler—I decided to take a fresh look at the data.

I discovered some surprises. Things I assumed were true—that petroleum wealth was linked to slow economic growth and weak government institutions—were probably wrong. Other findings held up, although in modified forms. Patterns that I thought I understood, like the relationship between oil and authoritarianism, and oil and civil war, were incomplete. Petroleum seemed to have a stronger and more harmful effect than other kinds of minerals. And I started to appreciate the role of factors I had overlooked—like the impact of petroleum wealth on economic opportunities for women, which had far-reaching consequences for women's political rights, population growth, and long-term economic growth.

Perhaps the biggest surprise was that the resource curse, as we know it today, is a new phenomenon. The oil-rich countries have long been distinctive; yet before 1980, there were relatively few political differences between oil-producing countries and non-oil-producing countries. The upheaval in global energy markets in the 1970s appears to have triggered the resource curse, by producing a drastic increase in the volume and volatility of government revenues in the oil-producing states. As I better understood the mechanics of the oil curse, I developed new ideas about how to alleviate it.

Over the course of writing this book I incurred an absurdly large number of debts. I received a generous grant from the Revenue Watch Institute in 2006 that allowed me to focus exclusively on writing the book for over a year. My gratitude to the Revenue Watch Institute goes far beyond the grant, though: serving on its advisory board has given me a more complete understanding of the challenges facing resource-rich countries and helped me appreciate the organization's remarkable work in dozens of countries. The institute has also brought me into contact with dozens of practitioners, scholars, and activists who have magnanimously shared their friendship and knowledge with me, including Karin Lissakers, Anthony Richter, Joe Bell, Anthony Venables, Bob Conrad, Antoine Heuty, Chandra Kirana, Julie McCarthy, Vanessa Herringshaw, and many others.

Over the years, I have had the privilege of meeting some of the scholars who pioneered the study of commodities and politics, including Bill Ascher, Richard Auty, Alan Gelb, Petter Nore, and Terry Karl; I hope my own research can build on theirs. My debt to another pioneering figure, Paul Collier, goes even further: his scholarship on natural resources, poverty, and political economy has inspired me since the beginning of my career. In 2000, he invited me to spend a year at the World Bank as a visiting scholar, and over the years drew me into many academic and policy initiatives. His research, generosity, and friendship have shaped this book in countless ways.

In 2009, I sent an early draft of this book to a handful of colleagues. Many were generous enough to give me their undiluted reactions. The suggestions of Pierre Englebert, Kevin Morrison, Desha Girod, Antoine

Heuty, Patrick Heller, Hiroki Takeuchi, and Ragnar Torvik were unusually helpful.

I sought out the comments of two friends in particular. Macartan Humphreys and Erik Wibbels are two of the smartest social scientists I know, and both have thought deeply about the politics of resource wealth. Each of them gave me remarkably detailed suggestions, which became essential guides to the final draft. Both have been generous to a fault with their time and friendship.

I benefited immeasurably from discussing pieces of my book-in-progress with scholars and students at many institutions, notably Brigham Young University, Georgetown University, MIT, the Rand Graduate School, the University of California at San Diego, the University of Pennsylvania, and Yale University. Organizers of the Lone Star National Security Forum—especially Eugene Gholz—were kind enough to devote a morning to dismembering my manuscript; Monica Toft's detailed insights caused me to rethink much of my argument. At Brigham Young University, Scott Cooper gave me invaluable feedback on what became a central part of my argument.

Since 2001, the University of California at Los Angeles has provided me with a marvelous intellectual home. The Department of Political Science—deftly chaired over the last decade by Mike Lofchie and Ed Keller—has been a source of both wonderful colleagues and close friends. I am especially grateful to Barbara Geddes, Dan Posner, Dan Treisman, and Jeff Lewis, all of whom guided me through unfamiliar territory as I tried to complete the book. The University of California at Los Angeles has also given me the chance to work with outstanding graduate students, many of whom helped me carry out the research that undergirds the book. These students include Mac Bunyanunda, Elizabeth Carlson, Paasha Mahdavi, Brian Min, Jeff Paris, Anoop Sarbahi, Ani Sarkissian, and Risa Toha. Ruth Carlitz, Paasha Mahdavi, and Eric Kramon combed through the penultimate draft, and helped make it more consistent and coherent.

For almost two decades, Tom Banchoff has been an indispensable friend and sounding board; his wisdom and encouragement have pulled me through the most difficult phases of the writing process. Key parts of the book emerged from long conversations with Andreas Wimmer; his wide-ranging comments on an earlier draft helped me drastically improve the manuscript. At Princeton University Press, my editor Chuck Myers has offered encouragement and guidance since the book's earliest incarnation, and graciously tolerated many missed deadlines. Dimitri Karetnikov turned confusing figures into elegant ones, and Cindy Milstein smoothed out my awkward prose.

I met my wife, Tina, shortly after I began to write this book. She did not help with any of the research or writing. Had we never met—and never had our beautiful son, Adam—I might have finished the book a little more quickly. But she has given me a better life than I ever imagined was possible, and I dedicate this book to her.

Abbreviations

AIOC   Anglo-Iranian Oil Company
EITI   Extractive Industries Transparency Initiative
ELN   Ejército de Liberación Nacional (Colombia)
FARC   Fuerzas Armadas Revolucionarias de Colombia
GAM   Aceh Freedom Movement (Indonesia)
GDP   gross domestic product
GMM   generalized method of moments
IMF   International Monetary Fund
IOC   international oil company
IPC   Iraqi Petroleum Company
NOC   national oil company
NGO   nongovernmental organization
OECD   Organization for Economic Cooperation and Development
OLS   ordinary least squares
OPEC   Organization of Petroleum Exporting Countries
PDVSA   Petróleos de Venezuela
PEMEX   Petróleos Mexicanos
PRI   Institutional Revolutionary Party (Mexico)

Country Abbreviations

Afghanistan	AFG	Congo, Republic of	COG
Albania	ALB	Costa Rica	CRI
Algeria	DZA	Côte d'Ivoire	CIV
Angola	AGO	Croatia	HRV
Argentina	ARG	Cuba	CUB
Armenia	ARM	Cyprus	CYP
Australia	AUS	Czech Republic	CZE
Austria	AUT	Denmark	DNK
Azerbaijan	AZE	Djibouti	DJI
Bahamas	BHS	Dominican Republic	DOM
Bahrain	BHR	Ecuador	ECU
Bangladesh	BGD	Egypt	EGY
Barbados	BRB	El Salvador	SLV
Belarus	BLR	Equatorial Guinea	GNQ
Belgium	BEL	Eritrea	ERI
Belize	BLZ	Estonia	EST
Benin	BEN	Ethiopia	ETH
Bhutan	BTN	Fiji	FJI
Bolivia	BOL	Finland	FIN
Bosnia	BIH	France	FRA
Botswana	BWA	Gabon	GAB
Brazil	BRA	Gambia	GMB
Brunei	BRN	Georgia	GEO
Bulgaria	BGR	Germany	DEU
Burkina Faso	BFA	Ghana	GHA
Burundi	BDI	Greece	GRC
Cambodia	KHM	Guatemala	GTM
Cameroon	CMR	Guinea	GIN
Canada	CAN	Guinea-Bissau	GNB
Cape Verde	CPV	Guyana	GUY
Central African Rep.	CAF	Haiti	HTI
Chad	TCD	Honduras	HND
Chile	CHL	Hungary	HUN
China	CHN	Iceland	ISL
Colombia	COL	India	IND
Comoros	COM	Indonesia	IDN
Congo, Dem. Rep.	ZAR	Iran	IRN

Iraq	IRQ	Norway	NOR
Ireland	IRL	Oman	OMN
Israel	ISR	Pakistan	PAK
Italy	ITA	Panama	PAN
Jamaica	JAM	Papua New Guinea	PNG
Japan	JPN	Paraguay	PRY
Jordan	JOR	Peru	PER
Kazakhstan	KAZ	Philippines	PHL
Kenya	KEN	Poland	POL
Korea (North)	PRK	Portugal	PRT
Korea (South)	KOR	Qatar	QAT
Kuwait	KWT	Romania	ROM
Kyrgyz Republic	KGZ	Russia	RUS
Laos	LAO	Rwanda	RWA
Latvia	LVA	Saudi Arabia	SAU
Lebanon	LBN	Senegal	SEN
Lesotho	LSO	Serbia	YUG
Liberia	LBR	Sierra Leone	SLE
Libya	LBY	Singapore	SGP
Lithuania	LTU	Slovak Republic	SVK
Luxembourg	LUX	Slovenia	SVN
Macedonia	MKD	Solomon Islands	SLB
Madagascar	MDG	Somalia	SOM
Malawi	MWI	South Africa	ZAF
Malaysia	MYS	Spain	ESP
Maldives	MDV	Sri Lanka	LKA
Mali	MLI	Sudan	SDN
Malta	MLT	Suriname	SUR
Mauritania	MRT	Swaziland	SWZ
Mauritius	MUS	Sweden	SWE
Mexico	MEX	Switzerland	CHE
Moldova	MDA	Syria	SYR
Mongolia	MNG	Taiwan	TWN
Morocco	MAR	Tajikistan	TJK
Mozambique	MOZ	Tanzania	TZA
Myanmar	MMR	Thailand	THA
Namibia	NAM	Togo	TGO
Nepal	NPL	Trinidad	TTO
Netherlands	NLD	Tunisia	TUN
New Zealand	NZL	Turkey	TUR
Nicaragua	NIC	Turkmenistan	TKM
Niger	NER	Uganda	UGA
Nigeria	NGA	Ukraine	UKR

United Arab Emirates	ARE	Venezuela	VEN
United Kingdom	GBR	Vietnam	VNM
United States	USA	Yemen	YEM
Uruguay	URY	Zambia	ZMB
Uzbekistan	UZB	Zimbabwe	ZWE

CHAPTER ONE

The Paradoxical Wealth of Nations

> It is the devil's excrement. We are drowning in the devil's excrement.
> —Juan Pablo Pérez Alfonso, former Venezuelan oil minister

> I wish your people had discovered water.
> —King Idris of Libya, on being told that a
> US consortium had found oil

SINCE 1980, the developing world has become wealthier, more democratic, and more peaceful. Yet this is only true for countries without oil. The oil states—scattered across the Middle East, Africa, Latin America, and Asia—are no wealthier, or more democratic or peaceful, than they were three decades ago. Some are worse off. From 1980 to 2006, per capita incomes fell 6 percent in Venezuela, 45 percent in Gabon, and 85 percent in Iraq. Many oil producers—like Algeria, Angola, Colombia, Nigeria, Sudan, and again, Iraq—have been scarred by decades of civil war.

These political and economic ailments constitute what is called the resource curse. It is more accurately a mineral curse, since these maladies are not caused by other kinds of natural resources, like forests, fresh water, or fertile cropland. Among minerals, petroleum—which accounts for more than 90 percent of the world's minerals trade—produces the largest problems for the greatest number of countries. The resource curse is overwhelmingly an oil curse.[1]

Before 1980 there was little evidence of a resource curse. In the developing world, the oil states were just as likely as the non-oil states to have authoritarian governments and suffer from civil wars. Today, the oil states are 50 percent more likely to be ruled by autocrats and more than twice as likely to have civil wars as the non-oil states. They are also more secretive, more financially volatile, and provide women with

---

[1] I use the term "oil" to refer to both oil and natural gas, and use "oil wealth," "petroleum wealth," "oil production," and "oil income" interchangeably. In appendix 1.1, I explain how I define and measure the value of a country's oil and gas production. I classify countries as "oil producers" or "oil states" if they generate at least a hundred dollars per capita (in 2000 dollars) in income from oil and gas in a given year. In 2009, there were fifty-six oil states scattered across all regions of the globe (see table 1.1).

fewer economic and political opportunities. Since 1980, good geology has led to bad politics.

The most troubling effects of this scourge are found in the Middle East. The region holds more than half of the world's proven oil reserves. It also lags far behind the rest of the world in progress toward democracy, gender equality, and economic reforms. Much of its petroleum wealth lies beneath countries plagued by decades of civil war, like Iraq, Iran, and Algeria. Many observers blame the region's maladies on its Islamic traditions or colonial heritage. In fact, petroleum wealth is at the root of many of the Middle East's economic, social, and political ailments—and presents formidable challenges for the region's democratic reformers.

Not all states with oil are susceptible to the curse. Countries like Norway, Canada, and Great Britain, which have high incomes, diversified economies, and strong democratic institutions, have extracted lots of oil and had few ill effects. The United States—which for much of its history has been both the world's leading oil producer and the world's leading oil consumer—has also been an exception in most ways. Petroleum wealth is overwhelmingly a problem for low- and middle-income countries, not rich, industrialized ones. This creates, unfortunately, what might be called "the irony of oil wealth": those countries with the most urgent needs are also the least likely to benefit from their own geologic endowment.

The resource curse was not supposed to happen. In the 1950s and 1960s, economists believed that resource wealth would help countries, not hurt them. Developing states were thought to have an abundance of labor, but a shortage of investable capital. Countries blessed with natural resource wealth would be the exception, since they would have enough revenues to invest in the roads, schools, and other infrastructure that they needed to develop quickly.[2]

Political scientists also believed in the virtues of resource wealth. According to modernization theory—the prevailing view in the 1950s and 1960s of political development, later revived in the 1990s and 2000s—increases in a country's income per capita would lead to improvements in virtually every dimension of its political well-being, including the effectiveness of its government, the government's accountability to its people, and the enfranchisement of women.[3]

In the 1950s, 1960s, and 1970s, the conventional wisdom was more or less correct. But in the 1970s, something went wrong in the oil states.

---

[2] See, for example, Viner 1952; Lewis 1955; Spengler 1960; Watkins 1963.
[3] Examples include Lerner 1958; Lipset 1959; Inkeles and Smith 1974; Adsera, Boix, and Payne 2003; Inglehart and Norris 2003.

Understanding the resource curse is important for countries that export petroleum, but it also matters for countries that import it to fuel their economies. Some argue that the location of oil in repressive, conflict-ridden countries is just an annoying coincidence. According to former vice president Dick Cheney, "The problem is that the good Lord didn't see fit to put oil and gas reserves where there are democratic governments."[4] But the problem is not divine intervention. These countries suffer from authoritarian rule, violent conflict, and economic disarray *because* they produce oil—and because consumers in oil-importing states buy it from them.

Petroleum is the world's largest industry. In 2009, $2.3 trillion worth of oil and gas was pumped out of the ground; petroleum and its by-products made up 14.2 percent of the world's commodity trade.[5] The global demand for petroleum will almost certainly continue to grow in the coming decades, despite overwhelming evidence that burning fossil fuels is destabilizing the planet's climate. To meet this demand, oil production is spreading to ever-poorer countries.

The 2001 US Energy Task Force, led by Cheney, called for the United States to diversify its sources of petroleum and reduce the country's dependence on the politically troubled states of the Middle East. Yet finding new oil suppliers in Africa, Asia, or Latin America has not improved US energy security. Instead, it is causing the resource curse to spread to new countries. Energy importers cannot circumvent the oil curse; they must help solve it.

This book takes a comprehensive look at the political and economic consequences of petroleum wealth, especially in developing countries.[6] Analyzing 50 years of data for 170 countries in all regions of the world, it finds little evidence for some of the claims made by earlier studies: that extracting oil leads to abnormally slow economic growth, or makes governments weaker, more corrupt, or less effective.[7] On some fronts, like reducing child mortality, the typical oil state has outpaced the typical non-oil one.

Yet this book also shows that since about 1980, oil-producing countries in the developing world have become less democratic and more

---

[4] Quoted in David Ignatius, "Oil and Politics Mix Suspiciously Well in America," *Washington Post*, July 30, 2000.

[5] BP 2010; UN Comtrade, database, available at http://comtrade.un.org/db/.

[6] This book focuses on petroleum, not other minerals. Among mineral resources, oil seems to have the strongest impact on the politics of the host country. Whether or not other minerals carry a similar curse is an important question, but one that goes beyond the scope of this book.

[7] As noted in the preface: mea culpa. Some of my own previous studies supported several of these claims.

secretive than similar states without oil. These countries have grown more likely to suffer from violent insurgencies, and their economies have provided women with fewer jobs and less political influence. They have also been afflicted by a more subtle economic problem: while they have grown at about the same rate as other countries, most have not grown as quickly as they should, given their natural resource wealth.

Geology is not destiny. Some oil producers have escaped each of these ailments. Nigeria and Indonesia have made transitions to democracy; Mexico and Angola have drawn large numbers of women into the economy and government; Ecuador and Kazakhstan have avoided civil wars; and Oman and Malaysia have had fast, steady, and equitable economic growth. The goals of this book are to explain *why* oil is typically a curse, why some countries have escaped the curse, and how more countries can turn their natural resource wealth from a curse to a blessing.

What Causes the Oil Curse?

Why does petroleum have such strange effects on a country's political and economic health? Some observers blame the foreign powers that intervene in oil-rich countries and manipulate their governments. Others fault the international oil companies that exploit these resources in pursuit of extraordinary profits.

Both arguments contain some truth, but neither stands up to scrutiny. The United States, Britain, and France have periodically invaded or supported coups in many oil-producing states—most recently, Libya. But they have been equally likely to invade countries without oil.[8] In recent decades, many oil-producing states—like Iran, Venezuela, Russia, Sudan, and Burma—seem to be unusually *immune* to pressures from Western states, and actively defy them, yet they still suffer from the same problems as other, more docile petroleum-rich countries.

For much of the twentieth century, international oil companies like Shell, British Petroleum, Exxon, and Mobil had remarkable influence over the fate of oil-producing countries in the developing world, and could justifiably be faulted for many of those countries' problems. But the oil companies' role has sharply diminished since the early 1970s, when most developing countries nationalized their oil industries. If foreign companies were the source of the problem, then nationalization should have been the cure. This book, though, shows that the events of

---

[8] On this issue, see de Soysa, Gartzke, and Lin 2009; Colgan 2010b; Sarbahi 2005.

the 1970s, *especially* nationalization, made the problems of the oil states a lot worse.

Most social scientists trace the oil curse to the governments of petroleum-producing states, although they agree on little else. Almost all studies focus on just one of the problems that seem to be linked to petroleum—like poor economic performance, the lack of democracy, or the unusual frequency of civil wars. They offer many explanations for these problems, faulting oil's alleged links to corruption, rent seeking, inequality, shortsighted policies, and weakened state institutions. These and other theories—some well founded, and others not—are discussed over the course of this book.

The Oil Curse argues that the political and economic problems of the oil states can be traced to the unusual properties of petroleum revenues. How governments use their oil revenues—to benefit the few or the many—is certainly important. But whether governments spend these funds wisely or foolishly, oil revenues have far-reaching effects on a country's political and economic well-being.

Petroleum revenues have four distinctive qualities: their scale, source, stability, and secrecy.[9] These qualities arose, or got worse, thanks to the rising power of state-owned oil companies.

The *scale* of oil revenues can be massive. On average, the governments of oil-producing countries are almost 50 percent larger (as a fraction of their country's economy) than the governments of non-oil countries. In low-income countries, the discovery of oil can set off an explosion in government finances. For example, from 2001 to 2009, total government expenditures rose by 600 percent in Azerbaijan and 800 percent in Equatorial Guinea. The sheer volume of these revenues makes it easier for authoritarian governments to silence dissent. It can also lead to violent insurrections, when the people who live in a country's oil-rich regions seek a larger share of these immense revenues.

The size of these revenues alone cannot account for the oil curse. Many peaceful, democratic European countries have bigger governments than many conflict-ridden, autocratic oil producers. The *source* of these revenues also matters. Oil-funded governments are not financed by taxes on their citizens but instead by the sale of state-owned assets—that is, their country's petroleum wealth. This helps explain why so many oil-producing countries are undemocratic: when governments are funded through taxes, they become more constrained by their

---

[9] Other scholars have also emphasized the importance of petroleum revenues, although they generally concentrate on different qualities. See, for example, Karl 1997; Jensen and Wantchekon 2004; Morrison 2007; Dunning 2008.

citizens; when funded by oil, they become less susceptible to public pressure.

Other problems can be traced to the *stability*—or rather, the insta-bility—of oil revenues. The volatility of world oil prices, and the rise and fall of a country's reserves, can produce large fluctuations in a government's finances. Governments are saddled with tasks they are seldom able to manage because of this financial instability, which can help explain why they frequently squander their resource wealth. Reve-nue instability also aggravates regional conflicts, making it harder for governments and rebels to settle their differences.

Finally, the *secrecy* of petroleum revenues compounds these prob-lems. Governments often collude with international oil companies to conceal their transactions, and use their own national oil companies to hide both revenues and expenditures. When Saddam Hussein was Iraq's president, more than half of his government's expenditures were channeled through the Iraqi National Oil Company, whose budget was secret.[10] Other countries have similar practices. Secrecy is a key reason why oil revenues are so commonly squandered, why oil-fueled dicta-tors can remain in power, since they can conceal evidence of their greed and incompetence; and why insurgents are generally reluctant to lay down their arms, because they distrust offers by the government to share their country's oil revenues more equitably.

Petroleum has other troublesome qualities. The extraction process typically creates few direct benefits, but many social and environmen-tal problems for the surrounding communities. Oil and gas facilities have large sunk costs, making them vulnerable to extortion. And when produced in large quantities, petroleum can affect a country's exchange rates and reduce the size of the manufacturing and agricultural sectors, which in turn can shut off economic opportunities for women. These features can give us further insights into the paradoxical effects of oil wealth, and I discuss them in future chapters.

But the most important political fact about oil—and the reason it leads to so much trouble in so many developing countries—is that the revenues it bestows on governments are unusually large, do not come from taxes, fluctuate unpredictably, and can be easily hidden.

Putting Oil into History

Oil revenues have not always had these properties, and oil wealth has not always been a curse.

[10] Alnasrawi 1994.

Until the 1970s, the oil-producing countries looked much like the rest of the world: they were just as likely to be ruled by dictators; they had civil wars at roughly the same rate as other countries; they offered women more or less the same kinds of opportunities; and their economic growth rates were both stable and well above the world average. After the 1970s, all of this changed.

This reversal was largely caused by a wave of oil industry nationalizations, in the 1960s and 1970s, which transformed the scale, source, and volatility of petroleum revenues. Before the 1970s, the world of petroleum was dominated by a handful of enormous companies—widely known as the "Seven Sisters"—that colluded to maintain control of world supplies.[11] In all but a few countries, the Seven Sisters owned or dominated the local subsidiaries that extracted and exported the host country's oil. They also controlled the shipping and marketing of almost all the world's petroleum, which enabled them to keep prices steady and capture most of the profits for themselves. The military and economic power of the United States and its European allies helped maintain this stable, highly unjust arrangement.

For the governments of oil-rich states like Iran, Iraq, Saudi Arabia, Libya, Algeria, Nigeria, and Indonesia, the power of these companies was intolerable, since it deprived them of control over their nation's assets—siphoning off profits, and forcing them to extract less oil, or more oil, than they believed would serve their nation's interests.

In the 1960s and 1970s, international petroleum markets were transformed by a series of closely related developments. Oil supplies begin to grow tighter, as rising demand outpaced new discoveries. The major oil exporters of the developing world started to collude through the Organization of Petroleum Exporting Countries (OPEC). The United States also became increasingly dependent on foreign supplies, as its domestic production began to decline while consumption soared. In addition, the Bretton Woods system of fixed exchange rates—which had contributed to keeping prices stable—fell apart.

Most importantly, virtually all oil-exporting countries in the developing world nationalized their petroleum industries, and then set up state-owned companies to manage them.[12] Everywhere nationalization was seen as a triumph, touching off glorious celebrations. The architect of Iraq's nationalization, Saddam Hussein, who at the time was the

[11] The seven companies were Standard Oil of New Jersey (later Exxon), Standard Oil of California (later Chevron), Anglo-Iranian Oil Company (later BP), Mobil, Texaco, Gulf, and Royal Dutch Shell. By 2010, they had been consolidated into four firms—ExxonMobil, BP, Shell, and ChevronTexaco—and were still among the world's largest publicly traded oil companies.

[12] Kobrin 1980; Victor, Hults, and Thurber 2011.

undersecretary general of the Revolutionary Command Council, became famous. The expropriation of Mexico's foreign oil companies—which occurred in 1938, before most others—is still commemorated with a national holiday.

In some ways, nationalization was a giant step forward for oil-producing countries. These countries gained greater control over their national assets. They began to capture a much larger share of the industry's profits. In the 1970s, they also were able to raise world prices to record levels, causing an unprecedented transfer of wealth from oil-importing states to oil-exporting ones.

Nationalization transformed the finances of oil-producing states. The size of government revenues grew dramatically, giving rulers access to unprecedented windfalls. Instead of collecting taxes and royalties from foreign companies, governments could fund themselves by selling oil through their national oil companies—which also helped them cloak these revenues in secrecy. World oil prices, and hence government finances, also started to fluctuate unpredictably.

The revolution in energy markets made the oil-rich governments larger, richer, and more powerful than they could have ever imagined. But for their citizens, the results were often disastrous. The powers once held by foreign corporations passed into the hands of their governments, making it easier for rulers to silence dissent and hold off democratic pressures. Ethnic minorities in oil-producing regions took up arms to fight for a larger share of the government's revenues. Moreover, in many states, the tidal wave of revenues produced new jobs for men but not for women. While citizens enjoyed booming economic growth in the 1970s, most of these gains disappeared after prices collapsed in the 1980s.

THE PETROLEUM FRONTIER

Changes in global energy markets are causing the oil curse to spread. In the next twenty-five years the global demand for oil and other liquid fuels will rise by an estimated 28 percent, and the demand for natural gas will increase by about 44 percent, if today's energy policies continue unchanged. While the United States is currently the world's leading petroleum importer, most of the new demand will come from developing countries, led by China and India.[13]

Companies are increasingly drilling in low-income countries in order to meet this rising demand. Historically, oil has been found in coun-

[13] Energy Information Administration 2010.

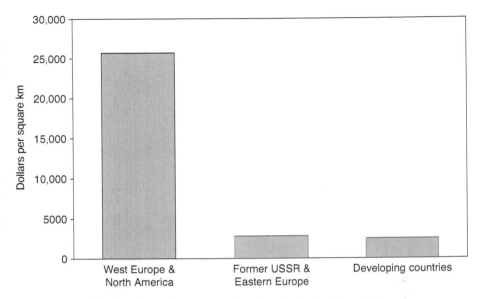

Figure 1.1. Foreign direct investment in extractive industries, 2007

These figures show the stock of foreign direct investment in "petroleum, mining, and quarrying" in 2007, expressed in dollars per square kilometer of territory.

Source: Calculated from data in United Nations Conference on Trade and Development 2009; World Bank, n.d.

tries that are already well off. Since the birth of the petroleum age in the mid-nineteenth century, rich countries have been about 70 percent more likely to produce oil than poor countries, not because they are sitting on top of more petroleum, but because they have more money to invest in locating and extracting it.[14] Today the rich democracies of North America and Europe have attracted about ten times more foreign direct investment in mining, per square kilometer, than the rest of the world (see figure 1.1).

In the new millennium, this has begun to change: the petroleum frontier has moved to ever-poorer countries. After the oil price shocks of the 1970s, the number of oil-producing states was relatively steady—hovering between thirty-seven and forty-four countries from 1976 to 1998 (see figure 1.2). From 1998 to 2006, the number of oil states rose from thirty-eight to a record fifty-seven. Almost all of the new producers

[14] Between 1857 and 2000, 63 percent of all oil-producing countries had average or above-average incomes in the year they began production. See appendix 1.1.

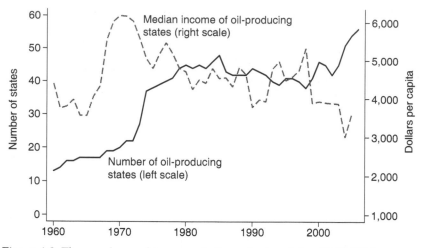

Figure 1.2. The number and income of oil-producing states, 1960–2006
These figures show the number of oil-producing countries (solid line), and their median income (broken line). States are defined as oil producers if they generate at least a hundred dollars per capita (in constant 2000 dollars) from oil and gas in a given year.
Source: Calculated from data in BP 2010; World Bank, n.d.

were low- and middle-income countries. As the number of producers rose, their median income fell sharply—from over fifty-two hundred dollars per capita in 1998 to just three thousand dollars in 2004—indicating that increasingly poor countries were joining the group.

In January 1999, oil was selling for just $10 a barrel; by June 2008, it had risen to $145 a barrel. Thanks to booming oil prices, companies found that the risks of working in poor, remote, and often badly governed countries were increasingly outweighed by the benefits of finding new reserves. Belize, Brazil, Chad, East Timor, Mauritania, and Mozambique have all become oil and gas exporters since 2004. In the next few years, as many as sixteen new countries—most of them in Africa, and almost all of them poor—are likely to join the list.[15] The vast majority of the world's new hydrocarbon supplies will come from developing countries in the next few decades.[16]

---

[15] Countries that may become new oil or gas exporters in the coming years include Cuba, Ghana, Guinea, Guinea-Bissau, Guyana, Israel, Liberia, Mali, São Tomé and Príncipe, Senegal, Sierra Leone, Tanzania, Togo, and Uganda. Indonesia and Tunisia—former exporters that had become importers—may also once again become petroleum exporters. On the scramble for Africa's oil resources, see Klare 2006.

[16] Energy Information Administration 2010.

This means that a flood of new hydrocarbon revenues is just starting to hit some of the world's poorest countries. If there were no resource curse, this would be spectacularly good news—a historically unique opportunity to escape from poverty. Yet the low-income countries that most desperately need money are also the most likely to be struck by the resource curse. Unless something is done, these windfalls will hurt, not help, people who live on the petroleum frontier.

LOOKING AHEAD

My analysis begins in chapter 2 by explaining why oil revenues have such unusual qualities. Some of these characteristics can be traced to the industry's distinctive economic properties: the ownership of oil and gas reserves by governments; the fact that these reserves can be depleted; the enormous up-front investments that are needed to extract them; the extraordinary profits they can generate; the harmful effect that their extraction can have on other kinds of businesses, by causing the currency to appreciate; their capacity to operate as economic enclaves; and the sensitivity of oil prices to small changes in supply and demand.

Many of these features have characterized the oil industry since the nineteenth century. But oil revenues were also shaped by a series of developments in the 1960s and 1970s: the tightening of global fossil fuel supplies; the demise of the Bretton Woods system of fixed exchange rates; the declining power of international oil companies, and the rise of OPEC; and a wave of nationalizations that gave oil-producing governments unprecedented wealth and influence. These and other changes made petroleum revenues larger and less stable than ever before, and help explain why many features of the resource curse only emerged in the 1980s.

Chapter 3 shows how the scale, source, and secrecy of oil revenues have helped keep authoritarian governments in power. Part of this story will sound familiar to political scientists. When dictators must finance themselves through taxes, they are met with demands for greater accountability; when they can fund themselves by selling off state-owned assets, like oil and gas, they can elude democratizing pressures. To this standard account I add some new elements. I demonstrate that oil has only had antidemocratic effects since the nationalizations of the 1970s; that oil tends to both keep authoritarian regimes in power and undermine low-income democracies; that oil revenues fail to trigger democratizing pressures, in part, because of their secrecy; and that authoritarian leaders are paradoxically more eager than democratic ones to keep domestic fuel prices low.

To illustrate how oil can keep authoritarian governments in power, chapter 3 looks at the case of the Soviet Union. To show how it can lead to the erosion of accountability in weak democracies, I use the example of post–Soviet Russia. An appendix provides a more careful look at the statistical relationships that are summarized in the chapter.

Some dimensions of the resource curse are surprising. Chapter 4 explains how oil wealth has reduced economic and political opportunities for women in many low- and middle-income countries—most important, in the Middle East and North Africa. This is partly due to the scale of oil revenues, which governments spend in ways that discourage women from joining the labor force, and partly because oil production can "crowd out" industries that would otherwise hire women as well as open pathways toward greater economic and political rights. One result is that women in the Middle East have made less economic and political progress than women in other world regions. Some observers claim that Islam is the real impediment to women's progress in the Middle East. I show that this cannot be the whole truth, since Middle Eastern women fare better in the region's oil-poor countries than its oil-rich ones.

To illustrate this argument, I compare three countries that are similar in many ways—Algeria, Morocco, and Tunisia—but only one of which (Algeria) produces significant quantities of petroleum. Oil has slowed the economic progress of women in Algeria, while women in Morocco and Tunisia have made much faster gains. Again, a statistical appendix offers a more deliberate look at the evidence.

Since the 1980s oil revenues have also heightened the danger of civil war, as explored in chapter 5. Among low- and middle-income countries, oil producers are more than twice as likely to have civil wars as non-oil producers. Some of these conflicts have been small, like the independence movement in China's Xinjiang Province or Mexico's Zapatista uprising. Others—like the wars in Angola, Colombia, and Sudan—have been ruinous.

The chapter contends that there are two kinds of petroleum-fueled conflicts: separatist wars waged by disenfranchised minorities in oil-producing regions, and conflicts led by rebels who fund themselves by extorting money from the oil industry. To trace the pathways that connect oil to insurrection, I use case studies of recent or near conflicts in Colombia, Congo-Brazzaville, Equatorial Guinea, Indonesia, Nigeria, and Sudan. The statistical links between oil and violent conflict are more carefully described in the appendix.

Chapter 6 looks at the economic effects of oil revenues, and how governments manage them. Many studies assert that oil has led to abnormally slow economic growth in developing states, which occurs because mineral wealth tends to damage state institutions—hurting bureaucratic efficiency, boosting corruption, and undermining the rule of law. Much of this "conventional wisdom" is wrong: while economic growth in the oil states has been unusually volatile, in the long run it has been neither faster nor slower than in the rest of the world. There is also little evidence that oil wealth tends to hurt state institutions. Claims to the contrary are typically based on what might be called the "Beverly Hillbillies fallacy" and the "fallacy of unobserved burdens."

The real problem is not that growth in the oil states has been slow when it should have been "normal" but rather that it has been normal when it should have been faster than normal, given the enormous revenues these governments have collected. Two factors can help explain this disappointingly average growth: the failure of the oil states to generate more jobs for women—which would have lowered fertility rates and population growth, and boosted per capita income growth; and the inability of their governments to cope with the extraordinary challenges created by revenue volatility.

The existence of the oil curse has far-reaching implications, which I discuss in the final chapter. It offers new insights into one of the oldest puzzles in the field of political economy: How are nations shaped by their natural environments? Social scientists have argued that countries are deeply affected by their placement on the continents, disease environment, and access to the sea. This book shows how, under certain conditions, a country's development path can also be shaped by its geologic endowment.

The oil curse should also remind us that more income is not always better, even for low-income countries: it depends on where the income comes from, and how it affects a country's politics. And understanding the oil curse can give us special insights into the Middle East, the region with the greatest abundance of petroleum wealth, and the most glaring shortages of both democracy and gender equality. This does not mean that the region's democracy and gender rights movements are doomed to failure. The effects of oil are formidable, but not immutable: much can be done to change the flow of petroleum revenues to governments, and reforms in the governance of oil can open the door to greater economic, social, and political rights.

The final chapter explains how countries might alleviate the oil curse by changing the troublesome qualities of their oil revenues. It describes an array of strategies to alter the size, source, stability, and secrecy of oil revenues, ranging from the simple (extracting it more slowly) to the exotic (using barter contracts, oil-denominated loans, and partial privatization). Since there are limits to what can be changed on the "revenue" side of the ledger, I also look at how governments can reform the ways they spend these revenues.

There is one remedy that can help everywhere: greater transparency in how governments collect, manage, and spend their oil revenues. Improved transparency could force governments to become more accountable to their citizens, reduce the danger of violent conflict, and shrink the economic losses caused by corruption. Transparency reforms in the oil-importing countries—whose voracious demand for fossil fuels is at the root of the resource curse—could have a powerful effect as well.

Reforms are most urgent for countries on the cusp of petroleum booms. Every few months, new oil and gas deposits are discovered somewhere in Africa, Latin America, the Middle East, or Asia. Many are found in countries that are poor, undemocratic, and ill equipped to manage large revenues. For the citizens of these countries, this book is a guide to what has gone wrong in the past—and what can be done differently in the future.

APPENDIX 1.1: A NOTE ON METHODS AND MEASUREMENTS

This book makes a series of arguments about the impact of a country's oil revenues on its political and economic development. It supports these claims with a mixture of quantitative and qualitative evidence, and by drawing on the work of other scholars.

The quantitative analysis is based on observational data from all countries since 1960.[17] There are important limits to the causal inferences that can be made using observational data, especially cross-national data. Since the book addresses questions that necessitate the use of observational data, I make a special effort to mitigate some of the problems that can compromise these inferences: the use of a causal variable that is itself affected by other variables in the model; statistical procedures that are unnecessarily complex and insufficiently transparent; correlations that are not robust but instead merely reflect quirks in the data, arbitrary methodological decisions, or the presence of a hand-

---

[17] I include all 170 countries that were sovereign in the year 2000, and had populations greater than 200,000. Countries enter the data set in either 1960 or their first year of independence, if in 1960 they were under colonial rule. Countries that disappeared between 1960 and 2000—South Vietnam, South Yemen, and East Germany—are excluded. I treat Germany as the successor state to West Germany, Vietnam as the successor to North Vietnam, Yemen as the successor to North Yemen, and Russia as the successor to the Soviet Union.

ful of highly influential observations; and a lack of clarity about the causal processes that connect the key variables.

MEASURING OIL

This book's most significant innovation is an improved measure of oil and gas wealth—one that overcomes the endogeneity problems of past measures, can be compiled in a reliable and transparent way, and is available for all countries and all years.

Most of the earlier studies exploring the resource curse used a country's dependence on hydrocarbon exports—that is, the value of its petroleum exports as a fraction of its gross domestic product (GDP)—as their independent variable.[18] But this variable has two key shortcomings—one conceptual, and the other a bias that may cause spurious correlations between oil and problems like authoritarian rule, civil war, and poor economic performance.

The conceptual flaw is that it only measures fuel that is exported, and it is hard to see why fuel that is sold domestically should not be counted. Governments earn oil revenues from both domestic and foreign sales. Even when fuel is sold domestically at subsidized prices, the true value of this oil—and hence the cost to the government of these subsidies—should be accounted for.

The measure may also be biased upward in poorer countries, which could produce spurious associations between oil export dependence and a variety of economic and political maladies that are highly correlated with low incomes. Even if two countries with the same population produce the same quantity of oil, the numerator—a country's oil exports—will be larger in the poorer country. Oil-producing countries typically consume a fraction of their oil domestically and export the surplus. Rich countries will consume more of their own oil, while poor countries will consume less of it, and hence export more of it. For example, on a per capita basis, the United States produces more oil than Angola or Nigeria, but Angola and Nigeria export more than the United States, because the United States is wealthier than Angola or Nigeria, and consumes all of its oil domestically. When we measure oil exports, we are indirectly measuring the size of a country's non-oil economy.

A similar problem occurs in the denominator. Even if two countries export the same quantity of oil, the poorer country will have a smaller

---

[18] For examples, see Sachs and Warner 1995; Collier and Hoeffler 1998; Ross 2001a.

GDP, and hence it will have a higher oil-exports-to-GDP ratio. This opens the door to several endogeneity problems. For example, having a high oil-exports-to-GDP ratio might cause slow economic growth (or corruption, or civil war), but it could also be a result of these ailments, since they tend to reduce a country's GDP. This makes it hard to interpret correlations between oil export dependence and conflict, for instance; both might be independently boosted by a country's poverty, producing a spurious correlation.

To surmount these problems, I measure the total value of oil and gas production instead of just exports, and divide it by a country's population, not its total exports or the GDP. The resulting variable, *oil income per capita*, can be used to evaluate a stark version of the oil curse: Does the value of a country's oil production—regardless of how well it is managed, and how it influences the rest of the economy—affect its politics?

The *oil income* variable also has a more intuitive meaning than the oil-exports-to-GDP ratio. If two countries with similar populations produce similar quantities of oil and gas—for example, Angola and Netherlands—they will have similar levels of *oil income* per capita (in this case, about five hundred dollars per capita in 2003). If we measured them by their oil-exports-to-GDP ratios, however, we would find that Angola's measure (0.789) is much higher than Netherlands' (0.056), because Angola is too poor to consume much of its own oil (making the numerator larger), and because its GDP is much smaller (making the denominator smaller).

The oil income variable has two important weaknesses. First, the distribution of values among states is highly skewed: most countries produce little or no oil, while a few produce enormous quantities, which can create problems when it is used in regressions. I take several steps to reduce this problem. I use the natural log of oil income in the regressions in chapters 3 and 5 (although not in chapter 4, for reasons I explain in appendix 4.1), to make the distribution of values less skewed. Since the log of oil income still has a nonnormal distribution, I retest all of my findings in chapters 3, 4, and 5 using a dichotomous measure of *oil income*, which identifies countries as oil producers when they have at least a hundred dollars per capita (measured in constant 2000 dollars) in income from oil and gas in a given year. In all the chapters, I employ cross-tabulations in which countries are again divided into oil and non-oil producers, to show that my inferences are not driven by extreme values in a small number of cases.

The second shortcoming is that *oil income* is not identical to the concept of oil wealth in my theory, even though it is closely related to it. Most of my arguments suggest that oil is politically harmful because of the revenues it generates for governments.[19] Unfortunately, the secrecy of these revenues makes them extraordinarily difficult to measure, except for certain countries in recent years. Even if complete and accurate information on oil revenues was available, this measure would have a disadvantage of its own: the size of a country's oil revenues is affected by the government's institutions and policies, and hence cannot be relied on to identify the causal effect of oil wealth on its governance. To obtain a measure of oil wealth that is more exogenous and available for more countries over a longer time period, I rely on the *oil income* measure.

Oil income can be readily calculated for all countries and years since 1960. Data on oil and gas production from 1970 to 2001 comes from the World Bank's Web site on environmental economics and indicators. Figures after 2001 are from the "BP Statistical Review of World Energy." Oil and gas production before 1970, and after 2001 for countries not covered by BP, are taken from the US Geological Survey's *Mineral Yearbook*. I take data on Soviet production—which is not well measured in the other data sets—from studies by Marshall Goldman and Jonathan Stern, and use data on oil and gas prices from the "BP Statistical Review."[20]

ENDOGENEITY

If *oil income* was randomly distributed among countries—and hence truly exogenous to a country's economic and political conditions—causal identification would be easy: statistically significant correlations between oil income and governance would strongly suggest that the former was causing the latter.

Unfortunately, the distribution of *oil income* is not random, which makes it important to understand why it varies over time and from country to country. The *oil income* variable is a function of three underlying factors: a country's geologic endowment, which determines the physical quantity and quality of petroleum that can be exploited; the investments made in extracting it, which affect how much will be discovered and commercially exploited at any given time; and the price of oil, which determines both the rate of extraction, and the

---

[19] This is not a problem for all parts of my argument. In a few cases, I maintain that income generated by petroleum can cause problems whether or not it is translated into government revenues—when it crowds out industries that usually hire women (chapter 4) or facilitates armed rebellions through extortion (chapter 5).

[20] Goldman 2008; Stern 1980.

amount of money that petroleum sales will generate. Both a country's geologic endowment and the global oil price should be unaffected by a country's economic and political features.[21] A country's economy and government, however, will influence the investments made in oil exploitation. Countries that are wealthier, more open to foreign investment, and provide better legal protections for investors are likely to attract more petroleum-sector investment.[22]

Although country-level data on petroleum investments are scarce and unreliable, regional-level data are available and informative. While the developing countries cover almost 60 percent of the world's landmass (outside Antarctica), they hold less than 20 percent of the world's stock of foreign direct investment in petroleum, mining, and quarrying. The rich democracies of Europe, North America, Australia, and New Zealand cover just 25 percent of the world's landmass, yet have almost 75 percent of the foreign direct investment stock in mining.[23] This indicates that the rich democracies have about ten times more foreign direct investment in all types of mining, per square kilometer, than either the developing states or those of the former Soviet Union and southeastern Europe (see figure 1.1). In fact, this understates the investment advantage of the rich democracies. While the developing countries are heavily dependent on foreign investment, including expensive Western technology, to develop their oil sectors, the rich democracies have more domestic investment available.

Since there is a better investment climate in the advanced industrialized countries (which also tend to be more democratic, peaceful, and have more female participation in government), we should expect, ceteris paribus, to see higher levels of *oil income* in countries that also more democratic. This also implies that if higher levels of oil income are correlated with authoritarianism, civil war, or the absence of women's rights, these relationships are unlikely to be spurious, and may understate oil's true effect.

Another way to check for exogeneity is to look at whether oil is more likely to be extracted from countries that were rich or poor ex ante, before they started to produce oil. Figure 1.3 shows the initial incomes of all 103 countries that began to produce petroleum between 1857 and

---

[21] Saudi Arabia might be a partial exception. Due to its unique role as a "swing producer," it may have the capacity to unilaterally affect global prices, at least in the short run.

[22] Christian Daude and Ernesto Stein (2007) find that countries with "better institutions"—including higher scores on measures of "government effectiveness" and "regulatory quality"—attract significantly more foreign direct investment, although they do not look separately at investment in petroleum. Rabah Arezki and Markus Brückner (2010) show that greater corruption tends to reduce oil production.

[23] United Nations Conference on Trade and Development 2009.

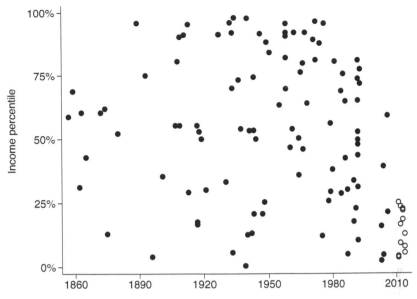

Figure 1.3. Incomes of new oil producers, 1857–2015
The dots show the per capita income of countries in the year they began to produce oil or gas, expressed as a percentile of all sovereign states in that year. Hollow dots in the lower-right corner represent countries that are expected to start production between 2010 and 2015.
Source: Calculated from data in Haber and Menaldo 2009; Maddison 2009.

2009, relative to other countries in the same year.[24] Countries above the fiftieth percentile, marked on the y-axis, had above-median incomes; those below the fiftieth percentile had below-median incomes.

Forty-one countries began to produce oil when their incomes were below the world median; four began production when they were at the world median; and fifty-eight countries began producing when their incomes were above the world median. This again suggests that oil and gas is more likely to be extracted from countries that are already rich, and hence more likely to be democratic and peaceful. Only since 2000 have low-income countries been more likely than high-income ones to start producing oil—reflecting the movement of the petroleum frontier to the poorest countries. In figure 1.3, hollow circles marks those countries that are expected to begin production between 2010 and 2015; all of them have low incomes.

[24] I use the income of whatever country ruled the extractive region when production began, even if the territories later changed hands or became independent. I am grateful to Steve Haber and Victor Menaldo for sharing their data on initial production dates.

TABLE 1.1
Oil- and gas-producing countries, 2009

These numbers show the estimated value of oil and gas produced per capita in 2009 in current dollars.

Countries	Oil income per capita (2009 dollars)
Middle East and North Africa	
* Qatar	24,940
* Kuwait	19,500
* United Arab Emirates	14,100
* Oman	7,950
* Saudi Arabia	7,800
* Libya	6,420
* Bahrain	3,720
* Algeria	1,930
* Iraq	1,780
* Iran	1,600
* Syria	450
Yemen	270
Egypt	260
Tunisia	250
Latin America and Caribbean	
* Trinidad	6,250
* Venezuela	2,130
* Ecuador	820
Suriname	680
* Mexico	610
* Argentina	530
Colombia	430
Bolivia	270
Brazil	240
Cuba	110

TABLE 1.1 (*continued*)

Countries	Oil income per capita (2009 dollars)
Sub-Saharan Africa	
Equatorial Guinea	12,310
* Gabon	3,890
* Angola	2,400
* Congo Republic	1,940
* Nigeria	370
Sudan	260
Chad	230
Cameroon	100
North America, Europe, Australia, and New Zealand	
* Norway	13,810
* Canada	2,530
Denmark	1,270
* Australia	790
* United States	730
* Netherlands	670
New Zealand	430
* Romania	170
* United Kingdom	150
Croatia	140
Ukraine	110
Southeast Asia	
* Brunei	11,590
East Timor	1,910
* Malaysia	860
Indonesia	140
Thailand	150
Papua New Guinea	120

TABLE 1.1 (*continued*)

Countries	Oil income per capita (2009 dollars)
Former Soviet Union	
* Turkmenistan	1,810
* Russia	2,080
* Kazakhstan	2,370
* Azerbaijan	2,950
* Uzbekistan	340
Ukraine	110

*Defined as a "long-term petroleum producer." This indicates that a country has produced at least a hundred dollars per capita in oil and gas income (using constant 2000 dollars) for at least two-thirds of the time since 1960, or if they became independent after 1960, for two-thirds of their sovereign years.

Sources: The calculations are based on BP 2010; US Geological Survey n.d.; World Bank n.d.

Some skeptics have suggested that authoritarian leaders, or the leaders of countries with civil wars, might be more desperate for revenues and thus likely to produce more oil than their more democratic and peaceful counterparts.[25] Yet outside Saudi Arabia, it is hard to find examples of leaders who have the capacity to adjust their country's oil production at will. Production rates generally are determined by geologic conditions, which limit how quickly the petroleum can be drawn out of the ground; and by oil prices, which determine how much oil in commercially marginal fields can be sold at a profit. Even if rulers could control these factors, we should expect democratic leaders—who face regular political competition and have high discount rates—to be equally or more desperate for revenues than authoritarian leaders.[26]

Oil income is not truly exogenous to a country's economic and political features, but it should be biased upward in countries that are more democratic, peaceful, and stable—and therefore biased against finding an oil curse.

[25] Haber and Menaldo 2009; Tsui 2011.

[26] In fact, a study by Gilbert Metcalf and Catherine Wolfram (2010) finds that democratic oil producers tend to extract their reserves more quickly than nondemocratic oil producers.

TRANSPARENCY AND ROBUSTNESS OF THE ANALYSIS

I have tried to analyze the data using the simplest and most transparent appropriate methods, including scatter diagrams, cross-tabulations, and difference-of-means tests.[27] Whenever feasible, I use tables and graphs to display both the countries that are consistent with a given pattern, and those that are not. I make a special effort to minimize the use of terms that are ambiguous or opaque. All of my data are included on my Web site for others to scrutinize, available at http://www.sscnet.ucla.edu/polisci/faculty/ross/. This book argues that transparency can encourage governments to better manage their oil revenues; maybe it can also encourage social scientists to be more careful in their analyses.

In the appendixes to chapters 3, 4, and 5, I use regression analysis to show that the chapter's key contentions can also be illustrated with more sophisticated methods. Even here I try to keep my models simple, heeding Christopher Achen's warning that "with more than three independent variables, no one can do the careful data analysis to ensure that the model specification is accurate and that the assumptions fit as well as the researcher claims."[28]

Scholars can make misleading inferences when their data sets are incomplete and the missing observations are "nonrandom." I make a special effort to construct complete or virtually complete data sets. Since it is often impossible to obtain data for all countries—economic data before 1980 for low- and middle-income countries are especially scarce—in the regression tables I report the fraction of observations in each estimation that are missing.

All of my key results are submitted to a battery of robustness tests to see whether the correlations depend on a small number of influential cases, the use of particular data sets, the omission of confounding variables (at least those that can be readily measured), or arbitrary methodological decisions. Since much of the world's oil is concentrated in the Middle East and North Africa, I report how my regression results are affected by both the inclusion of a dummy variable for the Middle Eastern region and, more drastically, dropping all Middle Eastern countries from the analysis. Most of my results survive these tests, but some do not.

Political scientists frequently report the "substantive" effect of their main explanatory variable on their dependent variable. Yet these figures

---

[27] According to Christopher Achen (2002, 442), "None of the important empirical generalizations in the discipline has emerged from high-powered methodological research. Instead, almost without exception, they were found with graphs and cross-tabulations." See also Shapiro 2005.

[28] Achen 2002, 446.

are only valid if we are estimating the true causal model, which we are not, and measuring our variables with great accuracy, which we often do not. Typically these numbers are sensitive to changes in our underlying assumptions, and can create a false impression of scientific precision. And since *oil income* is almost certainly biased upward in richer, more stable, and more democratic countries, my estimations will likely understate oil's true effect.

I find it more candid and transparent to report whether, for a given variable, the oil states have significantly different values than the non-oil states, and what those differences are. This should give readers a rough impression of the magnitude of oil's impact while avoiding misleading claims.

UNDERSTANDING CAUSAL PROCESSES

In chapters 3 through 6, I develop simple theoretical models to clarify my arguments about causal processes that connect oil to different outcomes. The model starts in chapter 3 with just two actors—a group of citizens who wish to improve their welfare, and a ruler who wishes to stay in office—to portray more explicitly how oil revenues should affect the ruler's ability stay in power. In chapter 4, I draw the distinction between male and female citizens, and show how a rise in oil income can discourage women from entering the labor force, and keep women economically and politically marginalized. The model in chapter 5 divides the population into two groups—those who live in a country's oil-producing region, and those who live outside it—and shows how oil wealth could increase the likelihood of an armed rebellion in the oil-producing region when incomes are low. Chapter 6 employs a somewhat looser set of models—mostly developed by other scholars—to highlight factors that can influence a ruler's capacity to make intertemporal trade-offs, and hence, manage a volatile flow of oil revenues over time.

When investigating causal mechanisms empirically, even the best statistical analysis can only take us so far. The problem is more acute when we use observational data, and our unit of analysis is as large and opaque as a country.[29] Hence, I also use brief case studies to show that the associations I report in the cross-national data can plausibly explain outcomes at the country level, and look more closely at causal processes that connect oil income to specific outcomes. The case studies

---

[29] For important discussions of these limitations, see Brady and Collier 2004; King and Zeng 2006; Przeworski 2007.

cover a wide range of countries, including Colombia, the Republic of Congo, Equatorial Guinea, Indonesia, Nigeria, South Korea, the Soviet Union and Russia, Sudan, and the US state of Louisiana.

In chapter 5, where I argue that a country's oil production can have a detrimental affect on women, I use the case study method more deliberately, comparing three countries that are similar in many ways (Algeria, Morocco, and Tunisia), but only one of which (Algeria) produces significant quantities of petroleum. I show how oil has slowed the economic progress of women in Algeria, while women in Morocco and Tunisia have made much faster gains.

Both the quantitative and qualitative analyses in this book have important limitations. I hope that making my analysis more transparent will help readers weigh the evidence for themselves.

CHAPTER TWO

The Trouble with Oil Revenues

> The spirit of a people, its cultural level, its social structure, the deeds its policy may prepare—all this and more is written in its fiscal history, stripped of all phrases. He who knows how to listen to its message here discerns the thunder of world history more clearly than anywhere else.
> —Joseph Schumpeter, "The Crisis of the Tax State"

JUST AS PEOPLE are affected by the kinds of food they eat, governments are affected by the kinds of revenues they collect. Since most governments receive the same kinds of revenues year after year, it is easy to overlook their significance. Only when there is a sharp change in these revenues, such as when oil is discovered, does their underlying importance become clear.

Oil revenues are marked by their exceptionally large size, unusual source, lack of stability, and secrecy. These four qualities reflect both the historic organization of the petroleum industry, and the revolutionary changes of the 1960s and 1970s that transformed the oil-producing world.

THE SCALE AND SOURCE OF OIL REVENUES

The petroleum industry generates a lot more government revenue than other kinds of industries. This makes the governments of oil-producing countries bigger than the governments of similar countries without oil.

Consider Nigeria, which became a major oil producer after the conclusion of the Biafra War in the late 1960s (see figure 2.1). From 1969 to 1977, the volume of oil that Nigeria produced grew by 380 percent, while the real price of oil almost quadrupled. The Nigerian government's total revenues—from oil and all other sources—rose from $4.9 billion to $21.5 billion over these eight years, after accounting for inflation. At the same time, government spending rose from about 10 percent to more than 25 percent of the Nigerian economy. Not only did the

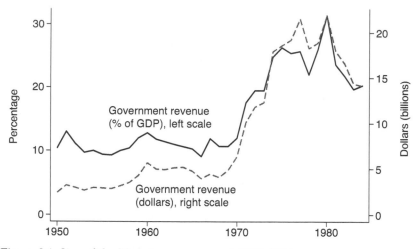

Figure 2.1. Size of the Nigerian government, 1950–1984

Sources: The figures on government revenues in dollars are from Bevan, Collier, and Gunning 1999; the figures on government revenues as a fraction of the GDP are from Heston, Summers, and Aten, n.d., table 6.2.

Nigerian government expand quickly; it expanded more quickly than the rest of the Nigerian economy.[1]

Azerbaijan and Equatorial Guinea became significant petroleum exporters in the early 2000s, at the same time that oil prices were rising. From 2001 to 2009, the value of government expenditures rose by 600 percent in Azerbaijan and 800 percent in Equatorial Guinea, after accounting for inflation.[2]

Because governments often conceal the true scale of their oil revenues, it is hard to accurately measure the state's size in oil-producing countries. But even bad data—which almost certainly understate the actual size of oil-rich governments—are suggestive. Figure 2.2 displays the oil incomes of 134 countries (on the horizontal axis), and the estimated size of their governments, as a fraction of their country's economy (on the vertical axis). As the upward-sloping line indicates, the more oil a country produces, the larger its government.

[1] Bevan, Collier, and Gunning 1999.

[2] Before accounting for inflation, government spending in Azerbaijan rose twelvefold and about thirteenfold in Equatorial Guinea. These estimates are based on the IMF's 2005 and 2010 article IV reports for the two countries.

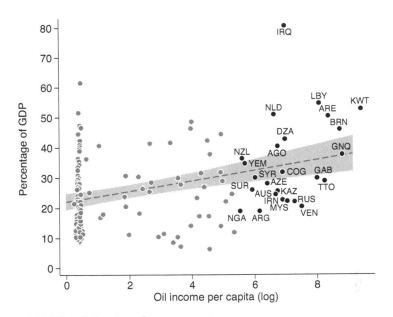

Figure 2.2. Oil and the size of government
The vertical axis shows the size of government revenues as a fraction of a country's GDP.
Source: The data on government revenue are from IMF article IV reports, for the most recent year (between 1997 and 2007) for which data are available; the figures on oil income are for the same year.

How much of a difference does oil make? One way to answer this question is to compare the governments of oil-producing countries with those of neighboring states with similar incomes but no oil (see figure 2.3). In these examples, the oil-funded governments are from 16 percent (Azerbaijan versus Armenia) to 250 percent (Algeria versus Tunisia) larger than the neighboring states without oil.

Another way to answer this question is compare the size of government in countries with significant oil income (which I define as a hundred dollars per capita in a given year, using constant 2000 dollars) with those that earn less, using simple cross-tabulations (see table 2.1). Again, the oil-producing states have dramatically larger governments—about 45 percent larger, on average.[3]

---

[3]In this table, and all subsequent tables with cross-tabulations, I use standard difference-of-means tests to indicate whether the oil-producing states are significantly different from the non oil-producing states.

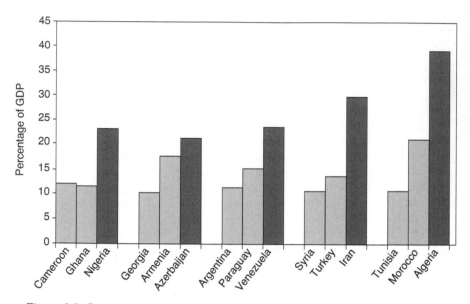

Figure 2.3. Government size in selected oil and non-oil states
The bars show the size of each country's government as a fraction of the country's economy. The darker bars are oil-producing states.
Source: The data on government revenue are from IMF article IV reports, for the most recent year (between 1997 and 2007) for which data are available.

Thanks to the scale of these revenues, petroleum wealth also has a powerful impact on the source of the government's funding. Most governments are funded by taxes. But as a country's oil wealth grows, its government becomes decreasingly reliant on taxes and increasingly reliant on "nontax revenues." Table 2.2 displays the link between a coun-

Table 2.1
Size of government, 2003

The numbers show the total government revenues as a percentage of GDP.

	Non-oil producers	Oil producers	Difference
Low income (below $5,000)	21.2	27.7	6.5**
High income (above $5,000)	32.8	44.6	11.8*
All countries	23.5	33.2	9.6**

*significant at 5%
**significant at 1%
Source: The calculations are based on IMF Article IV reports for 2003; for countries where these figures are missing, I used the most recent prior year for which IMF data were available.

TABLE 2.2
Taxes on goods and services, 2002

The numbers show the taxes on goods and services as a percentage of government revenue.

	Non-oil producers	Oil producers	Difference
Low income (below $5,000)	32.8	24.9	–7.9**
High income (above $5,000)	29.6	24.1	–5.5*
All countries	31.6	24.5	–7.1***

*significant at 10%, in a one-tailed t-test
**significant at 5%
***significant at 1%
Source: Calculations based on data from World Bank n.d.

try's oil industry and its government's dependence on taxes. In both low- and high-income countries, and in both autocracies and democracies, oil producers are about 30 percent less dependent than non-oil countries on taxes on goods and services.

It may seem unremarkable that when countries are more reliant on oil revenues, they become less reliant on taxes. But this understates the impact of oil revenues. The oil industry generates more revenues than other industries of similar size, and when governments receive more oil revenues, they tend to respond by collecting less revenue from taxes. As a result, the governments of oil-producing countries are not merely dependent on petroleum revenues; they are disproportionately dependent on them, and disproportionately liberated from taxes.[4]

If governments received funding from all industries in proportion to their contribution to the national economy, the government's finances would mirror the composition of the economy. If one-quarter of the nation's income came from oil, for instance, so would one-quarter of the government's revenues. But this is almost never the case, as figure 2.4 shows for the leading thirty-one hydrocarbon-rich countries. On average, the oil sector makes up 19 percent of the economy in these states, but funds 54 percent of the state's budget.

The link between higher oil revenues and lower taxes should not be surprising. Governments find it bureaucratically easier and politically more popular to collect revenues from their oil sectors than to collect taxes from the population at large. It also makes economic sense, at

[4]See Bornhorst, Gupta, and Thornton 2009; McGuirk 2010. This also means that governments in oil-producing countries would be even larger than they are if they kept taxes at "normal" levels.

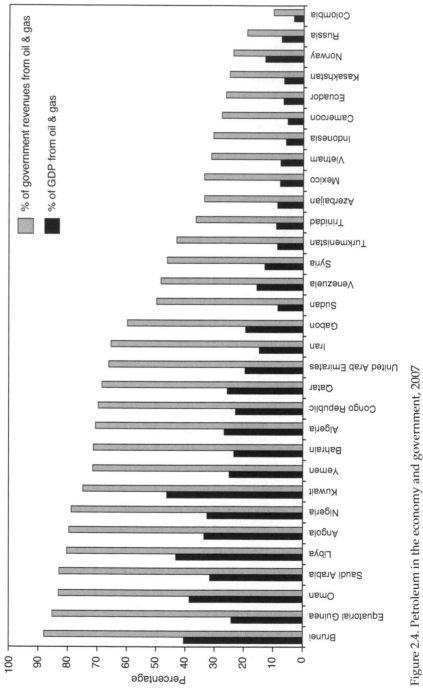

Figure 2.4. Petroleum in the economy and government, 2007

The dark bars show the value of petroleum as a fraction of the economy; the light bars show the value of petroleum revenues as a fraction of all government revenues.

Source: Bornhorst, Gupta, and Thornton 2009.

least up to a point. When the treasury is brimming with oil revenues, the government can transfer some of these funds to the public by cutting taxes. As we will see in later chapters, though, the government's dependence on oil revenues has far-reaching consequences for a country's politics and economy.

The distinctive size and source of oil revenues have their origins in the same unusual features of the petroleum world: the government's ownership of petroleum reserves; the industry's extraordinary profits, which since the 1970s have been largely captured by governments; and the industry's relatively small *direct* impact on the rest of the economy.

Government Ownership

In almost all countries, petroleum reserves are owned by governments. State ownership affects both the size and source of oil revenues. It gives governments a much larger claim on the industry's revenues, and allows them to collect these revenues directly, without having to tax private-sector companies.[5]

Governments have claimed ownership of mineral rights since at least the time of the Roman Empire, when mines and minerals belonged to the state by right of conquest. The Roman tradition of state ownership took root in early modern Europe, mostly through a series of royal decrees: in the German region by Frederick I, the Holy Roman emperor, in the twelfth century; in Britain, by King Richard I and King John in the late twelfth and early thirteenth centuries, and a 1689 act of Parliament; in Spain, through the 1383 decree of King Alfonso XI; and in France, through long-standing traditions that were codified in the Napoleonic Law of 1810.

This heritage is still reflected in the term "royalty," which according to the *Oxford English Dictionary* means both "the prerogatives, rights, or privileges" of a monarch, and "a payment made . . . by a producer of minerals, oil, or natural gas to the owner of the site."

When the modern age of oil production began in the early twentieth century, government ownership of subsoil minerals was well established in Europe. The British Crown already claimed ownership of gold and silver deposits; with the Petroleum Act of 1918, it established ownership of all petroleum deposits as well. From Europe, the principle of

---

[5]For heuristic purposes, I assume that governments collect all of their oil revenues through non-tax instruments like royalties, concession fees, and transfers from their national oil companies; in reality, governments also earn money from their oil sectors by taxing the private companies that work in the oil business. I return to this point in chapter 7.

sovereign ownership was passed on through colonial rule to the legal codes of countries around the world.[6]

Today, only one country allows the widespread private ownership of oil reserves: the United States.[7] When miners flocked to California during the gold rush in 1849, the United States had no applicable mining laws. To protect their rights and regulate disputes, miners had to establish their own rules. State and federal laws gradually recognized these local claims and regulations, and codified the right of anyone who improved a mine to purchase its title from the government at a reasonable price. This "bottom-up" process led to a system that is unusually favorable to private ownership and unique among the world's major oil producers.[8]

Generating Rents

While government ownership is important, it may or may not lead to large nontax revenues. Governments sometimes own other types of enterprises like steel factories and automobile plants that lose money. But thanks to the availability of extraordinary profits, or *rents*, the government's ownership of oil can be astoundingly profitable.

In most industries, firms typically earn a "normal" profit, determined by the laws of supply and demand. If their profits were much below this normal rate, some of the firms would leave the industry, which would raise profits for the remaining firms. If their profits were much above the normal rate, new companies would enter their industry to compete for these exceptional returns, which would drive profits down to normal levels. Companies in the oil business, however, can

---

[6]Elian 1979; Bunyanunda 2005.

[7]Not all US reserves are privately owned. The government owns the offshore oil reserves, which account for about a quarter of US production. Reserves beneath public lands can also be government owned.

Jones Luong and Weinthal (2010) point out that there are important differences in ownership patterns across countries. I return to the issue of ownership and privatization in the concluding chapter.

[8]On the evolution of US mining laws, see Libecap 1989. As Gavin Wright and Jesse Czelusta (2004, 11) point out, this does not mean that the United States had a well-functioning system of mineral rights:

> Much of the best US mineral land was transferred into private hands outside of the procedures set down by federal law. Nearly 6 million acres of coal lands were privatized between 1873 and 1906, for example, mostly disguised as farmland. Most of the iron lands of northern Minnesota and Wisconsin were fraudulently acquired under the provisions of the Homestead Act.

earn rents—profits above and beyond production costs, where the costs include a normal rate of return on the capital invested.

There are two broad conditions that generate rents in the petroleum or any other extractive industry. One is favorable geography, which gives some producers access to cheaper and better-quality oil than their competitors. Some reserves yield oil of relatively low quality at a high price and earn only a normal profit, but others yield high-quality oil at a low cost and hence will generate "differential" rents for the owner.[9] Since there is a limited supply of fields with low extraction costs and high-quality oil, new companies that enter the petroleum business cannot easily obtain these rents.

Producers can also earn "scarcity" rents when the demand for oil temporarily outpaces the supply. In theory, the supply of oil will eventually catch up with the demand, or the demand will eventually fall to meet the supply. But these adjustments can take years, either because oil supplies are growing scarce, or even if they are not scarce, because the price elasticity of the supply is relatively low, meaning that it takes a long time for producers to deliver more oil to the market in response to higher prices.

Figure 2.5 shows the magnitude of these rents in 2008 for eleven leading exporters. The black bars show the average cost of producing a barrel of oil, and the gray bars show its approximate price on the world market, reflecting differences in each country's oil quality. At the end of 2008, average extraction costs per barrel ranged from about US$1.80 in Saudi Arabia to US$31.40 in Canada, while prices ranged from US$38 in Canada to US$53 in Nigeria. The difference between these two figures was the rent, which ranged from about US$6 per barrel in Canada to US$42 per barrel in Nigeria.[10]

Scholars have long been fascinated by rents. In *Principles of Political Economy*, John Stuart Mill suggested that the concept of rent

> is one of the cardinal doctrines of political economy; and until it was understood, no consistent explanation could be given of many of the more complicated industrial phenomena. The evidence of its truth will be manifested with a great increase in clearness.[11]

[9] This type of rent—produced by innate differences in the quality or production costs of a good—is sometimes called "Ricardian" rent, since it was first described by nineteenth-century economist David Ricardo.

[10] The estimates of rents are admittedly rough; these figures are based on data produced by Kirk Hamilton and Michael Clemens (1999), and updated to account for inflation.

[11] Mill [1848] 1987, 16:3. Many social scientists argue that the pursuit of rents is the root of much evil, including economic waste, corruption, and violence. See, for example, Krueger 1974; Buchanan, Tollison, and Tullock 1980; Colander 1984. It is easier to construct theories about rents, however, than to test their validity.

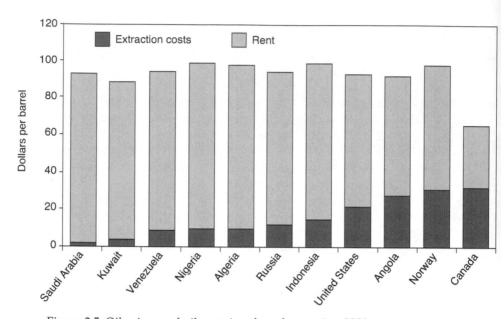

Figure 2.5. Oil prices and oil rents in selected countries, 2008
The height of the bars represent the price of exported oil from each country in January 2008. The darker sections show the extraction costs, and the lighter sections show the rents.

Sources: The oil prices are taken from the Energy Information Administration Web site, available at http://www.eia.doe.gov (accessed January 25, 2009); the extraction costs, adjusted for information, are taken from Hamilton and Clemens 1999.

Much of the politics of oil is shaped by the struggle between oil companies and governments for control of these rents. According to long-established principles, rents that come from the sale of an asset should belong to the asset's owner. I may hire a company to transport my collection of gold coins, which I store in a bank vault, to my house, but this does not entitle the transport company to keep some of the coins, once I pay the normal transport fee. Similarly, a government may give a company the right to extract oil from state-owned reserves, but this does not entitle the firm to retain any oil rents.

Before the changes of the 1960s and 1970s, the size of the oil firms and their ability to collude made it almost impossible for governments to collect the rents from oil companies that by right should have gone to the state. In theory, governments could have used market competition to force companies to pay rents—for example, by auctioning off concession rights to the highest bidder. In practice, the major oil companies refused to bid against each other, leaving host governments with little choice but to sign unfavorable contracts.

The oil companies had another advantage: their size and secrecy gave them innumerable ways to conceal their revenues from the government. The major companies were vertically integrated, meaning that they controlled every stage of the oil business: the same corporate entity that pumped crude oil out of the ground in one country would also transport it around the globe, refine it into gasoline, and ultimately pump it into the consumer's gas tank in another. This made it relatively easy for the companies to hide extra profits through transfer pricing—shuffling their revenues from an arm of the company that was subject to the jurisdiction of the host government to another arm that was not.

This allowed the major oil companies to earn exceptional returns on their investments in the non-Western countries. According to one estimate, in the mid-1950s the major oil companies were earning net profits of 60 to 90 percent on their investments in the Middle East and East Asia *after* their payments to host governments. Another study, carried out by the US Department of Commerce, found that in 1960, US petroleum companies had earned after-tax profits representing a 50 percent return on the book value of their investments in the Middle East, and a 29 percent return on their investments in Venezuela.[12] By any measure, these companies made extraordinary profits from their operations in developing countries.

Capturing Rents

In the 1950s, governments in the developing world nominally owned their nations' oil wealth, but most received only a fraction of the available rents. Often they could not even control how much oil was taken out of their soil and exported overseas. All of this was changed by the wave of nationalizations that swept the global oil industry in the 1950s, 1960s, and 1970s.

The first governments to nationalize their oil production were Argentina (1910), the Soviet Union (1918), Bolivia (1937), and Mexico (1938). Yet before World War II, nationalizations were rare. As late as 1950, the Seven Sisters controlled 98 percent of the world's traded oil, outside the United States and the Communist bloc.[13]

[12] Hartshorn 1962.
[13] Levy 1982.

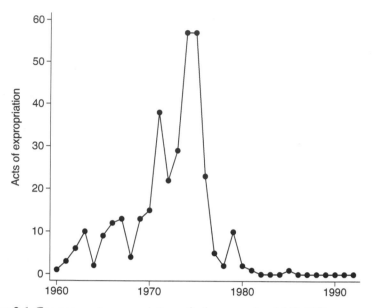

Figure 2.6. Government expropriation of oil companies, 1960–1993
The line indicates the number of significant "acts of expropriation" around
the world during each calendar year, defined as "formal expropriation, forced
sales, contract renegotiations, and extralegal interventions" in oil companies.
A single company may be subjected to several acts of expropriation over time.
Sources: Kobrin 1980; Minor 1994.

Between 1950 and 1970, however, the balance of power between oil
companies and host governments changed dramatically. As economic
historian Edith Penrose wrote in 1976,

> Exploration and production concessions granted in the early days
> have been repeatedly re-negotiated, invariably in favour of the coun-
> tries; where the concessions covered a very large proportion of a
> country's drilling area, they have been reduced in size; stiffer regu-
> lations respecting drilling requirements, reservoir maintenance and
> similar matters have been introduced; and financial arrangements of
> all kinds have improved in favour of the countries.[14]

The shift in power from corporations to governments culminated in a
wave of expropriations, which peaked between 1971 and 1976 (see figure 2.6). By 1980, almost all developing countries had nationalized their
petroleum industries and established national oil companies (NOCs) to

[14] Penrose 1976, 198.

manage them. According to Stephen Kobrin, "The net result was a revolutionary transformation of the international petroleum industry."[15] After 1985, the number of new expropriations fell sharply, not because sentiments had shifted, but because in non-Western countries, the governments had seized most of the available oil-sector assets.

The nationalizations of the 1960s and 1970s allowed governments to capture a higher share of the oil rents. In the 1950s, most major oil producers had "fifty-fifty" arrangements with international oil companies, which were supposed to give each party half of the profits from oil sales. But thanks to their size and vertical integration, the companies could readily conceal their profits from the host governments—leaving the governments uncertain if the companies were meeting their commitments. According to one study, expropriations raised the government's share of oil profits from 50 percent in the early 1960s to 98 percent by 1974.[16]

In gaining control over their oil industries, governments also gained control over the pace of oil production. The Seven Sisters had, in particular, stifled Iraq's oil industry. Despite its remarkable petroleum reserves—second only in size to Saudi Arabia's, and similarly cheap to extract—the foreign-owned Iraqi Petroleum Company (IPC) placed sharp limits on oil production in order to keep global prices from falling. After the Iraqi government nationalized the IPC in 1972, it more than doubled production over the next seven years.

WHAT CAUSED THIS WAVE OF NATIONALIZATIONS?

One factor was the rise of the nationalist sentiment in the developing world in the 1950s and 1960s that accompanied decolonization. These sentiments were entangled with antipathy toward foreign firms, whose local subsidiaries were often established during and closely associated with colonial rule. This made the nationalization of foreign oil companies popular.

In Mexico, for example, the expropriation of foreign oil companies in 1938 was received with such enthusiasm that the day it took place, March 18, has been celebrated as a holiday ever since. In 1951, Iranian prime minister Mohammed Mossadegh was compelled to nationalize the British-owned Anglo-Iranian Oil Company (AIOC) after his predecessor—who argued against nationalization—was assassinated. The takeover of the AIOC was greeted with exuberant celebrations and a special national holiday.[17]

---

[15] Kobrin 1980, 17. See also Jodice 1980; Minor 1994.
[16] Mommer 2002.
[17] Yergin 1991, 463.

Politicians linked to these nationalizations sometimes gained great acclaim. In Iraq, the takeover of the IPC was organized by the undersecretary general of the Revolutionary Command Council—Saddam Hussein—burnishing his public image and boosting popular support for the Baath Party. According to one biographer, the nationalization of the IPC became Hussein's "gateway to fame."[18]

Shortly after Libya's Muammar Qaddafi came to power in a 1969 military coup, he began to nationalize his country's oil industry. This led to a flood of new revenues, which allowed him to buy off powerful tribal chiefs, and fund his "revolutionary" agenda.

For all of their popularity, these nationalizations would not have been possible without a second development: the decline in the bargaining power of the major oil companies. Until the early 1960s, few governments dared challenge the oil majors, which tightly controlled the global oil trade. Any government that asserted control over its country's oil industry would be unable to sell its oil abroad, since the Seven Sisters controlled almost all distribution and marketing channels. Governments that nationalized paid a heavy price. After Mexico nationalized its oil industry in 1938, international companies boycotted its crude, denied it the use of tankers, and refused to sell it, a critical additive for gasoline.[19] When Iran nationalized the AIOC in 1951, it was slapped with a crippling embargo, and after two years of refusing to yield, the Mossadegh government was overthrown by a coup led by the US and British secret services. After the shah was restored to power, he effectively reversed the AIOC's nationalization.[20]

But in the 1950s and 1960s, the bargaining power of the major oil firms began to deteriorate. One reason was the rise of "independent" oil producers that reduced the market share of the oil majors; these included Getty Oil, Standard Oil of Indiana, the Italian state-owned ENI, and the Soviet Union. Equally important was the rise of smaller companies that could provide governments with specialized exploration, drilling, and engineering services that were once only available from the Seven Sisters.

Another factor was the 1960 founding of OPEC. At first, OPEC members simply shared previously secret information about their contracts with the oil companies. Over time they developed coordinated negotiating strategies, which ultimately improved the terms of their contracts.

Also important was the growing reluctance of the major Western powers—the United States, France, and Britain—to use military force to protect their economic interests abroad. The joint US-UK operation

---

[18] Coughlin 2002, 108.
[19] Krasner 1978.
[20] Mahdavi 2011.

to overthrow Iran's Mossadegh government in 1953 was considered a success at the time. But the next two decades witnessed humbling military setbacks for the major Western powers, including France in Vietnam and Algeria, Britain and France in the 1956 Suez Crisis, and the United States in Vietnam and Cambodia. By the late 1960s, the Western powers had grown reluctant to send their troops abroad to protect friendly regimes or overthrow hostile ones.

Finally, the bargaining position of the host governments improved over time thanks to the unusual qualities of the oil business. The extraction of oil requires large up-front investments, which are used to purchase highly specific assets—things like concessions, wells, pumping stations, and pipelines that cannot be easily moved to other places, or used for other purposes. Once companies make these investments, it becomes prohibitively expensive for them to withdraw, since they would have to leave these investments behind.

This presents companies with what economists call a "time-consistency" problem. Before the initial investments, companies are in a strong bargaining position and can negotiate highly favorable contracts with host governments. But once they make their investments, companies lose much of their bargaining power—leaving host governments free to abrogate any contract terms they dislike, with little fear that the companies will withdraw their investments.[21]

As long as the oil majors had exclusive control over the shipping and distribution of oil, and were backed by the military power of their home governments, they retained enough bargaining power to enforce their contracts with governments. When the rise of the independent oil companies broke the oligopsony of the Seven Sisters, and the Western powers grew reluctant to use force abroad, however, there was little to stop the host governments from breaking their contracts with the oil majors, and replacing them with their own national oil companies.

Since the 1970s, national oil companies have dominated the global petroleum supply. A handful of countries—notably Mexico and Libya—expelled foreign companies and foreign workers, and ran their petroleum industries with little international assistance. Yet in most countries the international oil companies (IOCs) continued to play a role, thanks to their access to capital, technical skills, and international marketing networks.

Today the relationships between NOCs and private companies vary widely in form.[22] In a handful of countries—mostly in the Middle

---

[21] Raymond Vernon (1971) refers to this problem as "the obsolescing bargain."

[22] For a discussion of the many forms that these contracts may take, see Johnston 2007. Paul Stevens (2008) suggests that there have been cycles of resource nationalism, especially in the Middle East.

TABLE 2.3
World's largest oil and gas firms, by market capitalization, 2005

Rank	Company	Ownership	Market capitalization (US$ billion)
1	ExxonMobil	Private sector	349.5
2	BP	Private sector	219.8
3	Royal Dutch Shell	Private sector	208.3
4	Gazprom (Russia)	Hybrid	160.2
5	Total	Private sector	154.2
6	Petrochina	State controlled	146.6
7	Chevron	Private sector	127.4
8	Eni	Private sector	111
9	ConocoPhillips	Private sector	80.7
10	Petrobras (Brazil)	Hybrid	74.7
11	Lukoil	Private sector	50.5
12	Statoil (Norway)	Hybrid	50.3
13	Sinopec (China)	State controlled	48.7
14	Surgutneftegaz (Russia)	Hybrid	45.8
15	ONGC (India)	State controlled	37.2

Source: PFC Energy, available at http://www.pfcenergy.com.

East—NOCs exercise day-to-day operational control of the industry and only hire international companies on service contracts to carry out specific tasks. In most other countries, governments have signed concession agreements, production-sharing agreements, or joint ventures with foreign companies, giving the companies greater control over day-to-day operations.

The business of oil is now run by a combination of NOCs, private-sector firms, and hybrid companies that combine state and private ownership. Most are so large and complex that it is difficult to know their true value. Companies that are publicly listed on a stock exchange can be measured by the market value of their outstanding stock. By this measure, the world's largest oil firms in 2005 were ExxonMobil, BP, and Royal Dutch Shell (see table 2.3). But firms that are wholly owned by states are not publicly listed. If we use an alternative measure—the size

TABLE 2.4
World's largest oil and gas firms, by proven reserves, 2005

Rank	Company	Ownership	Oil reserves (barrels)
1	Saudi Aramco	State controlled	262
2	National Iranian Oil Co.	State controlled	125
3	Iraqi National Oil Co.	State controlled	115
4	Kuwait Petroleum Corp.	State controlled	101
5	Abu Dhabi National Oil Co.	State controlled	98
6	PDVSA (Venezuela)	State controlled	77
7	Libya NOC	State controlled	39
8	Nigerian National Petroleum Corp.	State controlled	35
9	Lukoil	Private sector	16.1
10	Qatar Petroleum	State controlled	15.2
11	Rosneft (Russia)	State controlled	15
12	PEMEX (Mexico)	State controlled	14.6
13	Sonatrach (Algeria)	State controlled	11.8
14	ExxonMobil	Private sector	10.5
15	BP	Private sector	9.6

Sources: EIA Annual Energy Review 2007, available at http://www.eia.doe.gov, company reports; oil reserve figures are approximate and vary slightly by source.

of a company's proven oil reserves—nine of the top ten companies are NOCs (see table 2.4). A 2003 study found that NOCs controlled about 80 percent of global oil reserves and 75 percent of global production.[23]

Even before the nationalizations of the 1950s and 1960s, the governments of oil-producing countries were accruing large and sometimes even colossal petroleum revenues. But the shift toward national ownership enabled them to gain full control over their oil industries and initiate—and benefit from—the sharp increases in oil prices of the 1970s.

[23]McPherson 2003.

Oil and the Private Sector

Oil may boost the government's revenues, but why should it cause the state to grow more quickly than the rest of the economy? How come oil production does not lead to equally fast growth in the private sector? In fact, economic theories popular in the 1950s and 1960s suggested that resource booms typically produce a diversified pattern of growth in private enterprise.[24] Yet the private-sector benefits of oil booms largely come from increased government spending, especially in low-income countries. Understanding the reason helps explain why oil causes governments to grow *relative* to the private sector: while oil boosts the government's revenues, it does much less to help—and can even harm—other industries in the private sector.

There are three forces behind this odd pattern. The first is government ownership of oil reserves. If a country's subsoil assets were privately owned, extracting petroleum would enrich private companies more and governments less. The state's sovereign rights over oil deposits helps limit the impact of oil production on the private sector.

The second is the "enclave" nature of most oil projects. Even when the state controls the extraction, processing, and transportation of petroleum, we still might expect these activities to stimulate growth in other parts of a country's economy.

But the petroleum business typically operates in an enclave. In some cases, companies literally work in geographic enclaves—isolated, self-contained areas like offshore oil-drilling rigs. This is not always true, though. Sometimes the machinery of oil extraction stretches for hundreds or thousands of miles. According to one study, in 2006 Nigeria had 5,284 onshore and offshore wells, 7,000 kilometers of pipelines, 275 flow stations, ten gas plants, ten export terminals, four refineries, and three gas liquefaction plants.[25] Still, oil production generally takes place in an *economic* enclave, meaning it has few direct effects on the rest of the economy.[26]

To highlight this problem, consider for a moment a different type of economic activity: manufacturing. Growth in a country's manufacturing sector will stimulate growth in the rest of the economy through at least three pathways: its employees will buy goods and services produced by other firms (the "employment effect"); its employees will learn skills that they can take to future jobs (the "learning-by-doing" effect); and

---

[24]Spengler 1960; North 1955; Watkins 1963.

[25]Lubeck, Watts, and Lipschutz 2007.

[26]This problem, and the need for "fiscal linkages" to replace the missing "forward" and backward" linkages between the mineral sector and the rest of the economy, was first articulated in Hirschman 1958.

the manufacturing companies themselves will buy goods from other companies, to use as inputs for their products (the "backward linkage" effect). Studies in a wide range of countries have documented the scale and importance of these spillover effects.[27]

Yet none of these three pathways work well in the oil sector, for two reasons.

First, oil exploration and production are extraordinarily capital intensive: they use a lot of expensive equipment but relatively little labor.[28] Saudi Arabia is the world's largest petroleum producer, and oil and gas account for about 90 percent of the country's GDP. Yet the entire petroleum and minerals sector employs just 1.6 percent of the active labor force, and 0.35 percent of the total population.[29] The growing popularity of offshore drilling is making the industry even more capital intensive. A single deepwater platform can cost over $500 million to build and may rent for over $200 million a year. Once in place, however, it operates with fewer than two hundred people, often expatriates, who live aboard the rig.[30]

One way to measure capital intensity is to divide a company's investments in property and equipment by the number of workers it hires. A recent study of US businesses operating overseas found that textile companies made $13,000 worth of investments per employee, making it the industry with the lowest capital intensity. Oil and gas companies spent $3.2 million per employee, making it by far the most capital-intensive industry (see figure 2.7).[31]

Since the oil sector creates relatively few local jobs, both the employment and learning-by-doing effect tend to be small.

Second, oil producers buy relatively few inputs from local firms and thus generate few backward linkages to the local economy. Oil companies use a lot of equipment, but this equipment tends to be highly specialized and manufactured in high-income countries. Most deepwater drilling rigs, for example, are made in Singapore or South Korea. For

---

[27] Javorcik 2004; Moran 2007. In theory, companies can also create "forward linkages" by providing low-cost inputs for other industries, which would make them more competitive. In practice, studies rarely find these linkages to have much effect.

[28] In fact, this is one reason why oil triumphed over coal in the 1950s as the world's leading source of fuel. Since coal production was labor intensive, it was more susceptible to labor strikes and hence supply disruptions. Strikes among coal miners in the United States and Europe in the early postwar period encouraged many businesses to switch from coal to petroleum, which required fewer workers and was less vulnerable to strikes. See Yergin 1991, 543–45.

[29] International Labor Organization 2005.

[30] Williams 2006.

[31] Schultz 2006.

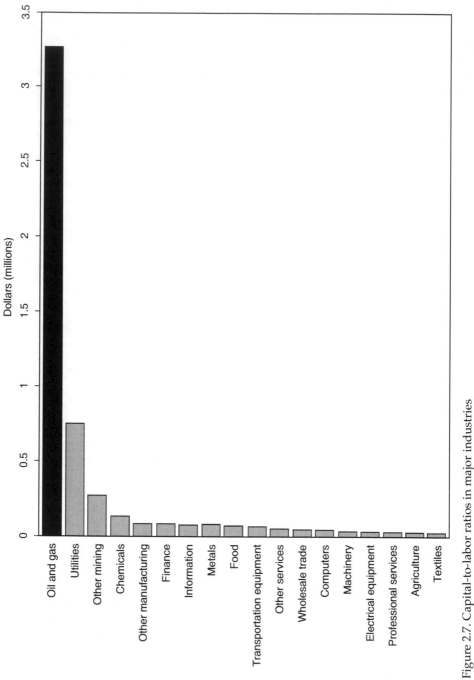

Figure 2.7. Capital-to-labor ratios in major industries

These bars show the amount of money (in million US$) invested per employee by US businesses operating overseas.

Source: Schultz 2006.

many companies, their main local "purchase" is the right to extract oil, which they buy directly from the government.

Thanks to these two qualities, oil production—and by extension, oil companies—can have a surprisingly small impact on the private sector, particularly in low-income countries. In the Republic of Congo, for instance, oil production has long accounted for about one-third of the economy. Yet a recent IMF study found that between 1960 and 2004, oil production had no direct impact on the growth of the non-oil economy.[32]

In his book *Crude World*, journalist Peter Maass describes his visit to a $1.5 billion natural gas facility in Equatorial Guinea that was built and operated by Houston-based Marathon Oil, and almost entirely staffed by foreign workers:

> The plant—like many oil installations in the developing world— could have been on the moon for all the benefit it offered local businesses. . . . Instead of buying cement from a Malabo company that might not deliver on time, Marathon built a small cement factory on the construction site. Raw materials were imported, and the factory would be dismantled when construction ended. The trailers in which (foreign workers) lived were prefab units—no local materials or local labor had been used to build them. The plant had its own satellite phone network, which was connected to the company's Texas network—if you picked up a phone you would be in the Houston area code, and dialing a number in Malabo would be an international call. The facility also had its own power plant and water-purification and sewage system. It existed off the local grid.[33]

Finally, oil often fails to boost private-sector growth due to the "Dutch Disease." The *Economist* magazine coined the term in November 1977 to describe the effect of natural gas exports on the Dutch economy. But the underlying syndrome was first noticed in the nineteenth century following the California gold rush of 1849 and the Australian gold rush of 1851.

William Newmarch, a banker (and ironically, an occasional writer for the *Economist*) argued that these gold-mining booms would stimulate other sectors of the US and Australian economies. But Irish economist John Elliot Cairnes made a surprising prediction: that a gold rush would not merely fail to stimulate the rest of the economy, as we might surmise from the enclave effect, but rather would *harm* other businesses by causing a drop in production. Cairnes's contention turned out to be

---

[32] Bhattacharya and Ghura 2006.
[33] Maass 2009, 35–36.

right, providing economists with some of their earliest insights into the Dutch Disease.[34]

Journalists sometimes use the terms Dutch Disease and "Resource Curse" interchangeably, to refer to all hardships that can be linked to resource exports. For economists, the term Dutch Disease has a narrower definition: it is the process that causes a boom in a country's natural resource sector to produce a decline in its manufacturing and agricultural sectors.

This decline is the result of two effects. The first is the "resource movement effect": as the resource sector booms, it draws labor and capital away from the agricultural and manufacturing sectors and raises their production costs. The second is the "spending effect": as money from the booming resource sector enters the economy, it raises the real exchange rate. A higher real exchange rate makes it cheaper to import agricultural and manufactured goods than to produce them domestically.

As a result, the manufacturing and agricultural sectors may lose a share of the domestic market, thanks to competition from cheaper imports, and they will find it harder to compete on world markets, thanks to higher production costs and the higher real exchange rate. Goods and services that cannot be imported (i.e., "nontradable goods," like construction, security, and education) are protected from these effects, and suffer no harm. A boom in resource exports therefore will lead to a drop in the relative size of the agricultural and manufacturing sectors, other things being equal.[35]

There is little doubt that the Dutch Disease is real. After the booms of the 1970s, the Dutch Disease hurt the agricultural and manufacturing sectors of many oil-exporting countries, including Algeria, Colombia, Ecuador, Nigeria, Trinidad, and Venezuela.[36] In Nigeria, the Dutch Disease caused the value of agricultural production to fall from the early 1970s to the mid-1980s, and it devastated industries built on the export of cocoa, palm oil, and rubber.[37] In Algeria, booming oil exports led to a drop in manufactured exports twice—first in the late 1970s, and again in the late 1990s and early 2000s.

From a purely economic perspective, the Dutch Disease is not as grave as its name implies. According to the theory of comparative advantage, a rise in oil and gas exports *should* crowd out other types of exports, since it connotes a shift in a country's comparative advantage.

[34] Bordo 1975.
[35] Corden and Neary 1982; Neary and van Wijnbergen 1986.
[36] Gelb and Associates 1988; Auty 1990.
[37] Bevan, Collier, and Gunning 1999.

If the income generated by the oil sector is greater than the income lost in manufacturing and agriculture—which should be true, according to simple economic models—the country should still be better off.[38]

The Dutch Disease can nonetheless be harmful if oil production has negative spillovers, or agriculture and manufacturing have positive spillovers, that might not show up in a simple economic analysis. If so, then a country with a larger oil sector along with a smaller agricultural or manufacturing sector might suffer in other ways—for example, by having more economic volatility, less democracy, fewer opportunities for women, and more violent conflict. Once these problems are factored in, the Dutch Disease becomes much more worrisome.

For the moment, though, notice how the Dutch Disease affects the size of the government as a fraction of the economy: since oil sectors are generally owned by governments, oil wealth expands the government; since agricultural and manufacturing sectors are typically in private hands, their declining profitability will reduce the size of the private sector. The Dutch Disease helps shift the country's economic activities from the private sector to the government.

What about the other major sector of the economy—the service sector? During oil booms, a country's service sector tends to thrive. Since it provides the economy with things that cannot be easily imported—like construction services, health care, and retail stores—the service sector should be unharmed by a rise in the exchange rate. In countries with exceptional oil wealth, most of the private sector is typically made up of service companies. According to World Bank data for 1990—the most recent year with relatively complete data—in the OPEC countries, 56 percent of the workforce was employed by the service sector; outside the OPEC countries, the average was 40 percent.[39] In oil-producing countries, these service companies often depend on government contracts—for example, to build state-funded projects like roads, bridges, and hospitals, and provide services to the oil industry.

In short, the Dutch Disease tends to make some industries (agriculture and manufacturing) smaller and more dependent on government help, and others (services) larger, partly through government contracts. Together with the enclave effect, the Dutch Disease helps explain why oil wealth does surprisingly little to aid other parts of the economy, and why the surviving businesses become more reliant on the government.

[38] Matsen and Torvik 2005.
[39] World Bank 2004.

THE STABILITY OF OIL REVENUES

The third feature of oil revenues is their instability: they can soar or plummet unexpectedly. This volatility is produced by a combination of three factors: changes in oil prices, changes in production rates, and the contracts between governments and oil companies, which can either smooth or heighten these fluctuations.

Changing Prices

In January 1861, scarcely a year after oil was discovered in Titusville, Pennsylvania, it sold for ten dollars a barrel; over the next twelve months the price dropped by 99 percent, to ten cents a barrel.[40] The price of oil has been oscillating ever since.

Much of this price volatility can be traced to a simple economic fact: in the short run, both the supply of and demand for petroleum are price inelastic. This means that neither suppliers nor consumers can quickly adjust to changes in prices by changing the amount of oil they supply or consume. When prices rise, for instance, it can take years for producers to extract more oil, since the up-front investments are so large and take many years to bear fruit.[41] It also takes months or years for consumers to reduce their fuel use—for example, by insulating their homes or buying more fuel-efficient vehicles.[42]

Thanks to these inelasticities, a minor change in supply or demand can have a major effect on prices. A small drop in the supply of oil—perhaps due to unexpected violence in Iraq, Libya, or Nigeria—can produce a spike in prices. Similarly, a modest rise in demand can cause prices to soar. Even the expectation of changes in supply and demand can cause prices to swing, thanks to the resulting purchases or sales by market speculators. The price of oil is more volatile than the price of 95 percent of all products sold in the United States.[43]

Oil markets have also had periods of stability. Figure 2.8 shows how the annual price of a barrel of oil, adjusted for inflation, changed between 1861 and 2009. During the industry's first century, prices gradually became steadier. The greatest stability occurred between 1935 and 1969, when the real price of oil rose or fell by an average of 5.9 percent

---

[40] Yergin 1991.

[41] If oil suppliers have unused production capacity, they can bring additional oil to the market more quickly. Even this can take months to accomplish, due to bottlenecks in refining and transportation.

[42] Smith 2009.

[43] See Kilian 2008; Regnier 2007.

Figure 2.8. Price of a barrel of oil, 1861–2009
Oil prices are in constant 2005 dollars.
Source: BP 2010.

a year, and there was just one year (1947) when prices changed by more than 20 percent. But since 1970, the price of oil has changed by an *average* of 26.5 percent a year. Before the 1970s, no one bothered to forecast oil prices, since they changed so little; after 1973, oil price forecasting became a major enterprise, albeit one with a dismal track record.[44]

The return of price volatility around 1970 was the result of three factors.

The first was the wave of nationalizations that swept the oil-producing countries in the 1960s and 1970s. From the 1930s to the 1960s, the companies that dominated the international oil trade were able to keep global prices stable by boosting or cutting production to match changes in demand.[45] When there was a global oil glut in the 1960s, they limited production in the Persian Gulf, particularly in Iraq, and accepted lower profits to keep prices from collapsing. But the rising power of oil-producing governments in the 1960s and 1970s deprived these

[44]Some economists suggest that since 1973, oil prices approximate a "random walk"—meaning that the best predictor of next year's price is this year's price, but that even this prediction is spectacularly inaccurate. See Engel and Valdés 2000; Hamilton 2008.
[45]Levy 1982.

companies of their control over global petroleum supplies, and hence their ability to keep prices stable.

The nationalizations of the 1960s and 1970s caused the petroleum industry to become—for the first time in a century—*less* vertically integrated. The international companies that controlled global shipping and marketing no longer controlled production. The state-owned companies that now controlled production were free to sell their oil to the highest bidder, taking advantage of the new "spot market" that allowed investors to buy and sell individual oil shipments.[46] Since market forces instead of long-term contracts increasingly determined oil prices, prices could fluctuate freely to reflect shifts in supply and demand.

The second factor was the demise of the Bretton Woods system of fixed exchange rates. In the decades after World War II, the Bretton Woods system limited changes in the value of national currencies and hence helped dampen fluctuations in commodity prices, which were usually denominated in dollars. When the fixed exchange rate system broke down in 1971, the value of the dollar began to fluctuate. This made international commodity prices, which were denominated in dollars, much more erratic.[47]

Finally, the rise in volatility was the result of increasingly tight oil supplies. From the 1940s to the 1960s, the discovery of massive new oil fields—largely in the Middle East—allowed global production to grow as quickly as global consumption. But by 1970, the industry's production capacity was expanding more slowly, even though the demand for oil continued to boom.

The position of the United States was especially influential. From the 1860s to the mid-1970s, the United States was both the world's leading oil producer and its leading consumer.[48] But in October 1970, US production reached its historic peak and then began a steady decline; at the same time, US consumption continued to grow rapidly (see figure 2.9). US imports began to soar as a result, doubling from 1969 to 1973. Until 1970, the world had enough spare capacity to smoothly meet rising demand; after 1970, oil producers could no longer respond to rising demand by raising production, and instead raised prices.

All of these forces came together in 1973–74, when the real price of oil tripled. They doubled again in 1978–79. In the currency of the day, the price of oil rose from $1.80 a barrel in 1970 to over $36 a barrel in 1980.

---

[46] Leonardo Maugeri (2006) provides an especially good account of the emergence of the spot market.

[47] Cashin and McDermott 2002.

[48] Except for 1898 to 1901, when czarist Russia briefly outproduced the United States, according to Goldman 2008.

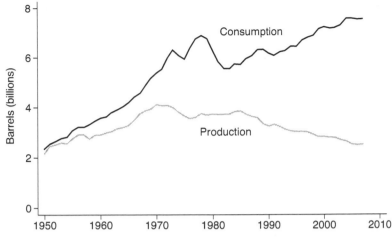

Figure 2.9. US petroleum production and consumption, 1947–2007
The lines show US consumption (upper line) and US production (lower line) in billions of barrels per year.
Source: Energy Information Administration, available at http://www.eia.doe.gov (accessed January 15, 2009).

According to contemporary observers, the 1973–74 oil shock was caused by the boycott organized by OPEC's Arab members, in response to the Yom Kippur War between Israel and its neighbors. But this explanation was incomplete. Two earlier Arab boycotts—one after the 1956 Suez Crisis, and the other following the 1967 Six-Day War—had little impact on global prices. The 1973–74 Arab oil boycott was different because the international oil companies had lost their capacity to boost production in the fields they once controlled, and because the United States had lost its position as the world's swing producer.[49]

In the 1970s, many policymakers believed that the world had entered a new era of chronically high oil prices. The 1972 Club of Rome report, *The Limits to Growth*, predicted that primary commodities would become increasingly scarce in the coming decades, giving the resource-rich countries a privileged slot in the international system.[50] According to economist John P. Lewis, the Club of Rome report "froze the attention of the public-affairs community of the world as nothing had before." Old arguments offered by a handful of economists in the 1950s

[49] Tetreault 1985.
[50] Meadows et al. 1972.

and early 1960s about the disadvantages of mineral wealth were seemingly disproved.[51]

Yet what looked like a new era of high oil prices turned out to be a new era of price volatility. Prices shot up in the 1970s, but from 1980 to 1986 the real price of oil dropped by more than two-thirds, as Western countries reduced their consumption and the Saudi government boosted production.

From 1986 to 1999, oil prices were relatively stable once again. Some industry observers argued that the oil shocks of the 1970s and the crash of the early 1980s were aberrations. In 2000, two leading analysts wrote that "long-term trends point to a prolonged oil surplus and low oil prices over the next two decades.[52] In the new millennium, though, oil prices boomed once more, rising from below $10 a barrel in January 1999 to over $145 a barrel in July 2008, before collapsing to less than $40 a barrel just five months later.[53]

Changing Production

A nation's oil revenues can also fluctuate due to changes in production. For example, when a country begins to extract oil or gas, rising production can lead to a flood of new revenues—which can overwhelm the government's capacity to use them wisely, as chapter 6 will point out.

Of course, production can also fall. Since countries have a limited stock of petroleum reserves, in the long run the number of barrels they pump from the ground will decline. Not every petroleum-rich country needs to worry about running out of oil in the foreseeable future. Those with the largest reserves, including Saudi Arabia, Kuwait, Iraq, and Iran, have enough to maintain their production levels for many decades, perhaps even centuries (see figure 2.10). But most oil-producing countries have smaller reserves, whose depletion could lead to falling incomes. Countries whose incomes are already low and that are dependent on revenue from their petroleum sectors face the greatest dangers. Several major oil and gas producers, including Indonesia, Ecuador, and Gabon, depleted most of their petroleum reserves in the 1980s and 1990s, although each enjoyed a reprieve due to subsequent discoveries. Other countries, like Syria, Bahrain, and Yemen, are expected to run out of petroleum in the near future.

[51]Lewis 1974, 69. See, for example, Prebisch 1950; Singer 1950; Nurske 1958; Levin 1960; Hirschman 1958. These and other studies are reviewed in Ross 1999.

[52]Jaffe and Manning 2000.

[53]These are spot market prices for Brent crude in current dollars, according to data posted on the Energy Information Administration Web site, available at http://www.eia.doe.gov (accessed April 13, 2010).

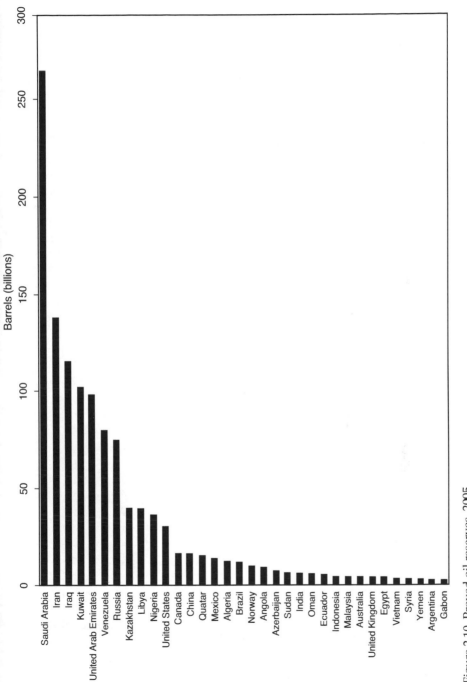

Figure 2.10. Proved oil reserves, 2005
These bars represent proved oil reserves, in billions of barrels; natural gas is not included.
Source: BP 2010.

In one way, changes in oil production are less worrisome than changes in prices, since they can be anticipated years in advance and do not cause the same level of uncertainty. But in another way they are more worrisome, because they create an additional problem for governments—the problem of compensating for the depletion of the country's mineral assets.

Countries whose income comes from depleting their natural resources are undergoing a fundamentally different process than those whose income comes from the production of goods and services. To better understand these differences, it is helpful to distinguish between income and wealth. An individual's income is their salary, while their wealth is the money they have saved. A country's income is the total value of the goods and services that it produces in a given year, while its wealth is its accumulated assets.

All countries have four types of wealth: physical capital, which includes roads, buildings, and other infrastructure; human capital, meaning the size, quality, and education of the labor force; social capital, which consists of the country's shared values, norms, and civic organizations; and natural capital, which is made up of its land, forests, and minerals.[54] Physical, human, and social capital all are renewable resources. If properly nurtured, they can generate income indefinitely.

Income from oil, however, comes almost entirely from a country's natural capital.[55] Some types of natural capital, like soil and forests, can be sustained indefinitely when properly maintained. Yet oil is a limited resource, and once exploited, cannot be regenerated. It is a nonrenewable form of wealth. When a country extracts and sells its oil, it is reducing its total stock of natural capital. Unless it replaces these assets with other forms of capital, such as roads and schools, the depletion of its oil will lead to a drop in the country's income.

Destabilizing Contracts

Changes in prices and production can partly explain why oil revenues are unstable, but the contracts that governments sign with oil companies also play a role. Contracts determine how much of the money generated by oil sales will go to the government, and how much to the private companies that help them extract, refine, and ship their petroleum.

[54] These categories roughly correspond to the classic division of factors of production into "land" (natural resources), "labor" (human and social capital), and "capital" (physical capital).

[55] Strictly speaking, the money earned from the sale of minerals should not even be classified as income but rather as revenues from the sale of assets. For an insightful analysis of this issue and how it often leads to confusion, see Heal 2007.

These contracts can either smooth out or aggravate the volatility caused by changing prices and production rates.[56]

To understand why these contracts matter, it is useful to think of the price of oil as having both fixed and variable components. Imagine that the price of oil fluctuates over time between $20 and $120 a barrel, with an average price of $70. The fixed component of the price is $20—since the price never falls below this point—while the variable component ranges from zero to $100, with an average value of $50.

If a contract divides the income from an oil well into these two components, whatever entity receives the fixed component will experience none of the price volatility, and whatever entity receives the variable component will experience all of it. In fact, the holder of the variable component will experience even more volatility than changes in the price would suggest. While the overall price of oil varies by a factor of six (from $20 to $120), the variable component might vary by a factor of one hundred (from $1 to $100). In the long run, the variable component generates more income than the fixed one, since its average value is $50, but coping with this volatility can be costly.

Until the 1950s, oil contracts gave governments a more or less fixed portion of the oil revenues, and the international companies a larger but more variable portion. While companies gained most of the benefits from oil extraction, they also incurred most of the risks, including that of price fluctuations. For example, a 1948 contract between Getty Oil and the Saudi Arabian government gave the government a fixed royalty of fifty-five cents a barrel, regardless of the world price—which at the time was about two dollars a barrel.[57] The Saudi government gained a steady and predictable income, but missed out on large windfall profits when prices were high. Getty sometimes gained large windfall profits, but also bore the risks of price fluctuations. This was one reason that the major companies worked so hard to stabilize prices by boosting or cutting production: because they bore most of the costs of price volatility.

When governments nationalized their oil sectors in the 1960s and 1970s, the terms of these contracts were largely reversed. Today foreign companies receive a relatively fixed part of the oil profits, while governments collect a larger, but more variable part. One study of an Angolan oil contract showed that a 50 percent rise in the price of oil would lead to an 82 percent increase in government revenues, but only

[56] These contracts are part of country's overall tax regime—the mix of taxes, royalties, and other fees that the government uses to collect revenues. The tax regime also affects the stability of government revenues: property taxes along with unit or ad valorem taxes produce a relatively steady stream of revenues; profit and income taxes create a more volatile flow of revenues (Barma, Kaiser, Le, and Viñeula 2011).

[57] Yergin 1991.

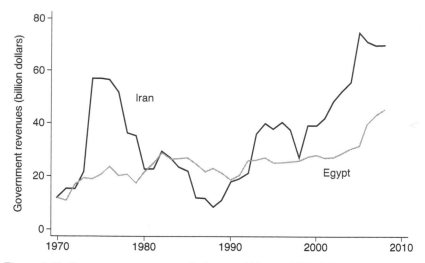

Figure 2.11. Government revenues in Iran and Egypt, 1970–2009
Sources: Central Bank of Egypt, annual reports; Central Bank of Iran, annual reports.

a 9 percent rise in revenues for the international oil company; a drop in oil prices would also produce an exaggerated fall in government revenues.[58] When the market booms, governments benefit disproportionately; when it collapses, they also lose disproportionately.[59]

Contracts affect revenue stability in other ways too. When a contract is finalized, governments frequently receive an immediate "signing bonus," which acts as a onetime windfall. Companies recoup the cost of these bonuses and other early investments by paying lower taxes or royalties during the early years of production. After receiving a signing bonus, a government thus may collect little oil income for the next few years—causing a boom and bust in government revenues, even if prices and production levels are steady.

Governments have little control over oil prices, but they have a lot of control over contracts. Yet instead of designing contracts that stabilize their revenues, most governments now sign contracts that seem to further destabilize their revenues.

Together these three features—changing prices, changing production, and destabilizing contracts—make the budgets of oil states un-

---

[58] Shaxson 2005.
[59] Michael Shafer (1983) made this point long ago, in analyzing the disastrous consequences for both Zambia and the Democratic Republic of Congo of nationalizing their copper industries.

usually volatile. Figure 2.11 compares government revenues in oil-rich Iran to oil-poor Egypt. In 1970, their governments each collected about $12 billion in revenues (in constant 2009 dollars). Since then, Iran's revenues have grown faster, but have also been more volatile—more than tripling from 1972 to 1974, falling by more than 80 percent from 1974 to 1988, then rising quickly but erratically from 1988 to 2005. Egypt's revenues have also grown, but more slowly and smoothly.

THE SECRECY OF OIL REVENUES

Oil revenues are unusually easy for governments to conceal. Many democracies make their oil revenues known to the public: Brazil, New Zealand, Norway, and the US state of Alaska are models of revenue transparency.[60] But most undemocratic oil producers, and some partially democratic ones like Iran and Venezuela, take advantage of the slippery nature of oil revenues to keep them out of the public view. One analysis found that "secrecy in the extractive industries is so commonplace that until recently, neither states nor companies have felt compelled to develop sophisticated arguments to defend it."[61]

Secrecy is intrinsically hard to measure. There is no easy way to document how much money a government is concealing from the public. Still, many country-level studies show that the finances of resource-rich countries are unusually opaque.[62] A recent analysis of Cameroon, for example, found that just 46 percent of its oil revenues between 1977 and 2006 were transferred to the budget; the remaining 54 percent could not be accounted for.[63] A 2010 survey of budget policies in ninety-four countries around the world found that the national budgets of hydrocarbon-dependent countries were dramatically less transparent than those of other countries.[64]

The exceptional secrecy of the oil states can be traced in part to their use of unreported off-budget accounts. Oil-funded governments often use these accounts to keep a large fraction of their spending off the

---

[60]See Revenue Watch Institute 2010.

[61]Rosenblum and Maples 2009, 12.

[62]On the secrecy and misuse of petroleum revenues in Angola, Cambodia, Congo-Brazzaville, Equatorial Guinea, Kazakhstan, and Turkmenistan, see reports by Global Witness, a London-based NGO, available at http://www.globalwitness.org. On similar problems in Chad and Nigeria, see reports by another NGO, Publish What You Pay, available at http://www.publishwhatyoupay.org.

[63]Gauthier and Zeufack 2009.

[64]International Budget Partnership 2008. I describe this survey more fully in chapter 3.

books, sometimes hidden in the crevices of national oil companies, whose finances are withheld from public scrutiny. For instance:

- Before he was overthrown in 1998, Indonesia's President Suharto used the national oil company, Pertamina, to covertly distribute benefits to his supporters. At its height, Pertamina controlled about one-third of the government's budget and was shielded from public disclosure.[65]
- During Saddam Hussein's rule, more than half of Iraq's national budget was funneled through the Iraqi National Oil Company, whose budget was secret.[66]
- In Azerbaijan, about half of the government's budget runs through the national oil company, known as SOCAR. The actual sum, once again, is secret.
- A large fraction of the Angolan government's budget goes through Sonangol, its national oil company. The amount has never been publicly disclosed, but a 1995 IMF analysis suggested it was about 40 percent of total government spending.[67]
- Mexico's ruling party from 1929 to 2000, the Institutional Revolutionary Party (PRI), relied heavily on funding from the national oil company, Petróleos Mexicanos (PEMEX).[68] During the 2000 elections, PEMEX reportedly funneled more than a hundred million dollars to the PRI reelection campaign through the oil workers' union.[69] The election was preceded by a sudden increase in PEMEX's discretionary disbursements to "civic associations, schools, foundations, agricultural communities, fishing cooperatives, unions, and municipal governments" in politically important regions.[70]
- When Libya's civil war broke out in early 2011, Colonel Muammar Qaddafi survived international sanctions by using "tens of billions" in cash that had been secretly hidden in Tripoli to fund loyalists and hire mercenaries. According to the *New York Times*, intelligence officials said it was hard to distinguish between the assets of the Libyan government, including its sovereign wealth fund, and the Qaddafi family's assets.[71]

---

[65] Crouch 1978.
[66] Alnasrawi 1994.
[67] Human Rights Watch 2004.
[68] Ascher 1999; Greene 2010.
[69] Schroeder 2002.
[70] Even after Mexico's transition to democracy in 2000, PEMEX donations have risen sharply in election years (Moreno 2007).
[71] Risen and Lichtblau 2011.

While the most egregious examples of off-budget financing come from authoritarian governments, the same syndrome can occur in partially democratic states. The Iranian government transfers oil profits to politically powerful figures through *bonyads*—semipublic enterprises that are nominally outside the government's purview and shielded from public disclosures.[72]

The example of Venezuela is even more telling. In the 1980s and 1990s, Venezuela's Petróleos de Venezuela S.A. (widely known by its acronym, PDVSA), was one of the world's most politically independent and well-managed national oil companies. In the early 2000s, President Hugo Chávez stripped PDVSA of its independent authority and replaced its top officials with loyal followers. He then placed PDVSA in charge of administering a new set of social programs, closely tied to his political machine. By 2004, two-thirds of PDVSA's budget went to social programs, not petroleum-related activities. As its social programs grew, PDVSA's transparency fell. After 2003, its financial disclosures dropped sharply, and independent observers found its activities increasingly difficult to monitor.[73]

The NOCs of Western democracies can be equally corrupt. In the mid-1990s, a series of audits revealed that France's national oil company, Elf Aquitaine, had been an important source of campaign financing for political parties, especially the Gaullist Rally for the Republic. John Heilbrunn notes that

> prosecutors uncovered evidence that a few managers at Elf had embezzled approximately 400 million Euros that they used to finance campaigns, bribe foreign politicians, and enrich themselves. In 2003 trials began for thirty-seven people implicated in the scandal. The scandal embroiled several former ministers and the French constitutional council's president, as well as former German president Helmut Kohl, Gabonese president Omar Bongo, and Congolese president Denis Sassou-Nguesso.[74]

Two of the industry's features, discussed above, help explain why oil revenues are so easy to conceal. Since oil reserves are state-owned property, companies can only gain access to them by negotiating detailed contracts with the government, often through national oil companies. These contracts are notoriously complex, but ultimately determine how much companies will pay.[75] Since the terms of these contracts are

[72] Brumberg and Ahram 2007; Mahdavi 2011.
[73] Mares and Altamirano 2007; International Crisis Group 2007.
[74] Heilbrunn 2005, 277.
[75] Johnston 2007; Radon 2007.

typically secret, it is nearly impossible for observers to know the size of these payments. Even though international companies could disclose the payments they make to governments, they rarely do so.[76] If oil reserves were not state owned, these negotiations would be unnecessary: companies would be able to buy oil rights the same way they buy land rights, and oil companies would be subject to the same tax laws as other companies.

The other feature is the prevalence of national oil companies, which have dominated the industry since the 1970s. State-owned enterprises of all kinds—in agriculture, manufacturing, and services—were far more common until the 1980s. In the 1980s and 1990s, however, most countries privatized a large fraction of their state-owned companies, which were widely seen as inefficient, corrupt, and a drain on government resources. In low-income states, the fraction of total employment accounted for by state-owned enterprises dropped from 20 percent in 1980 to 9 percent in 1997; it fell from 13 to 2 percent in middle-income countries.[77]

Yet in the oil business, there has been little movement toward privatization. In fact, high oil prices in the 2000s led to new nationalizations in Venezuela, Bolivia, Ecuador, and Russia.[78] In many undemocratic countries, NOC budgets are exempt from parliamentary oversight. The parliament's role in undemocratic states is of course already limited. Still, most authoritarian governments submit regular budget statements to their parliaments and the public; the budgets of NOCs are nevertheless typically excluded or summarized so tersely that little is revealed about their finances.

If benevolent accountants ran governments, the unusual qualities of oil revenues might not matter. But governments are ruled by self-interested politicians, who are deeply influenced by the kinds of funds at their disposal. States whose revenues are massive, unstable, opaque, and do not come from taxes, tend to have some strange qualities.

---

[76] Transparency International 2008.
[77] Guriev and Megginson 2007.
[78] Guriev, Kolotilin, and Sonin 2010; Duncan 2006; Kretzschmar, Kirchner, and Sharifzyanova 2010.

CHAPTER THREE

More Petroleum, Less Democracy

> The problem is that the good Lord didn't see fit to put oil and
> gas reserves where there are democratic governments.
> —former vice president Dick Cheney, 2000

IN JANUARY 2011, prodemocracy protests broke out across the Middle
East. For decades, the Middle East has had less democracy, and more
oil, than any other world region. This is no coincidence: oil-funded rulers have long used their petrodollars to entrench themselves in power
and block democratic reforms. Although protesters took to the streets
in almost every Arab country, they found it much easier to overthrow
rulers in oil-poor countries, like Tunisia and Egypt, than rulers in oil-
rich states, like Libya, Bahrain, Algeria, and Saudi Arabia.

Oil has not always been an impediment to democracy. Until the
1970s, oil producers were just as democratic—or undemocratic—as
other countries. But from the late 1970s to the late 1990s, a wave of democracy swept across the globe, bringing freedom to countries in virtually every region—except the petroleum-rich countries of the Middle
East, Africa, and the former Soviet Union. From 1980 to 2011, the democracy gap between the oil and non-oil states grew ever wider.

This chapter explains how oil has kept autocrats in power by enabling
them to increase spending, reduce taxes, buy the loyalty of the armed
forces, and conceal their own corruption and incompetence. Petroleum
does not *inevitably* block democratic freedoms: a handful of oil-rich
developing countries have still made transitions to democracy—most
recently, Mexico and Nigeria. Yet among the oil states—both in the
Middle East and beyond—transitions to democracy have been exceedingly rare. Oil and democracy do not easily mix.[1]

---

[1] Students of Middle Eastern politics have long been familiar with oil's corrosive effects on government accountability. Important studies of oil and authoritarian rule in
the Middle East include Mahdavy 1970; Entelis 1976; First 1980; Skocpol 1982; Beblawi
and Luciani 1987; Crystal 1990; Brand 1992; Anderson 1995; Gause 1995; Chaudhry 1997;
Vandewalle 1998; Okruhlik 1999; Herb 1999; Lowi 2009. Yet for many years, the largest
and most influential studies of global democracy said little about oil, and often avoided
the Middle East entirely. See, for example, O'Donnell, Schmitter, and Whitehead 1986;
Diamond, Linz, and Lipset 1988; Inglehart 1997; Przeworski et al. 2000.

The Sources of Democracy

No topic receives more attention from political scientists than democracy. But there is no consensus on the answers to many key questions, including what causes dictatorships to become democratic, and what causes democracies to become dictatorships. Even simple questions, like how democracy should be defined and measured, are widely debated.

Still, scholars agree on some key things.

Most would probably agree with Adam Przeworski and his colleagues that to qualify as a democracy, a country minimally must meet at least four conditions: the government's chief executive, whether a president or prime minister, must be elected; its legislature must be elected; there must be at least two large political parties that can freely compete in elections; and at least one incumbent government must have been defeated and then replaced by an elected successor.[2]

Scholars also agree that the number of democracies has grown over time (see figure 3.1). In the 1970s, the world had three dictatorships for every democracy. By the early 1990s, the number of democracies surpassed the number of dictatorships. Today almost 60 percent of the world's countries are democracies.

Explaining this trend toward democracy is more difficult, and different studies emphasize different causes. Putting aside the issue of oil, some of the key factors are:

- *Higher incomes.* Many studies find that when authoritarian states have higher incomes, they become more likely to transit to democracy.[3]
- *Slow economic growth.* According to some researchers, autocratic governments are more likely to become democracies in the face of economic crises.[4]
- *Geographic and temporal proximity.* Samuel Huntington famously observed that democratic transitions have occurred in "waves": neighboring states have frequently moved toward (or away from) democratic rule at about the same time—like in Latin America in the 1980s, Africa and Central and Eastern Europe in the 1990s, and even parts of the Middle East today. More recent studies have documented and developed explanations for these clustering effects. Other things being equal, one country's transition to democ-

---

[2] Przeworski et al. 2000.
[3] Lipset 1959; Londregan and Poole 1996; Epstein et al. 2006.
[4] Haggard and Kaufman 1995; Przeworski et al. 2000; Epstein et al. 2006.

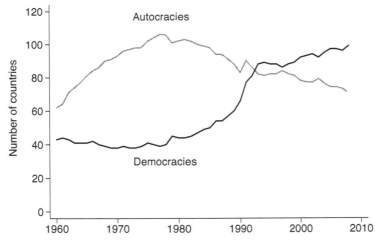

Figure 3.1. Number of democracies and autocracies, 1960–2008
The gray line is the number of autocratic countries in the world; the black line is the number of democracies.
Source: Calculated from data in Cheibub, Gandhi, and Vreeland 2010.

racy raises the likelihood that its neighbors will undergo a similar change.[5]

- *Islamic culture.* Many argue that Islamic culture and traditions are impediments to democracy, and that this explains why almost all countries in the Middle East and North Africa have long been undemocratic.[6]

Not all studies agree that these factors matter. Recent books by Carles Boix as well as Daron Acemoglu and James Robinson stress the role of inequality; a study by Acemoglu, Robinson, and their colleagues Simon Johnson and Pierre Yared emphasizes the quality of colonial rule and accumulation of historical idiosyncrasies.[7] Research on this issue is vibrant and controversial.

WHY SHOULD OIL MATTER?

Even after we account for all of the factors above, oil makes a difference: the more petroleum that an authoritarian country produces, the

[5] Huntington 1991; O'Loughlin et al. 1998; Gleditsch and Ward 2006.
[6] Salamé 1994; Hudson 1995; Midlarsky 1998; Fish 2002.
[7] Boix 2003; Acemoglu and Robinson 2005; Acemoglu et al. 2008.

less likely it will make the journey to democracy. Chapter 2 shows that producing oil has a potent effect on government revenues, but why should these revenues affect government accountability? To answer this question, we need a theory of democracy that looks at the role of fiscal issues.

Social scientists already know a lot about how politicians manipulate government finances, and how citizens respond to this manipulation, thanks to the study of political budget cycles. Many studies demonstrate that the fiscal policies of governments tend to fluctuate in tandem with elections, as politicians boost spending and cut taxes to win voters' support. Scholars have observed these cycles in a wide range of democracies, including in the United States, the advanced industrialized states more generally, and in Latin America. Budget cycles also occur in authoritarian states: even when elections are not competitive, autocrats still use the budget to boost their popularity at election time.[8]

Collectively, these studies imply that citizens tend to support governments with larger budgets and lower taxes. But what does this tell us about democratization?

We can glean some additional hints from studies that link the collection of taxes to the emergence of democratic governments. Some scholars argue that when autocrats raise taxes, it tends to trigger popular demands for representative government.[9] Evidence for this link comes from historians, who suggest that representative government arose in early modern Europe when monarchs in England, France, Spain, Austro-Hungary, and the Netherlands were compelled to relinquish part of their authority to parliaments, in exchange for the right to levy new taxes.[10]

Most US citizens are familiar with a different example. In the thirteen British colonies that became the United States, opposition to British taxes—especially the 1765 Stamp Act, which imposed a tax on many printed materials—catalyzed the movement for independence. Even though the tax was eventually repealed, the fact that King George had "impos(ed) taxes on us without our consent" was cited in the 1776 Declaration of Independence as one of the rebellion's key grievances, and ultimately led to the foundation of a sovereign government that was pledged to democratic principles.[11]

---

[8] On budget cycles in the United States, see Tufte 1978; Hibbs 1987. In the advanced industrialized states more generally, see Alesina, Roubini, and Cohen 1997. In Latin America, see Ames 1987. In authoritarian states, see Block 2002; Magaloni 2006; Blaydes 2006.

[9] Brennan and Buchanan 1980; Bates and Lien 1985; North 1990.

[10] See Schumpeter [1918] 1954; Hoffman and Norberg 1994; Morrison 2009.

[11] See Morgan and Morgan 1953; Bailyn 1967. Although the phrase "no taxation without representation" is closely identified with the American Revolution—and is today printed on automobile license plates in Washington, DC—it is not found in the Declaration of In-

In a 2004 study, I showed that in a modified version, the same dynamic still holds. The original claim implies that citizens only care about keeping their taxes low and that a dictator who raises taxes will be forced to democratize. Looking at tax levels in all countries from 1971 to 1997, I found no support for this assertion. But my statistical analysis found evidence to support a modified contention: that citizens object to paying higher taxes *if they do not receive commensurate benefits*.

This suggests that citizens care about *both* their taxes and government benefits. They do not necessarily want to minimize their tax burden, regardless of the consequences for their benefits. Nor do they wish to maximize their government benefits, regardless of what they must pay in taxes. Instead, they wish to simultaneously minimize the taxes they must pay while maximizing the benefits they receive. If taxes rise but government benefits do not, or if government benefits fall but taxes do not, citizens will protest.

This implies that citizens do not want minimal government but rather an efficient government—one that provides them with the greatest "bang for their buck." Authoritarian governments that kept taxes low *as a percentage of government spending* were more likely to avoid democratic transitions.[12]

The idea that a rise in taxes relative to government spending can produce democratizing rebellions is closely related to the notion of a political budget cycle. They both imply that citizens will support governments that provide them with more benefits and lower taxes, and try to replace ones that supply fewer benefits with higher taxes. If these tax rebellions occur in dictatorships, they can bring about transitions to democracy.

A FISCAL THEORY OF DEMOCRACY

These studies can tell us a lot about the impact of oil wealth on democracy. Since oil boosts the size of government revenues, it typically increases government benefits. Thanks to their unusual source—since

---

dependence or Constitution. John Adams used the phrase in what became known as the "Braintree Instructions," an influential statement against the Stamp Act in 1765, but it had already been in use in Ireland for a generation (McCullough 2001). Ironically, in 1820 the US Supreme Court appeared to reject the no taxation without representation claim when it ruled in *Loughborough v. Blake* that the federal government had the right to impose taxes on US territories that had no representation in Congress.

[12] Ross 2004a. Bryan Jones and Walter Williams (2008) show that this pattern is true in the United States today: voters express greater support for the government when the benefits-to-taxes ratio rises, which unfortunately tends to encourage politicians to run budget deficits.

these revenues do not come from taxes—governments can keep taxes low. The secrecy of oil revenues is also important. Yet before examining its role, let us take a more careful look at the logic that connects a country's oil wealth to the accountability of its government.

To make the argument about oil and democracy more explicit, it is useful to employ an informal model—that is, to describe these links in a simplified imaginary world.[13] The model includes a group of citizens who act collectively and can be treated as a single actor, and a ruler who controls the government. In each of the next three chapters I augment this model, using it to illustrate how oil revenues might lead to other outcomes, such as civil war, reduced opportunities for women, and inadequate economic policies.

Suppose that a ruler whose goal is to stay in power leads the government. To this end, the ruler uses his fiscal powers to build political support—by both spending money on patronage and public goods, and keeping taxes low. If the ruler fails to maintain enough support, a challenger will replace him, either through elections, if the country is a democracy, or a popular rebellion, if it is a dictatorship.

Citizens are concerned with their economic well-being, both now and in the future. Their support for the ruler is determined by the government's impact on their incomes: they favor governments that take little from them (in the form of taxes), but give them much (like patronage and public goods). If their government provides them with large benefits and low taxes, they will support the ruler; if it provides them with few benefits and high taxes, they will try to replace him.[14]

Under these conditions, what would happen to an authoritarian government in a country without oil? Assume for the moment that the government can run neither a surplus nor a deficit. Since all of the government's revenues come from taxes, there is a one-to-one ratio between the taxes it collects and the benefits it distributes. Suppose that when the economy is strong, the government is able to provide large enough benefits, with low enough taxes, to maintain public support; but when the economy slows, the government is forced to cut benefits or raise taxes, which causes the ruler to lose popularity.

If this imaginary country were a democracy, citizens could replace the ruling party through elections; but if it is an autocracy, they have no constitutional process for replacing a ruler they oppose—which means

[13] For a more formal treatment of this issue that differs from this account in important ways, see Morrison 2009.

[14] Theories of democracy and authoritarianism commonly focus on the distribution of patronage resources. See Gandhi and Lust-Okar 2009; Bueno de Mesquita and Smith 2010. Some also incorporate the autocrat's capacity to use violent repression—a factor that I omit. See Wintrobe 2007.

they must resort to strikes, demonstrations, or riots to force a leader from power.

Throwing out a dictator does not automatically turn a country into a democracy. But if we assume that citizens are forward-looking, they might look for ways to facilitate the removal of future governments should they become equally unpopular—in other words, to push for democratic reforms. Democratic reforms might also arise if a poorly performing dictator agrees to constraints on his powers to forestall his removal. Over time, the proclivity of citizens to overthrow low-performing autocrats, and their wariness about the performance of future autocrats, should lead to a process of democratization.[15]

Now consider the impact of oil. Oil production leads to a rise in nontax revenues—enabling governments to deliver more benefits to citizens than they collect in taxes. In countries without oil (or other sources of nontax revenues), governments can only push total benefits above total taxes by running budget deficits—a strategy that may work at election time, but is typically unsustainable over the long run. But oil-rich countries can indefinitely provide more benefits than they collect in taxes, allowing them to maintain popular support and avoid democratizing rebellions. While autocracies without oil gradually become democratic, autocracies with oil can remain autocratic.[16]

So far the model rests on an important assumption: that citizens care a lot about how their government uses its tax revenues, but are indifferent to how it spends its oil revenues. But is this true? Anyone familiar with oil-rich countries knows that their citizens care passionately about getting their fair share of these revenues. Chapter 2 notes that people in oil-rich states have strongly supported the nationalization of foreign oil companies to ensure that the oil rents are not sent abroad. As we will see in chapter 5, they sometimes take up arms to gain a larger fraction of these revenues. In his analysis of Persian Gulf monarchies, Michael Herb points out,

> It is sometimes suggested that the citizens of the oil monarchies feel gratitude to their rulers for giving them the money, and that this gratitude translates into political support. Yet gratitude results from the

---

[15] There are other ways to explain how the overthrow of an unpopular dictator might lead to a democratic transition—for instance, if there was no alternative figure with enough popular support or coercive power to reestablish a dictatorship (see Olson 1993).

[16] It may seem odd that citizens would reward or punish their rulers for events beyond the government's control, like high or low world oil prices. Yet recent studies suggest this is how voters behave. Christopher Achen and Larry Bartels (2004) show that US voters are less likely to support incumbents after droughts, floods, and shark attacks—unfortunate events that incumbents had no control over.

receipt of a gift. The Gulf Arabs, however, think that they themselves, as citizens, own the oil, *not* the ruling families. . . . Few are particularly grateful on receipt of something they think is theirs in the first place.[17]

Most people in oil-producing countries seem to recognize that they have a right to benefit from their nation's mineral wealth. It makes little sense to pretend that they do not care.

Perhaps people do not really care about their government's spending-to-*taxation* ratio but rather its spending-to-*revenue* ratio. In countries without oil, all of the government's revenues come from taxes—hence, its spending-to-revenue ratio is identical to its spending-to-taxation ratio, and the original model is unchanged. But citizens in oil-producing countries know that their governments have another source of revenue, and they care about how it is spent. If they believe their government delivers too few services, given the size of its revenues, they will rebel.

There is, however, a catch. Chapter 2 explains that oil revenues are unusually easy for governments to conceal, since they are set by secret contracts and often channeled through off-budget accounts. Citizens know their governments receive *some* petroleum revenues; they do not know *how much*.

So far I have assumed that citizens have "complete information" about their government. They have a good idea of what it spends, which is plausible, since they can observe its programs and projects, and they have a good idea of what it collects in taxes, which makes sense because they must pay these taxes.[18]

Citizens in oil-producing countries, though, cannot directly observe how much their government collects in oil revenues. They must rely on the government and media for their information. If they live in a democracy, this information is probably available.[19] If they live in an autocracy, their government can conceal some of these revenues, and if citizens fail to realize the magnitude of their government's oil revenues, they will mistakenly conclude that it is performing well, using its relatively modest revenues to deliver a generous array of goods and services. By hiding some of their oil revenues, rich autocrats can increase their government's *perceived* spending-to-revenue ratio.

---

[17] Herb 1999, 241.

[18] While people cannot observe each other's income taxes, they can observe the general level of taxes on goods and services, which constitute a larger fraction of tax revenues in low- and middle-income countries. Public discourse about the shared tax burden is often part of both popular and political culture. See, for example, Scott 1976.

[19] On the transparency of democratic governments, see Rosendorf and Vreeland 2006.

All autocrats, whether or not they have oil revenues, probably benefit from secrecy. But autocrats in the oil states have more to gain from secrecy, because it allows them to fool their citizens into underestimating the size of the government's revenues. This implies that autocrats in the oil states will be more inclined to camouflage their budgets and impose tight restrictions on the media than autocrats in non-oil states.

In short, rulers in general and autocrats in particular remain in power when citizens believe that their governments are delivering a lot of benefits relative to their revenues. In non-oil countries, this means that they are receiving sufficient benefits from their taxes. In oil countries, this means that they are receiving sufficient benefits from both their taxes and the government's oil revenues. Since citizens can observe taxes but not petroleum revenues, autocrats in oil-producing countries can boost their own popularity by concealing a portion of their oil revenues from the public.

What happens if governments lose their capacity to hide the flow of petrodollars? Greater transparency could spark democratic uprisings, if citizens start to notice that the ruler is squandering the nation's petroleum wealth. Whether or not these uprisings succeed may depend on an additional factor: the loyalty of the armed forces. Richard Snyder's 1992 study of uprisings against "neopatrimonial dictatorships" points out that the unity and loyalty of the military can determine the fate of popular revolutions.[20] Here again, the size of the state's oil revenues may help block transitions to democracy: when autocrats are better financed and directly control the distribution of benefits to the military, they are more likely to retain the backing of the armed forces and extinguish any rebellions.

A LOOK AT THE DATA

In this chapter's appendix, I use multivariate regressions to look at the statistical relationship between oil and democracy. But the basic links between oil and democracy can be illustrated with simple cross-tabulations and graphs.

There is strong evidence that when autocracies have more oil, they are less likely to transit to democracy. Table 3.1 shows the central pattern. The numbers in the cells represent the percentage of authoritarian states that transited to democracy in an average year. The first column

---

[20] Snyder 1992.

TABLE 3.1
Transitions to democracy, 1960–2006

These numbers show the percentage of authoritarian states that became democratic in an average year.

	Non-oil producers	Oil producers	Difference
All countries and periods	2.22	1.19	−1.02**
By income			
Low income (below $5,000)	2.41	1.52	−0.89*
High income (above $5,000)	1.35	0.73	−0.63
By period			
1960–79	1.13	1.33	0.20
1980–2006	3.18	1.14	−2.04***
By region			
Latin America	4.30	11.27	6.96***
All other regions	1.93	0.43	−1.50***

*significant at 10%, in a one-tailed t-test
**significant at 5%
***significant at 1%
Source: Calculated from data in Cheibub, Gandhi, and Vreeland 2010.

shows the non-oil states, the second depicts the oil states, and the third captures the difference.[21]

The first row shows that authoritarian states without oil had a 2.2 percent chance each year of transiting to democracy; authoritarian states with oil had just a 1.2 percent chance. The next two rows show that the pattern affects rich and poor oil producers alike, although it only reaches statistical significance among poor states.

Some studies argue that the net impact of oil wealth (or oil dependence) on democracy is ambiguous: while it may hinder democratic transitions through some channels, it promotes democratization through others.[22] These numbers suggest that oil's net impact on democratization has been strongly negative.

---

[21] I use the database in Przeworski et al. 2000—updated in Cheibub, Gandhi, and Vreeland 2010—to determine whether a country is democratic or authoritarian, and when it transits from one to the other.

[22] Herb 2004; Dunning 2008; Goldberg, Wibbels, and Mvukiyehe 2009.

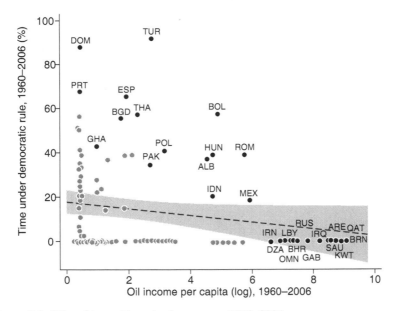

Figure 3.2. Oil and transitions to democracy, 1960–2006
Each point represents a country that was under autocratic rule in 1960, or if it achieved independence after 1960, was under autocratic rule in its first year of independence. The vertical axis represents the percentage of its subsequent history that it dwelled under democratic rule. Countries with higher percentages made early transitions to democracy, and remained democratic; countries at the bottom never made democratic transitions.
Source: Calculated from data in Cheibub, Gandhi, and Vreeland 2010.

Another way to look at the data is with a scatterplot that includes all countries that could have made transitions from authoritarianism to democracy between 1960 and 2008, including all 64 countries that were under authoritarian rule in 1960, plus the 50 countries that became independent after 1960 and were under authoritarian rule in their first year of independence. Figure 3.2 displays the petroleum income of these 114 countries, along with their progress—or lack thereof—toward democracy. The values on the horizontal axis represent their average oil income between 1960 and 2008; the values on the vertical axis denote the percentage of the time (since either 1960 or their first year of independence) that these initially authoritarian countries dwelled under a democratic government. Those that were continuously authoritarian have a score of zero; those that transited to democracy early and stayed democratic have scores approaching one hundred.

TABLE 3.2
Democratic transitions among oil-producing countries, 1946–2010

This table depicts the countries with the greatest oil wealth to make the transition from authoritarian to democratic rule since 1946. The transition is coded as a failure if the country subsequently reverted to authoritarian rule, and as a success if it remained democratic as of 2010. The oil income figures are for the year of transition.

Country	Year	Oil income	Outcome
Venezuela	1958	1,717	Success
Nigeria	1979	1,007	Failure
Ecuador	1979	773	Failure
Congo Republic	1992	563	Failure
Mexico	2000	442	Success
Argentina	1983	428	Success
Peru	1980	336	Failure
Bolivia	1982	307	Success
Ecuador	2002	280	Success
Bolivia	1979	264	Failure

Source: Calculated from data in Cheibub, Gandhi, and Vreeland 2010.

The downward-sloping line shows the overall relationship between oil and authoritarian durability: the greater a country's oil income was, the less likely it transited to (and stayed) democratic.[23] Countries that transited to democracy early and remained democratic, like the Dominican Republic, Turkey, Portugal, and Spain, had little or no oil. A handful of countries with modest oil and gas wealth, such as Bolivia, Romania, and Mexico, had more recent (and sometimes more erratic) transitions to democracy. But no country with high levels of oil and gas income successfully became a democracy between 1960 and 2010.

Thankfully, oil wealth does not *necessarily* stop democratization. Table 3.2 lists the top-ten oil producers, ranked by oil income, to move from authoritarian to democratic rule since 1946. Venezuela's 1958 transition is at the top of the list. The next three oil producers to democratize were Nigeria (1979), Ecuador (1979), and the Republic of Congo (1992); all

[23] The shaded area represents the 95 percent confidence interval.

of these transitions were later reversed. Nigeria and Ecuador subsequently returned to democracy, but only after their oil income fell to much lower levels. This highlights the unusual quality of Venezuela's success. Since Venezuela's 1958 transition, no country with more oil income than Mexico in 2000 has become and remained democratic.

Oil and Democracy over Time

As chapter 2 showed, there was a dramatic rise in the size of oil revenues in the 1970s, thanks to both skyrocketing prices and the nationalization of foreign oil companies. The increase in oil revenues coincided with a drop in the likelihood that oil states would become democratic.

Let me return for a moment to table 3.1. When the whole forty-seven-year period in the first row is taken into consideration, the oil-producing states are about 40 percent less likely than the non-oil-producing states to transit to democracy. But if we divide the 1960–79 period from the 1980–2006 one (rows four and five), we see a striking difference. Before 1980, the oil states and the non-oil states were equally likely—or rather, equally unlikely—to become democracies; the difference between these two groups is not statistically significant. Since 1980, the democratization rate among non-oil producers has almost tripled; the democratization rate among oil producers has remained the same. The non-oil states are now almost three times more likely to become democracies.

We can also revisit figure 3.1, which shows the steady rise in the number of democracies since the 1970s. When we separate the long-term oil producers from the rest of the world—in figure 3.3—we see a much different pattern: while the rest of the world has democratized, there has been little change among the long-term oil and gas producers.[24] The celebrated "third wave" of democratic transitions in the 1980s and 1990s left most of the oil states untouched. Almost all the increase in global democracy since 1979 has come from the non-oil states.

---

[24] It is sometimes hazardous to generalize about the characteristics of "oil states," since membership in this group changes over time. To get around this problem, I periodically focus on the thirty-five countries that can be classified as "long-term oil producers." I code countries as long-term producers if they generated at least a hundred dollars per capita (in constant 2000 dollars) in petroleum income for two-thirds of the years between 1960 and 2006, or if they became sovereign after 1960, for two-thirds of their sovereign years. These countries are marked with asterisks in table 1.1. In chapter 6, I look at the economic performance of these long-term producers.

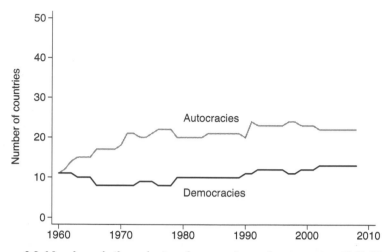

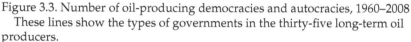

Figure 3.3. Number of oil-producing democracies and autocracies, 1960–2008
These lines show the types of governments in the thirty-five long-term oil producers.

Source: Calculated from data in Cheibub, Gandhi, and Vreeland 2010.

This means that petroleum-rich countries have made up a growing fraction of the world's remaining authoritarian states. In 1980, oil producers constituted just over 25 percent (27 of 103) of the world's autocracies; by 2008, they made up over 40 percent (30 of 74). For democracy advocates, the effects of oil have become increasingly salient.[25]

Did oil have *any* antidemocratic effects before 1980? It is hard to be certain. According to the regression analysis in appendix 3.1, it depends on how you measure democracy. Using one indicator, oil had significant but milder antidemocratic effects between 1960 and 1980 once other variables are controlled for; using a different indicator, oil had no effect at all.[26]

Perhaps figure 3.4 can provide a simpler answer. It compares the average democracy scores of long-term oil producers to all other countries over time. Democracy scores range from one to ten, with higher scores indicating greater democracy. The numbers are based on a widely used measure of democracy, called Polity IV.[27] Until the early 1980s, the oil and non-oil states had virtually identical scores; since then, the gap between the two has steadily grown wider.

[25] See, for example, Diamond 2008.
[26] Marshall and Jaggers 2007; Przeworski et al. 2000.
[27] Marshall and Jaggers 2007.

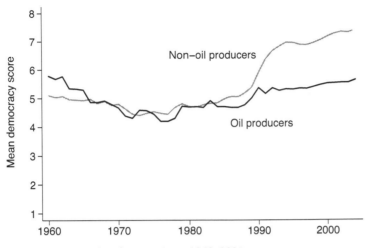

Figure 3.4. Democracy levels over time, 1960–2004

These lines show the mean Polity scores of long-term oil producers (black line) and non-oil producers (gray line). Polity scores have been rescaled to range from one to ten, with higher numbers indicating greater democracy.

Source: Calculated from data in Marshall and Jaggers 2007.

Spending and Revenues

There is also *some* evidence that authoritarian governments with higher government spending-to-revenues ratios will be less likely to democratize. Unfortunately, accurate figures on spending and revenues are scarce, which makes this argument hard to evaluate. And according to the model, what matters most is the *perception* of the government's revenues, not the government's actual ones—and without surveys, these perceptions cannot be measured.[28]

Still, the existing data on government spending and revenues is suggestive. Figure 3.5 compares the government spending-to-revenues ratios of authoritarian states that have never transited to democracy (the first column) with those that subsequently became democratic (the second column); countries that have never transited have ratios almost twice as high. The third column records the spending-to-revenues ratios of this second group in the year before their transitions to democracy; their ratios were even lower.

Do oil-backed dictators really spend these extra revenues to buy public support, or is it simply lost to corruption? The secrecy of oil

---

[28] I discuss these data problems at greater length in the appendix to chapter 3.

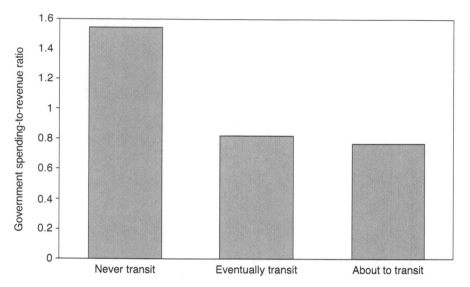

Figure 3.5. Government spending-to-revenue ratios in autocracies, 1970–2008
   These bars represent a government's reported consumption spending as
a fraction of its reported revenues. All measurements are for authoritarian
countries, and compare countries that never transited to democracy (left bar),
eventually transited to democracy (middle bar), and were one year away from
transiting to democracy (right bar).
   Sources: Calculated from fiscal data in World Bank n.d.; democracy data in Cheibub,
Gandhi, and Vreeland 2010.

revenues makes this a hard question to answer,[29] but there is considerable evidence nonetheless that oil-backed autocrats spend a lot of
money to satisfy popular demands. Countries with great per capita oil
wealth, like the oil-rich kingdoms of the Arabian Peninsula, provide
their citizens with a remarkable portfolio of free benefits, such as free
education through college, free health care, and subsidized food and
housing. When oil prices crashed in the 1980s, the Saudi government
tried to raise taxes and cut many subsidies, but after widespread public
criticism, it withdrew both measures.[30] In response to the popular uprisings in 2011, almost all governments in the Middle East offered their
citizens new subsidies. In the oil-rich states, these offers were more generous, and outside of Libya, appeared to be more effective.

[29] Wasteful public spending—on expensive but useless "white elephant" projects—
may have hidden political benefits. See Robinson and Torvik 2005.
[30] Chaudhry 1997. Many other factors besides oil have contributed to the survival of
the Saudi monarchy. See Herb 1999; Hertog 2010.

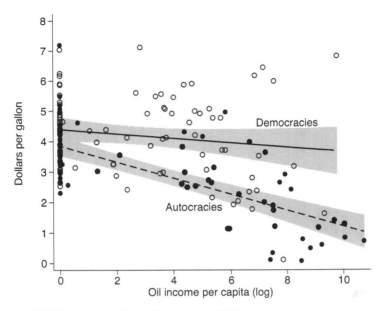

Figure 3.6. Oil income and gasoline prices, 2006
The hollow dots represent democratic countries, and the solid dots represent autocratic countries.
Sources: Calculated from data on gasoline prices in Gesellschaft für Technische Zusammenarbeit 2007; democracy data in Cheibub, Gandhi, and Vreeland 2010.

Many oil-funded governments subsidize fuel prices, even though these subsidies can be ruinously expensive, economically wasteful, and environmentally disastrous. In partially democratic Iran, gasoline and electricity subsidies cost the government—in revenues it would have otherwise collected, had the energy been sold at market prices—a remarkable 20 percent of the GDP in 2007–8, or the equivalent of about $3,275 for a family of four.[31]

It should be no surprise that citizens in oil-producing countries like cheap gasoline. But it *is* surprising that these subsidies tend to be larger in authoritarian states—where governments should be more insulated from public opinion—than in democratic ones.

Figure 3.6 displays the correlations between oil income and gasoline prices for both autocracies and democracies. The horizontal axis shows a country's oil income, while the vertical axis shows the price (in dollars) of a gallon of gasoline in 2006. Solid circles represent undemocratic

---

[31] International Monetary Fund 2008.

countries, and hollow circles represent democratic ones. In both types of states, countries that produce more oil tend to subsidize the price of gas more heavily. But the trend is stronger among authoritarian states (bottom line), and they tend to have lower gasoline prices. The most extreme example is Turkmenistan, where a highly repressive government provides the public with gasoline at two cents a gallon, plus free electricity.

Why would dictators spend so heavily on fuel subsidies? One reason may be that the removal of these subsidies can trigger public demonstrations, which are more likely to endanger authoritarian leaders than democratic ones. The September 2007 protests in Burma began with rallies against the reduction of fuel subsidies; they quickly turned into demonstrations against the military junta. Cameroon's February 2008 riots started out as protests against the removal of fuel subsidies, but escalated into a campaign to stop a constitutional amendment that would allow the incumbent president to remain in office. In April 2010, crowds that initially gathered to protest higher fuel prices ultimately toppled Kyrgystan's president. Authoritarian leaders have good reason to keep gas prices low.

Secrecy

Even though it is hard to measure, government secrecy seems to play a special role in keeping oil-funded autocrats in power.

One way to gauge the secrecy of a country's finances is by using the Open Budget Index, which measures the fiscal transparency of eighty-five national governments, based on an analysis of ninety-one observable features of their budgets, including the frequency with which they disclose important budget documents, the comprehensiveness of these documents, and the role played by the government's auditors. Governments are scored on a scale that runs from zero to a hundred, with higher scores indicating greater budget transparency.[32]

Table 3.3 shows the ratings of both oil producers and nonproducers in 2008. Overall, the oil countries have more or less the same ratings as the non-oil countries. But when democracies and autocracies are viewed separately, there is a conspicuous pattern: among autocracies, the oil-producing states have less budget transparency; among democracies, the oil states have somewhat greater transparency, although the latter difference is not statistically significant.

Figure 3.7 plots the budget transparency scores of the authoritarian states on the vertical axis, and their oil income on the horizontal axis.

---

[32] The International Budget Partnership produces the Open Budget Index. For more on this remarkable index, see http://www.openbudgetindex.org.

TABLE 3.3
Budget transparency, 2008

Budget transparency scores range from zero to a hundred, with higher scores indicating greater transparency.

	Non-oil Producers	Oil Producers	Difference
All countries	39.6	39.9	0.3
Democracies only	43.3	56.5	13.2
Autocracies only	33.4	18.9	−14.5*

*significant at 5% in a two-sample Wilcoxon-Mann-Whitney test
Source: Calculated from the data in International Budget Partnership 2008.

The greater the oil wealth is, the more secretive the budget. The budget secrecy of the African oil producers is especially pronounced: four of the region's five most opaque governments—Angola, Chad, Nigeria, and Cameroon—are significant petroleum exporters. The five most transparent countries—South Africa, Botswana, Zambia, Uganda, and Namibia—have little or no petroleum.

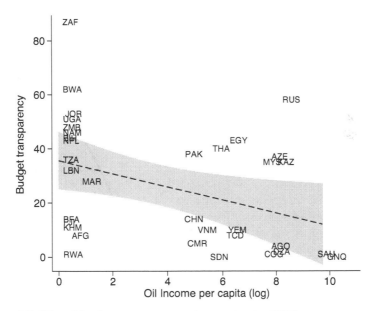

Figure 3.7. Oil and budget transparency in autocracies, 2008
Budget transparency scores range from zero to one hundred, with higher scores indicating greater transparency. This figure only includes autocratic countries.
Source: Data on budget transparency is from International Budget Partnership 2008.

Table 3.4
Press freedom, 2006

The press freedom scores range from one to a hundred, with higher scores indicating greater freedom of the press. The scale has been reversed from the original so that higher scores signify better outcomes.

	Non-oil producers	Oil producers	Difference
All countries	54.0	44.5	−9.5***
Democracies only	65.7	67.0	1.3
Autocracies only	35.5	25.8	−9.7***

*significant at 10%, in a one-tailed t-test
**significant at 5%
***significant at 1%
Source: Calculations from data in Freedom House 2007.

Restrictions on the media can be examined using the freedom of the press index, which ranks all countries on a scale of one (complete censorship) to one hundred (complete press freedom).[33] As table 3.4 shows, when all countries are pooled together—both democracies and autocracies—there is significantly less press freedom in the oil states. Yet when democracies are separated from autocracies, oil wealth has no obvious effect on press freedom among democracies (row two); among autocracies, however, oil is associated with greater censorship. Dictatorships funded by oil are more secretive than those funded by taxes.

There is one further piece of evidence on government openness. My argument about oil and democracy implies that governments will be relatively eager to report how much they spend (since expenditures are popular), but more reluctant to report how much they collect in revenues. It also implies that oil states will be especially reluctant to disclose their revenues. Table 3.5 displays the fraction of countries in 2006—the most recent year for which World Bank data are relatively complete—that produced information on their revenues and expenditures. Two patterns stand out: all countries were more likely to publicly disclose their expenditures than their revenues; and even though the oil producers published their expenditures at the same high rate as the

[33] Georgy Egorov, Sergei Guriev, and Konstantin Sonin (2007) first established the link between oil and the lack of press freedom. Antoine Heuty and Ruth Carlitz (2009) carefully examined the tendency for resource-dependent countries to have less budget transparency. The freedom of the press index is compiled by Freedom House and available at http://www.freedomhouse.org/template.cfm?page=16. I have reversed the scale to make it consistent with other measures of government quality.

TABLE 3.5
Availability of fiscal data, 2006

These numbers show the percentage of countries that provided the World
Bank with data on "Government Revenues" and "Government Consumption"
for 2006.

	Non-oil producers	Oil producers	Difference
Data on government revenues	64	50	−14*
Data on expenditures	90	89	−1

*significant at 10% in a two-sample Wilcoxon-Mann-Whitney test
Source: Calculated from World Bank n.d.

non-oil producers, they were substantially more secretive about their
revenues.

THE SOVIET PETROSTATE

The most widely recognized examples of oil-backed autocracies are
found in the Middle East, North Africa, and sub-Saharan Africa. Less is
known about the Soviet Union, which was the world's second-largest
petroleum producer for much of its history, and whose government relied on oil revenues to boost popular support at critical junctures.

Chapter 2 explains how most oil-rich governments had little control
over their petroleum industries before the 1970s. The Soviet Union,
however, nationalized its oil industry just after the 1917 Russian Revolution. The resulting oil revenues helped the Soviet government to
finance a vast array of social projects and subsidize the spectacularly
inefficient Soviet economy. Yet oil production was unable to keep up
with the expanding economy, and by the early 1950s, according to one
expert, a limited oil supply had become the Achilles' heel of the Soviet
economy.[34]

In the 1960s, the discovery of productive new wells in Siberia turned
the Soviet Union into a major oil exporter. When prices began to soar after 1973, the Kremlin was suddenly flooded with cash. Oil accounted for
80 percent of Soviet hard currency earnings between 1973 and 1985.

According to historian Stephen Kotkin, the Soviet leadership used
the oil windfall of the 1970s and early 1980s to fund the invasion of Afghanistan, fortify its East European allies, and bankroll a vast military
buildup. Domestically,

[34] Hassmann 1953, 109.

oil money also went into higher salaries and better perks for the ever-expanding Soviet elite. And oil financed the acquisition of Western technology for making cars, synthetic fibres, and other products for consumers, as well as Western feed for Soviet livestock. In the future, the inhabitants of the Soviet Union would look back fondly on the [Leonid] Brezhnev era, recalling the cornucopia of sausages that had been available in state stores at subsidized prices. Oil seemed to save the Soviet Union in the 1970s, but it merely delayed the inevitable.[35]

After oil prices peaked in 1980, they fell by over 70 percent over the next six years; so did Soviet oil revenues, producing the economic and political crisis that ultimately led to the Soviet government's collapse. As Clifford Gaddy and Barry Ickes suggest,

> The entire Soviet system was built on the assumption of a persistent stream of available resource rents to keep it going. Once this fundamentally nonviable structure had been created, continued injection of resources was required to sustain it.[36]

In 1985–86, Soviet leaders tried to boost revenues by boosting output, but the most productive wells had been overused, and despite increasingly desperate measures, oil production began to fall, compounding the crisis. From 1986 to 1991, oil production dropped 25 percent—offsetting a modest rise in prices, and leaving the government desperately short of hard currency.

The Soviet economic crisis helped convince Mikhail Gorbachev—who became general secretary of the Communist Party in March 1985—to adopt both economic reforms that relaxed state control of the economy (perestroika), and political reforms that allowed for competitive elections for many local and national offices, a freer press, and greater freedom of association (glasnost).

Yet without enough hard currency to provide citizens with key public goods, especially food, neither perestroika nor glasnost were enough to sustain the Soviet system.[37] At the September 17, 1990, meeting of the Council of Ministers, the government's highest officials implored each other to find ways to boost oil production to stave off economic and political disaster. Yuri Maslyukov, the chair of Gosplan (the state planning agency), explained,

---

[35] Kotkin 2001, 16.

[36] Gaddy and Ickes 2005, 569.

[37] Many scholars now believe that Perestroika itself led to the demise of the Soviet system. I am grateful to Daniel Treisman for pointing this out.

We understand that the only source of hard currency is of course oil, so I will make this proposal. I feel that we must . . . take the most determined measures to achieve additional oil production, whatever the conditions may be for the riggers. . . . I have the presentiment that if we do not make all of the necessary decisions now, then we may spend next year in a way that we haven't even dreamed of. . . . Things can end most critically in the socialist countries. This will lead us to a real crash, and not just for us, but for our entire system.[38]

Without oil revenues to finance the socialist economy—providing citizens, however inefficiently, with virtually all their material goods—the government's authority dwindled until December 1991, when it collapsed altogether. At the industry's peak in 1980, the Soviet Union was producing about $3,100 per capita in oil and gas income. This income had fallen by 1991 by about two-thirds, to around $1,050 per capita.

Tragically, the end of the Soviet Union did not mean the end of the now-Russian economic crisis. When prices fell to $10 a barrel in 1998, Russia's oil income fell to about $475 per capita—down about 85 percent from its 1980 peak—and the government went bankrupt and defaulted on billions of dollars in domestic loans.

THE LATIN AMERICAN EXCEPTION

An important study by Thad Dunning shows that Latin America seems to be unaffected by the antidemocratic powers of petroleum.[39] Consider once again table 3.2, which displays the ten-top oil producers that have transited to democracy since 1950. All five of the countries that made successful transits were in Latin America: Venezuela (1958), Bolivia (1982), Argentina (1983), Mexico (2000), and Ecuador (2002). Conversely, all of Latin America's oil producers (like almost all of its non-oil producers) are now democracies. The cross-tabulations in the bottom rows of table 3.1 tell the same story: in Latin America, countries *with* oil were more than twice as likely to democratize; in the rest of the world, countries *without* oil were more than four times more likely to democratize.

There are several ways to account for the Latin American anomaly. Dunning argues that oil only impedes democratization in countries with low levels of inequality. But in countries with high inequality levels, like those in Latin America, oil hastens democratization by

---

[38] Quoted in Gaidar 2008, 164.
[39] Dunning 2008.

alleviating the concern of wealthy elites that democracy will lead to the expropriation of their private wealth.[40]

The reasoning is compelling but hard to test with much precision, since global data on inequality are scarce, and inequality is measured in ways that differ from country to country. Moreover, inequality data are missing for many of the world's oil-producing countries. The greater a country's oil income, the less information it typically discloses about its inequality levels.[41]

An alternative explanation could be that oil only hinders democracy in countries with no previous democratic experience.[42] According to the model earlier in this chapter, oil makes dictators more popular, in part because they can conceal the true scale of their government's oil revenues. Maybe if a country has been under democratic rule in the past, dictators will find it harder to hide these revenues: citizens will already know, from their previous access to a free press, the true scale of their country's petroleum wealth, making them more skeptical about a dictator's claims.

If this were true, oil wealth would only block democratic transitions in countries whose citizens had never been exposed to democratic rule. Indeed, most of Latin America's oil producers, including Argentina, Bolivia, Brazil, Chile, Colombia, Ecuador, and Peru, had earlier spells of democracy. Mexico, which did not, was the slowest to democratize. The largest African oil producer to transit to democracy, Nigeria, had democratic experience in its early days as an oil producer. There is also statistical evidence in the appendix that the Latin America anomaly can be at least partly accounted for by the prior democratic experience of most Latin American oil producers.

Whatever the cause, Dunning is right: oil is associated with more democracy in Latin America, but less democracy in the rest of the developing world.

Does Oil Wealth Hurt Democracies?

Does oil wealth cause democracies to become less democratic? At first glance, the model seems to suggest "no": if oil boosts the popularity of the government in place, it should reinforce both autocracies and

---

[40] Ibid.

[41] This is another feature of the unusual secrecy of the oil states.

[42] I am grateful to Tulia Faletti for proposing this idea.

democracies. And several statistical studies find that oil revenues tend to help democracies stay democratic.[43]

But a closer look suggests a more complicated answer. According to the model, oil helps empower *incumbents*, regardless of whether the country is authoritarian or democratic. We can assume that empowered autocrats want their countries to remain autocratic, since this helps them stay in power. Empowered democratic incumbents may not necessarily want their countries to remain democratic, however. In fact, they might try to remain in power longer by making their countries more autocratic.

Not all democracies should be equally susceptible to this danger. Rich democracies tend to place more effective constraints on executive power, due to the greater influence of their parliaments and courts; less wealthy democracies typically have weaker legislatures, weaker courts, and weaker constraints on executive power. In wealthy oil-producing democracies, checks and balances that keep incumbents from accruing too much power should counterbalance the economic power that oil brings to the incumbent. But in poor and middle-income democracies, oil wealth may help incumbents accumulate enough political influence to dismantle the checks and balances that would otherwise keep their government democratic.

This implies that oil wealth can make low-income democracies less democratic. There may be too few oil-producing democracies with low and middle incomes to test this claim with much confidence. Nevertheless, there is some weak evidence to support it in table 3.6, which shows the annual rate of democratic failures—meaning the annual likelihood that a democratic government will turn into a dictatorship—for all countries from 1960 to 2008. Overall, democratic failures were *less* common in oil-producing countries, although the difference is not statistically significant (row one). Even when we divide countries by wealth (rows two and three), democratic failures in the oil states are not significantly different from democratic failures in the non-oil states.

We still need to account for time. Earlier we saw that oil had stronger antidemocratic effects after the transformative events of the 1970s. Rows four and five show that democratic failures were dramatically less frequent in the oil states from 1960 to 1979. Since 1980, they have become slightly more frequent in the oil states, but again the difference is not statistically significant.

When we put these two factors together—looking at lower-income democracies since 1980 (row six)—democratic failures become notably more frequent among the oil states, although the difference falls just

[43] Smith 2007; Morrison 2009.

TABLE 3.6
Transitions to authoritarianism, 1960–2006

These numbers show the percentage of countries that changed from democratic to authoritarian rule in a given year.

	Non-oil producers	Oil producers	Difference
All countries and periods	1.9	1.17	−0.72
By income			
Low income (below $5,000)	3.32	2.97	−0.35
High income (above $5,000)	0.28	0.46	0.18
By period			
1960–1979	3.7	0.74	−2.95**
1980–2008	1.08	1.3	0.21
By income and period			
Low income, 1980–2006	1.86	3.33	1.46

*significant at 10%, in a one-tailed t-test
**significant at 5%
***significant at 1%
Source: Calculated from data in Cheibub, Gandhi, and Vreeland 2010.

short of statistical significance in a one-tailed t-test. I show in the appendix that once we control for confounding variables, the link between
oil and democratic failures—especially in lower-income countries, and
especially after 1980—becomes statistically significant.[44]

The number of oil-producing democracies outside the rich industrialized states is small, which makes it hard to be sure that these correlations are meaningful. But at the case study level, there are indications
that oil has strengthened the hand of democratically elected incumbents, and enabled them to roll back democratic constraints.

Some of the most surprising evidence comes from the United States.
Much of the US oil industry is regulated by states, not the federal government, which means that state governments can receive substantial
oil revenues. If oil and gas wealth has empowered US politicians, it
would be most visible at the state level. Studies by Ellis Goldberg, Erik

[44] This is consistent with Nathan Jensen and Leonard Wantchekon's work (2004), which
shows that oil has indeed led to democratic failures in sub-Saharan Africa. Perhaps this is
because incomes in the region are relatively low.

Wibbels, and Eric Mvukiyehe as well as Justin Wolfers have found that in states with greater oil revenues, incumbent governors are more likely to be reelected, and tend to defeat their opponents by wider margins.[45]

The most extreme case may have been in Louisiana beginning in the 1920s, where Governor Huey Long accrued unprecedented political influence through a kind of petropopulism. After raising taxes on oil companies, Long used the resulting revenues to fund new roads and hospitals, free textbooks for schoolchildren, and patronage for the legislators and local politicians who backed him. The state's largess gave Long great popularity and extraordinary powers, including the power to censor unsympathetic newspapers, financially cripple local governments in parts of the state that opposed him, and personally hire and fire state employees, all the way down to the level of deputy sheriffs and schoolteachers.[46] Thanks to Louisiana's oil revenues, Long—and his relatives who succeeded him—"more nearly matched the power of a South American dictator than that of any other American state boss."[47]

The erosion of democracy in Louisiana in the 1920s and 1930s foreshadowed the deterioration of democracy in many lower-income democracies in recent years. The 2000–8 boom in oil prices helped give popularly elected leaders in many oil-rich states the capacity to strip away restrictions on their power:

- In Azerbaijan, President Ilham Aliyev sponsored a March 2009 referendum to remove term limits that would have otherwise forced him to step down. The opposition boycotted the referendum, which according to the government was approved by over 90 percent of the voters.
- Nigeria's 2007 elections gave the incumbent People's Democratic Party an overwhelming victory, including the presidency and large majorities in the house and senate. Both domestic and international observers reported widespread fraud in favor of the People's Democratic Party. According to the International Crisis Group, the elections were the most fraudulent in the country's history.[48]
- The reelection of Iran's President Mahmoud Ahmadinejad in June 2009 was viewed by many observers—both foreign and domestic—as flawed by widespread voting irregularities. The Ahmadinejad government relied heavily on the Revolutionary Guards to put

[45] Goldberg, Wibbels, and Mvukiyehe 2009; Wolfers 2009.
[46] Williams 1969.
[47] Key 1949, 156. For more on the history of oil politics in Texas and Louisiana, see Goldberg, Wibbels, and Mvukiyehe 2009.
[48] The March 2011 elections were much cleaner. On other African cases, see Posner and Young 2007.

down the resulting protests. The government had given businesses owned by the guards a large number of government contracts, including a number of no-bid petroleum contracts worth billions of dollars.[49]

- Over the last decade, Venezuelan president Chávez capitalized on rising oil prices to fund projects that increased his popularity among key constituencies, including low-income families and the military. He then took advantage of this support to eliminate independent checks on his authority—for example, by replacing disloyal judges on the Supreme Court and imposing new restrictions on the media.[50] In February 2009, Chávez won a national referendum to remove term limits on public officials, enabling him to remain in office indefinitely.

RUSSIA REVISITED

Just as the case of the Soviet Union shows how oil revenues can prolong authoritarian rule, the case of Russia since 1998 illustrates how oil revenues can endanger a weak democracy by boosting the popularity of an elected incumbent, who gradually removes checks and balances on their own authority.

In Russia, the drop in oil and gas revenues helped precipitate the government's 1998 bankruptcy. But the weakness of the government's finances also opened the door to greater civil liberties, freedom of the press, and meaningful political competition—if not quite a full democracy. Once the Russian oil industry began to recover in 2000, democracy began to deteriorate. The broad pattern is evident in figure 3.8, which displays the country's democracy level along with its petroleum income between 1960 and 2007.

Between 2000 and 2006, Russia's booming petroleum sector helped fuel a remarkable economic recovery: real incomes rose by 48 percent, unemployment fell from 9.8 to 6 percent, and the government's oil revenues rose by a factor of more than seven, from $14.3 to $107 billion (in constant 2000 dollars).[51]

Part of the petroleum sector's growth was caused by rising production: from 2000 to 2006, oil production rose by 43 percent and natural

[49] Wehrey et al. 2009.

[50] International Crisis Group 2007.

[51] International Monetary Fund 2007. Paavo Suni (2007) uses simulations of the Russian economy to show that rising oil and gas prices are responsible for much of Russia's economic boom. Without the leap in prices, Russia's GDP growth in 2006 would have been below 1 percent instead of greater than 6 percent.

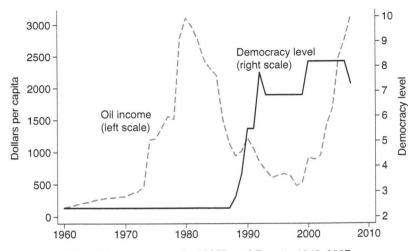

Figure 3.8. Oil and democracy in the USSR and Russia, 1960–2007

The solid line shows democracy levels in the Soviet Union and Russia, according to the Polity IV data set. The broken line shows oil income per capita, in constant 2000 dollars. Polity scores have been translated to a 1–10 scale, with 10 representing full democracy.

Source: Calculated from data in Marshall and Jaggers 2007.

gas production grew by 12 percent. Most of the revenue boom, however, was caused by higher prices: from 2000 to 2006, the price of oil doubled and the price of natural gas rose more than 150 percent. Thanks to the ensuing windfall, old debts were paid off and budget deficits were replaced by surpluses. The highest marginal tax rate on corporations was cut from 35 to 24 percent; the top rate on individuals was cut from 35 to 13 percent.[52]

These higher budgets and lower tax rates reflected Vladimir Putin's ability to reassert state control over the oil sector, which had been largely privatized in the early 1990s.[53] Placing this colossal wealth in the private sector contributed to the weakening of the Russian state, which found it difficult to collect taxes from the largest corporations, and hence to fund public services and balance the budget. Privatization also brought great political influence to the owners of these firms. Boris Berezovsky, the head of the oil giant Sibneft, created a media empire

---

[52] It may not be accurate to describe these changes as "tax cuts": due to better enforcement, these changes led to an increase in tax revenues. I am grateful to Dan Treisman for pointing this out.

[53] Long before he became a politician, Putin developed strong ideas about how Russia should manage its natural resources. See Balzer 2009.

and was deeply involved in Kremlin politics. Mikhail Khodorkovsky, the head of the oil group Yukos and one of the world's wealthiest people, reportedly offered Russia's two liberal parties, Yabloko and Soyuz Pravykh Sil (Union of Right Forces), a hundred million dollars to jointly oppose Putin, and he successfully blocked efforts in the parliament in 2001 and 2002 to increase taxes on petroleum producers. The mayor of Nefteyugansk, the headquarters of Yukos' major production unit, was murdered after he criticized the failure of Yukos to pay taxes.[54]

After splitting with Putin, Berezovsky fled to London in 2001. Two years later the Russian government arrested Khodorkovsky, and eventually sentenced him to an eight-year prison term for tax evasion and fraud. It also forced the sale of Yukos—at a heavily discounted price—to Rosneft, a state-run oil company.[55] In 2006, it coerced international oil companies to cede control over a major project on Sakhalin Island to state-controlled Gazprom. These and other measures brought a significant fraction of Russia's oil and gas wealth back under the state's influence, either directly through state-controlled companies or indirectly through more effective government regulation.

The Kremlin's greater control over the allocation of oil rents along with the skyrocketing size of those rents gave Putin sufficient popularity to rescind many of the political liberties of the 1990s. By the time he assumed the prime minister position in 2008—transferring the presidency to Dmitry Medvedev, his handpicked successor—Putin had curtailed freedom of the press, restricted freedom of assembly for government opponents, and weakened the parliament.

As Michael McFaul and Kathryn Stoner-Weiss suggest,

> With so much money from oil windfalls in the Kremlin's coffers, Putin could crack down on or co-opt independent sources of political power; the Kremlin had less reason to fear the negative economic consequences of seizing a company like Yukos (a leading private oil company) and had ample resources to buy off or repress opponents in the media and civil society.[56]

Russia's oil boom contributed to the deterioration of Russian democracy by increasing the government's financial resources, at least once Putin reasserted state control over the industry. The resulting cascade of revenues allowed Putin to simultaneously boost government spending and cut tax rates, which helped make him extraordinarily popular:

[54] Goldman 2004; Rutland 2006.
[55] Myers and Kramer 2007.
[56] McFaul and Stoner-Weiss 2008.

just before leaving office, polls taken by the highly respected Levada Center showed that 85 percent of the public approved of his performance.[57] With petroleum prices at record levels, Putin used his personal popularity to reverse many of the democratic reforms of the 1990s and draw Russia back toward one-party rule.[58]

Despite its drift away from democracy, in one way Russia looked like an exception: until 2010 it had significantly greater budget transparency than any other oil-producing authoritarian state. In figure 3.7, Russia is the only country that is able to combine formidable oil wealth and meaningful budget transparency. Unfortunately, in April 2010 much of this transparency disappeared when now–Prime Minister Putin signed a decree that suspended the publication of information about the assets, revenues, and expenditures of Russia's two oil funds as well as the government's oil and gas revenues.[59] The suspension was to remain in effect until 2013—well after Russia's next elections.

In oil-producing countries, transitions to democracy are exceedingly rare. Petroleum wealth has not always been an impediment to democracy, and its antidemocratic powers could recede in the future. Over the last three decades, however, the political benefits of oil have been largely captured by dictators, not citizens.

APPENDIX 3.1: A STATISTICAL ANALYSIS OF OIL AND DEMOCRACY

This appendix uses multivariate regressions to illustrate the statistical association between oil income and three outcomes—democratic transitions, democratic failures, and support for democracy.[60]

---

[57] See http://www.russiavotes.org.

[58] Scholars differ on the role of petroleum in contemporary Russian politics. M. Stephen Fish (2005) argues that Russia's oil, gas, and mineral wealth has made its government less democratic, but for somewhat different reasons: it caused high levels of corruption in the 1990s, which led citizens to favor a more autocratic government that was more effective at curbing corruption; and it has facilitated "economic statism," giving the government much stronger control over the economy. According to Treisman (2010), oil's impact on Russian democracy has been quite small.

[59] See http://www.revenuewatch.org/news-article/russia/russia-suspends-most-oil-and-gas disclosures.

[60] This is a relatively simple analysis. For more innovative studies of oil and democracy, which use instrumental variables to estimate the effects of oil wealth on democracy, see Ramsay 2009; Tsui 2011. Another innovative study, by Eoin McGuirk (2010), uses micro-level data from public opinion surveys in fifteen African countries and finds that more

The model in chapter 3 implies the following five patterns, which can be stated as hypotheses:

Hypothesis 3.1: When authoritarian governments have more oil income per capita, they will be less likely to transit to democracy.

Hypothesis 3.2: Oil income should be more likely to impede democracy after 1980 than before 1980.

Hypothesis 3.3: When authoritarian governments have higher ratios of government spending to perceived government revenues, they will be less likely to transit to democracy.

Hypothesis 3.4: When oil-rich authoritarian governments place more restrictions on the media and have less transparent budgets, they will be less likely to transit to democracy.

Hypothesis 3.5: When low-income democracies have more oil income per capita, they will be more likely to transit to authoritarianism.

DEMOCRATIC TRANSITIONS

To see if a country's oil income is correlated with the likelihood that it will transit to democracy, I use two alternative measures of regime type: a dichotomous democracy-autocracy measure, which I examine with a logit estimator; and a twenty-one-point measure, which I look at with an ordinary least squares (OLS) estimator.

Maximum likelihood estimators like logit allow us to estimate the likelihood of a discrete event. This makes it an appropriate way to determine whether oil income is correlated with the probability that an authoritarian state will transit to democracy. I use the OLS model to see if petroleum income is correlated with more subtle changes in regime types. It is also useful as a robustness check. The disadvantage of the OLS model is that entails looking at the link between oil income and regimes of all types, ranging from fully democratic to fully authoritarian. Hence, we cannot use it to distinguish between oil's effect on democratic transitions and its effect on democratic failures.[61]

Dependent Variable

The dependent variable in the logit estimations is *democratic transition*, a dummy variable that takes the value "one" in the year that a country changes from authoritarian to democratic rule, and "zero" otherwise. It is taken from the dichotomous democracy-autocracy measure devel-

---

natural resource wealth has led to weakened tax enforcement, which in turn has reduced the demand for free and fair elections.

[61] This shortcoming was first pointed out in Ulfelder 2007.

oped by Przeworski and his colleagues, and updated by José Cheibub, Jennifer Gandhi, and James Vreeland.[62]

For the OLS estimations, the dependent variable is *polity*, which is drawn from the Polity IV data set, and ranges from −10 (full autocracy) to 10 (full democracy).[63] To simplify the interpretation, I have rescaled the values to run from 1 to 10, with higher values indicating greater democracy. Both the Cheibub-Gandhi-Vreeland and Polity data cover all 170 countries that were sovereign in the year 2000, and had populations greater than 200,000. The logit estimations cover the years 1960–2006, while the OLS estimations cover the years 1960–2004.

Independent and Control Variables

The independent variable of interest is the natural log of a country's per capita oil income. *Oil income (log)* denotes the value of a country's oil and gas production in constant 2000 dollars divided by its midyear population, and is described more fully in appendix 1.1. Since the distribution of oil income across countries is highly skewed—most countries in any given year produce no oil or gas—I instead take its log value.

In both the logit and OLS models, I include the variable *income*, which measures the natural log of income per capita based on data from the World Development Indicators, with missing observations filled in with figures from the Penn World Tables.[64] Most prior studies of democratization suggest that income is a critical factor: when incomes rise, so does the likelihood that a state will be democratic.[65]

The logit model also includes a variable to account for duration dependence. *Regime duration* is the natural log of the number of continuous years since 1946 that a country has been under authoritarian rule; it represents the underlying hazard rate. In the robustness section, I show that the results are unaffected by differing assumptions about the hazard rate.

[62] Przeworski et al. 2000; Cheibub, Gandhi, and Vreeland 2010. They define regimes as democracies if they meet all of the following conditions: the chief executive is elected, the legislature is elected, there are at least two political parties, and at least one incumbent regime has been defeated. My analysis in many ways follows that of Jay Ulfelder (2007), who uses an event history design to test a similar pair of hypotheses, but develops his own dichotomous autocracy-democracy measure. Our substantive results are similar.

[63] Marshall and Jaggers 2007.

[64] Heston, Summers, and Aten n.d.

[65] Londregan and Poole 1996; Boix and Stokes 2003; Epstein et al. 2006. Since a country's income is affected by its oil wealth, including it in the model can lead to biased estimates of oil's true impact. I describe a more general version of this problem in chapter 6 as the "Beverly Hillbillies fallacy." Because I have already illustrated the bivariate relationship between oil and democracy in chapter 3 (using difference-of-means tests and scatterplots), I am less concerned about this bias here.

To reduce serial correlation in the OLS models, I employ an AR1 process, include a lagged dependent variable as a control, and only use observations from every fifth year, beginning in 1960.[66]

Both the logit and OLS models also include a series of period dummies—one for each five-year period, beginning in 1960—to control for temporal patterns and contemporaneous shocks.

After exploring a core model that includes just two control variables (adhering to Achen's "rule of three," at least if the period dummies are not counted), I add three additional controls to see if the results are robust to their inclusion.[67] The first is a variable to account for a country's prior history of democracy. Several studies suggest that when states have previous experience with democracy, it boosts the likelihood of a subsequent transition to democracy.[68] The dummy variable *prior democracy* takes the value "1" if a country was previously under democratic rule for at least one year since 1946.

The second is *economic growth,* which is measured as the year-to-year change in a country's income per capita. According to several studies, economic growth helps autocracies survive.[69]

The third additional control is the variable *Muslim population,* which represents the Muslim fraction of a country's population, and is taken from David Barrett, George Kurian, and Todd Johnson's work, with values for missing countries taken from the CIA World Factbook online.[70] Several scholars argue that states with larger Islamic populations are less likely to become democratic.[71]

All of the right-hand-side variables (except for the period dummies, and *prior democracy*) are lagged either one year (in the logit models) or one five-year period (in the OLS models). The regressions were run with Stata 11.1.

Results

Table 3.7 displays the results of the logit estimations. To simplify the display, I omit the constants and period dummies.

Column one includes only the two control variables. While the coefficients are in the expected directions, neither variable attains statistical

---

[66] See Acemoglu et al. 2008; Aslaksen 2010.

[67] Achen 2002.

[68] See, for example, Gassebner, Lamla, and Vreeland 2008.

[69] Haggard and Kaufman 1995; Przeworski et al. 2000; Epstein et al. 2006; Gassebner, Lamla, and Vreeland 2008.

[70] See Barrett, Kurian, and Johnson 2001; http://www.cia.gov/library/publications/the-world-factbook.

[71] Midlarsky 1998; Fish 2002; Donno and Russet 2004.

TABLE 3.7
Transitions to democracy, 1960–2006

This table reports logit estimates of the likelihood that an authoritarian state will undergo a democratic transition in a given year. All of the variables except *prior democracy* are lagged a single year. Each estimation includes a series of five-year period dummies (not shown). The robust standard errors are in parentheses.

	(1)	(2)	(3)	(4)	(5)	(6)
Income (log)	0.139	0.332*	0.406	0.124	0.256	0.225
	(0.150)	(0.171)	(0.254)	(0.134)	(0.168)	(0.162)
Regime duration	−0.00174	−0.0457	−0.122	−0.438***	0.00964	0.387*
	(0.178)	(0.181)	(0.303)	(0.141)	(0.181)	(0.229)
Oil income (log)	—	−0.179**	−0.0783	−0.129**	−0.292***	−0.197**
		(0.0787)	(0.114)	(0.0594)	(0.0921)	(0.0897)
Oil income (log)* Latin America	—	—	—	—	0.673***	0.415***
					(0.152)	(0.143)
Prior democracy	—	—	—	—	—	1.915***
						(0.465)
Economic growth	—	—	—	—	—	−0.0536***
						(0.0168)
Muslim population	—	—	—	—	—	−0.720
						(0.551)
Years	All	All	1960–79	1980–2006	All	All
Number of countries	125	125	89	121	125	125
Observations	3,639	3,507	1,297	2,210	3,507	3,422
Missing observations	10.5%	13.7%	23.5%	6.6%	13.7%	15.8%

*significant at 10%
**significant at 5%
***significant at 1%

significance. Column two includes *oil income,* which is negatively correlated with the likelihood of a democratic transition and statistically significant at the 0.05 level. This is consistent with $H_{3.1}$, which states that higher levels of oil income will reduce the likelihood of a transition to democracy.

In columns three and four, I look separately at the 1960–79 and 1980–2006 periods. In the first period (column three), the size of the *oil income* coefficient drops sharply and loses all statistical significance. In the second period, the *oil income* coefficient regains its size and statistical significance. This is consistent with $H_{3.2}$, which suggests that oil's antidemocratic effect has grown since the 1970s.[72]

Column five includes a variable interacting *oil income* with a dummy for Latin America, to explore Dunning's finding that oil hastened democratization in Latin America while impeding it elsewhere.[73] The variable is statistically significant at the 0.01 level, consistent with Dunning's assertion. Moreover, its inclusion causes both the absolute value and statistical significance of the *oil income* variable to grow—implying that once oil's democracy-enhancing effects in Latin America are accounted for, oil's democracy-impeding effects in the rest of the world are larger than previously estimated.

Column six shows the model when the other three controls—*prior democracy, economic growth*, and *Muslim population*—are included. The *prior democracy* and *economic growth* variables are significantly correlated with *democratic transitions* in the expected directions, and their inclusion causes the *oil income* coefficient to drop by about one-third, but *oil income* remains significantly correlated with *democratic transitions.*

Table 3.8 shows the estimation results from the OLS models.[74] The first column includes only *income* and the lagged dependent variable;

---

[72]Almost a quarter of the observations for the 1960–79 period are missing, mostly due to missing income data. The missing data problem is equally worrisome in table 3.8, columns three, six, and seven. Since these missing data are almost certainly nonrandom, they may bias my results in ways that are difficult to predict.

[73]Dunning 2008. Since there is little reason to expect that the Latin American states are otherwise distinctive, I do not include a Latin America dummy in the model. If nonetheless placed in the model, or in the OLS model (table 3.8, column five), it is not statistically significant, and its inclusion has little or no effect on the other variables.

[74]The OLS model is much like the generalized least squares model in Ross 2001a, which also had a lagged dependent variable, a similar set of control variables, a series of period dummies, and a five-year lag for the right-hand-side variables. There are three key differences: the data now cover more countries (170 instead of 113) and years (1960–2004 instead of 1971–97); the causal variable is now *oil income (log)* rather than oil exports as a fraction of the GDP; and instead of using annual observations, I take observations from every fifth year to reduce autocorrelation.

TABLE 3.8
Democracy levels, 1960–2004

This table shows OLS regression coefficients; the dependent variable is a country's polity score, rescaled to run from 1 to 10. Observations are made at five-year intervals. All estimates include a lagged dependent variable and a full set of period dummies (not shown), and use an AR(1) process. All of the other explanatory variables are lagged for a single period. The robust standard errors are in parentheses.

	(1)	(2)	(3)	(4)	(5)	(6)	(7)
Polity (lagged)	0.652*** (0.0232)	0.620*** (0.0236)	0.698*** (0.0355)	0.697*** (0.0270)	0.616*** (0.0235)	0.432*** (0.0289)	0.151*** (0.0369)
Income (log)	0.348*** (0.0529)	0.508*** (0.0590)	0.487*** (0.0904)	0.354*** (0.0636)	0.518*** (0.0577)	0.439*** (0.0649)	−0.0628 (0.266)
Oil income (log)	—	−0.165*** (0.0287)	−0.100** (0.0455)	−0.152*** (0.0298)	−0.205*** (0.0297)	−0.136*** (0.0352)	−0.0755 (0.0832)
Oil income (log)* Latin America	—	—	—	—	0.223*** (0.0515)	0.0961 (0.0590)	0.570*** (0.199)
Prior democracy	—	—	—	—	—	1.474*** (0.192)	—
Economic growth	—	—	—	—	—	−0.858 (0.807)	—
Muslim population	—	—	—	—	—	−1.022*** (0.256)	—
Fixed effects?	No	No	No	No	No	No	Yes
Years	1960–2004	1960–2004	1960–80	1985–2004	1960–2004	1960–2004	1960–2004
Number of countries	170	170	124	170	170	170	167
Observations	1,032	1,032	414	618	1,032	903	862
Missing observations	14.1%	14.1%	21.1%	8.7%	14.1%	24.9%	28.3%

*significant at 10%
**significant at 5%
***significant at 1%

both are highly significant, as are the period dummies (not shown). In column two, I add *oil income*; it is also highly significant and negatively correlated with *polity*, consistent with $H_{3.1}$.

Columns three and four cover the periods 1960–80 and 1985–2004, respectively. *Oil income* is significantly correlated with *polity* in both periods, although the size of the *oil income* coefficient is about 50 percent larger in the latter period. This is consistent with $H_{3.2}$, which suggests that the antidemocratic effects of oil grew after the 1970s.

The model in column five includes the interaction term *oil income*Latin America* to once again show the Dunning effect. It is positively correlated with *polity*, and its inclusion once more increases the size of the *oil income* coefficient. In column six, the addition of three further control variables reduces the size of the *oil income* coefficient by about one-third, but *oil income* remains significantly associated with lower *polity* scores. The inclusion of the other controls—notably, *prior democracy*—also causes the *oil income*Latin America* coefficient to drop by more than 50 percent and lose statistical significance. This is consistent with my argument that oil may have hastened democratic transitions in Latin America because these states had prior democratic experience, which undermined the revenue secrecy that is essential to oil's democracy-inhibiting effect.

When country fixed effects are introduced (column seven), *oil income* loses statistical significance—as does *income* and the period dummies. There are several ways to explain this result. *Oil income* may have long-term effects on regime type, which are readily apparent in cross-national comparisons, but harder to detect in the short term, and hence do not appear in the within-country correlations.[75] This reflects a well-known drawback of fixed-effects models: they make it difficult to detect correlations when the dependent variable changes slowly—as does the *polity* variable.[76] To address this problem, Silje Aslaksen suggests using the system generalized method of moments (GMM) estimator developed by Richard Blundell and Stephen Bond, which outperforms the more-common first-difference GMM estimator in Monte Carlo simulations when the key variables change slowly.[77] Using this estimator, Aslaksen finds that a country's oil income is indeed correlated with authoritarian rule, even in the presence of country fixed effects.

---

[75] A study by Jeffrey Colgan (2010b) suggests that while oil income hurts democracy in the long run, short-term fluctuations in oil income have little immediate effect.

[76] Beck, Katz, and Tucker 1998.

[77] Aslaksen 2010; Blundell and Bond 1998. Charlotte Werger (2009) and Treisman (2010) also find that oil is linked to less democracy in fixed-effects models.

A paper by Stephen Haber and Victor Menaldo finds that the relationship between oil wealth and democracy disappears in models that include country fixed effects along with a lagged dependent variable, and employ the Arellano-Bond GMM estimator.[78] Aslaksen suggests that when the key variables—like oil income and democracy—are highly persistent, the Arellano-Bond estimator suffers from a weak instruments problem and is inferior to the Blundell-Bond system GMM estimator.

DEMOCRATIC FAILURES

The variables in the model for democratic failures are similar to those in the model for democratic transitions. The dependent variable, *democratic failure*, is a dummy variable that denotes a transition from democratic to authoritarian rule, and is once again taken from the Cheibub-Gandhi-Vreeland data set. The core model includes controls for the log of income per capita and a variable to account for duration dependence (*regime duration*), which is the natural log of the number of continuous years (since 1946) that a country has been under democratic rule.

Since democratic failures are rare events—there were just fifty such transitions from 1960 to 2006, out of 2,816 possible country years—using a standard logistic estimator could produce biased estimates. I thus use the rare-events logit estimator developed by Gary King and Langche Zeng, and cluster the standard errors by country.[79]

In the estimates reported in table 3.9, column one shows only the control variables. Both *income* and *regime duration* seem to reduce the likelihood that democracies will break down. Column two includes the *oil income* variable, which is positively correlated with *democratic failures* and statistically significant at the 0.05 level.

According to $H_{3.5}$, oil should be linked to the likelihood of a democratic breakdown in low-income, but not high-income, countries. To demonstrate this pattern, in columns three and four I look separately at countries with incomes below (column three) and above (column four) five thousand dollars per capita. *Oil income* is only correlated with the likelihood of *democratic failure* in lower-income countries.

If the antidemocratic powers of oil grow over time, as $H_{3.2}$ suggests, *oil income* should have a stronger effect after 1980 than before 1980. I

[78] Haber and Menaldo 2009.

[79] King and Zeng 2001. Rare-events logit might also be appropriate for estimating the likelihood of democratic transitions, which are comparably infrequent. When the models in table 3.7 are reestimated with rare-events logit, the results are virtually identical.

Table 3.9
Transitions to authoritarianism, 1960–2006

This table portrays rare-event logit estimates of the likelihood that a democratic state will undergo a transition to authoritarian rule in a given year. All explanatory variables are lagged for one year, and standard errors are clustered by country. The robust standard errors are in parentheses.

	(1)	(2)	(3)	(4)	(5)	(6)
Regime duration (log)	−0.342** (0.168)	−0.342** (0.169)	−0.240 (0.164)	−0.892** (0.452)	−0.417* (0.242)	−0.280 (0.209)
Income (log)	−0.641*** (0.142)	−0.717*** (0.144)	−0.580*** (0.177)	−2.480*** (0.651)	−0.689*** (0.172)	−0.960*** (0.218)
Oil income (log)	—	0.121** (0.0564)	0.113* (0.0630)	0.129 (0.174)	0.0949 (0.117)	0.242*** (0.0752)
Income group	All	All	Below $5,000	Above $5,000	All	All
Years	All	All	All	All	1960–79	1980–2006
Number of countries	105	105	76	46	60	103
Observations	2,673	2,673	1,301	1,372	728	1,945
Missing observations	1.6%	1.6%	~2%	~1%	4.7%	0.4%

*significant at 10%
**significant at 5%
***significant at 1%

estimate the model in column five using only data from 1960 to 1979, and the same model in column six using data from 1980 to 2006. Consistent with the hypothesis, *oil income* is only correlated with democratic failures since 1980.

Robustness

Table 3.10 summarizes a series of robustness tests for each of these three models: the logit model predicting democratic transitions (column one), the OLS model predicting *polity* scores (column two), and the rare-events logit model predicting democratic failures (column three).

TABLE 3.10
Democracy: Robustness tests

These figures are the coefficients of the *oil income* variable in each of the
models described. See the text for details.

	Transitions to democracy	Democracy levels	Transitions to authoritarianism
Core model	−0.292***	−0.205***	0.242***
Simple regime duration	−0.293***	—	0.255***
Add regime squared	−0.294***	—	0.265***
Dichotomous oil income	−1.88***	−1.04***	1.03**
Drop key countries	−0.229**	−0.152***	0.216**
Drop all Middle East	−0.179*	−0.123***	0.242***
Add regional dummies	−0.160*	−0.138***	0.230**

*significant at 10%
**significant at 5%
***significant at 1%

Each column displays the values and statistical significance of the *oil income* coefficient under different conditions.

The first row shows the *oil income* coefficient in each of the core models. The core model for predicting *democratic transitions* is drawn from table 3.7, column five, and includes controls for *income, regime duration, oil income*Latin America*, and a set of period dummies. The core model for estimating *polity* is taken from table 3.8 column five, and is nearly identical to the logit model, but includes a lagged dependent variable in place of *regime duration* to offset duration dependence. The rare-events logit model estimating the likelihood of *democratic failures* is taken from table 3.9 column six, and includes controls for *income* and *regime duration*, and is restricted to the 1980–2006 period.[80]

In both the core logit and rare-events logit models, I have used a base hazard rate (*regime duration*, measured as the natural log of the number of years of continuous authoritarian or democratic rule) that is some-

[80] When tested with the full 1960–2006 data set, the correlation between *oil income* and *democratic failures* is less robust. Restricting the other two models to the 1980–2006 period increases the size of the *oil income* coefficients, and has no effect on their robustness.

what arbitrary. Hence, in row two I replace the previous *regime duration* variable with the simple number of years of continuous authoritarian or democratic rule; in row three I add another variable to each model, measuring the square of the number of continuous authoritarian or democratic years, to account for a possible nonlinear effect. The *oil income* coefficients remain large and statistically significant.

These results could be biased by the nonnormal distribution of the *oil income* variable, even though I am always using its log value. In row four, I therefore try a dichotomous version of *oil income*, which takes the value "1" when countries earn more than a hundred dollars per capita in oil income (using constant year 2000 dollars) and zero otherwise. In all three models, the dummy variable is significantly correlated with less democracy. Perhaps the links between oil and democracy are driven by a handful of oil-rich countries and do not represent a broader, global pattern. To see if this is true for the models predicting *democratic transitions* and *polity*, in row five I drop all observations of the seven oil-producing authoritarian states on the Arabian Peninsula: Saudi Arabia, Kuwait, Qatar, the United Arab Emirates, Bahrain, Oman, and Yemen. *Oil income* remains statistically significant in both models, although the coefficients drop by about 25 percent.

For the model predicting *democratic failure*, I drop the three countries with the largest oil incomes where democracy has failed since 1980: Congo-Brazzaville (where democracy failed in 1997), Ecuador (2000), and Nigeria (1983). The size of the *oil income* coefficient drops by about 15 percent, yet remains statistically significant at the 0.05 level.

It is still possible that the association between oil and dictatorships is not causal but instead produced by the concentration of oil wealth in the Middle East, where democracy also happens to be rare. In row six, I check for this possibility by dropping all Middle Eastern countries from the data set. All of the oil variables remain statistically significant. In row seven I use a different approach, adding to the models a series of dummy variables for six world regions: the Middle East and North Africa, sub-Saharan Africa, Latin America, Asia (including East, South, and Southeast Asia), the former Soviet Union, and the traditional Organization for Economic Cooperation and Development (OECD) states (Western Europe, North America, Japan, Australia, and New Zealand). *Oil income* continues to be significantly associated with less democracy, although in the *democratic transitions* model only at the 0.10 level.

These tests suggest that the correlation between *oil income* and a country's regime type is robust in several important ways: it is unchanged by plausible modifications in the underlying hazard rate, the removal of influential countries from the data set, the use of a dichotomous measure of *oil income,* and the inclusion of regional dummies.

Causal Mechanisms

Chapter 3 indicates that oil income is tied to authoritarianism through two pathways: by causing a high ratio of government spending to perceived government revenues, and by leading to greater government secrecy, including a lack of budget transparency and restrictions on the media.

The first mechanism is the most difficult to measure. High-quality data on both government revenues and expenditures are scarce, especially for oil-rich states, and the model suggests that *perceived* government revenues, not *actual* ones, are what matter—yet these perceptions cannot be gauged without contemporaneous surveys. Official figures on government consumption spending and revenues are available for many countries from the World Development Indicators, although their accuracy is questionable, and observations are missing for a substantial number of countries and years.

Still, looking at these flawed data might be instructive. I showed in figure 3.5 that countries that eventually transited to democracy had higher spending-to-revenue ratios than those that did not. Unfortunately, the *spending-to-revenue ratio* variable cannot be employed in the logit model because the data are too scarce. In the reduced sample of countries and years for which the variable is available, *oil income* is no longer correlated with democratic transitions.

It can be used in the OLS model, although only with a cross-section (not a panel) of countries. To increase the number of country observations, I take the mean values for the spending-to-revenue ratio from 2000 to 2004, using only those years where data are not missing. For consistency, I also use the mean 2000–2004 values for the other variables (*income, oil income*, and *polity*). The resulting *spending-to-revenue ratio* is available for 111 of 170 possible countries; about one-third of the data are missing. The scarcity of these indicators is still a problem. As table 3.5 depicts, oil states are especially reluctant to release their revenue data, which implies that the missingness is nonrandom and likely to bias my estimations.

Table 3.11, column one, shows the baseline model, including only observations for which the *spending-to-revenue ratio* is not missing. The *spending-to-revenue ratio* is added to the model in column two, and is significantly and negatively correlated with *polity:* the more a government spends, relative to its revenues, the less democratic it is. While this is consistent with $H_{3.3}$, another feature of the estimation is not: adding the *spending-to-revenue ratio* to the model does not reduce the size or significance of the *oil income* coefficient. While this could indicate a flaw in the model, the *spending-to-revenue ratio* is too weak an indicator

TABLE 3.11
Transitions to democracy: Causal mechanisms

This table shows OLS regression coefficients; the dependent variable is a country's Polity score. In columns one and two, country values are averaged over the 2000–2004 period; in columns three and four, they are for 2004 only. The estimations in columns five and six, which use time series cross national data, the explanatory variables are lagged for a single year, and include a lagged dependent variable (not shown). The robust standard errors are in parentheses.

	(1)	(2)	(3)	(4)	(5)	(6)
Income (log)	0.756***	0.630***	0.988***	0.595***	0.0549***	0.0527***
	(0.118)	(0.132)	(0.171)	(0.191)	(0.0151)	(0.0151)
Oil income (log)	−0.248**	−0.253**	−0.260**	0.441***	−0.0240***	0.0156
	(0.110)	(0.111)	(0.103)	(0.156)	(0.00824)	(0.0155)
Government spending-to-revenues ratio	—	−1.949**	—	—	—	—
		(0.916)				
Oil income (log)*budget transparency	—	—	—	−0.0100***	—	—
				(0.00199)		
Oil income (log)*press freedom	—	—	—	—	—	−0.772***
						(0.255)
Years	2000–2004	2000–2004	2004	2004	1990–2004	1990–2004
Number of countries	111	111	83	83	168	168
Observations	111	111	83	83	1,658	1,658
Missing observations	34.7%	34.7%	51.2%	51.2%	33.9%	33.9%
R-squared	0.195	0.223	0.240	0.405	0.954	0.954

* significant at 10%
** significant at 5%
*** significant at 1%

to draw strong inferences—especially since the estimate is based on a cross-section of countries.

It is also hard to measure government secrecy. According to $H_{3.4}$, oil-backed dictatorships are less likely to transit to democracy because their budgets are more opaque and they place greater restrictions on the media.

The best-available measure of revenue transparency is the Open Budget Index, described in chapter 3, which ranks countries on a scale of zero to one hundred based on the transparency of the central government's budget documents. Unfortunately, it is only available for up to eighty-three countries, for just one or two years, beginning in 2006. Again, the scarcity of these data should make us cautious in our inferences.

Table 3.11, columns three and four, show a pair cross-national OLS estimations looking at the relationship between a variable interacting *oil income* with *budget transparency*, and a country's *polity* score. I use an interaction term since the hypothesis suggests that a lack of transparency in the presence of oil wealth has special, democracy-inhibiting effects. To make the results easier to interpret, I have reversed the scale of the original Open Budget Index so that higher scores indicate less transparency. Rising values of the interaction term thus indicate more oil and less transparency, both of which should have antidemocratic effects.

Column 3 portrays the core model before adding the interaction term, using only observations for the eighty-three countries rated by the Open Budget Index in 2008. Column 4 shows the same model and observations, after adding the interaction term. Consistent with the hypothesis, the interaction term is negatively correlated with *polity*, and its inclusion has a powerful effect on the *oil income* coefficient—causing it to change signs from significantly negative to significantly positive. This implies that *oil income* only hurts democracy when it coincides with greater budget secrecy.[81]

A different type of political transparency can be gauged with the Freedom of the Press Index developed by Freedom House, which evaluates the freedom of the print, broadcast, and internet media on a scale of one to one hundred. Unlike the *spending-to-revenue ratio* and *oil income*budget transparency* variables, data on media freedom are available for virtually all countries in the data set and include annual figures

---

[81] Adding *budget transparency* separately, as an additional control variable, has no substantial effect on these results.

beginning in 1990. This makes it possible to use a cross-national time-series OLS model.[82]

Like above, I reverse the Freedom of the Press Index so that higher scores indicate less freedom and then interact this with *oil income*. In table 3.11, column five, I show an OLS regression that includes just the control variables—*income* and *oil income*, and a lagged dependent variable—and uses an AR1 process to cope with autocorrelation; the data cover 168 countries from 1990 to 2004. In column six, I add the interaction term. It is negatively correlated with *polity*, and its inclusion once more has a large impact on the *oil income* measure, causing the coefficient to reverse signs and lose statistical significance. This again implies that *oil income* is only linked to less democracy when it is paired with exceptional government secrecy.[83]

These estimations offer limited support for hypothesis 3.3, which highlights the importance of a country's government spending-to-revenue ratio. They provide somewhat stronger support for hypothesis 3.4, which emphasizes the role of government secrecy. Still, the poor quality of the spending and revenue indicators, and the large number of missing countries in both these and the budget transparency data, make it hard to be confident about these results. The data on press freedom are more extensive and more complete, and can be interpreted with somewhat greater confidence: when placed in a simple OLS model, the results are consistent with the claim that in oil-producing countries, government secrecy plays a special role in hindering democracy.

These estimations suggest that most of the hypotheses in chapter 3—all but $H_{3.3}$—are consistent with patterns in the data:

- In authoritarian states, greater oil income is associated with a lower chance of transiting to democracy.
- In *lower-income* democracies, greater oil income is correlated with an increased chance of transiting to authoritarianism.
- Both of these patterns have only been evident since about 1980.
- Latin America is an exception; in this region, oil income is correlated with a higher likelihood of transiting to democracy.
- Government secrecy seems to account for a significant portion of oil's democracy-inhibiting effects.

[82] Since the data only cover fifteen years (1990–2004), I use annual observations in this model rather than taking observations from every fifth year, as I do in the core model (table 3.8). While this increases the number of observations for each country, it also becomes harder to mitigate serial correlation.

[83] Adding *press freedom* as an additional control has little effect on these results.

The most important correlations—between oil income and measures of democracy—are also reasonably robust, especially when we account for the anomalous status of Latin America, and focus on the post-1980 period.

There is also limited support for the remaining hypothesis: countries with higher ratios of government spending to government revenues tend to be less democratic, although this pattern cannot be linked to the oil-autocracy correlation. The scarcity and low quality of data on government spending and revenues, and the absence of measures of perceived government revenues, make it difficult to draw strong inferences—either favorable or unfavorable—about this hypothesis.

CHAPTER FOUR

Petroleum Perpetuates Patriarchy

> The utilization of Arab women's capabilities through political and economic participation remains the lowest in the world in quantitative terms, as evidenced by the very low share of women in parliaments, cabinets, and the work force and in the trend towards the feminization of unemployment. . . . Society as a whole suffers when a huge proportion of its productive potential is stifled, resulting in lower family incomes and standards of living.
> —*Arab Human Development Report*, 2002

As COUNTRIES GET RICHER, women typically gain more opportunities—both economic opportunities in the workplace, and political opportunities to serve in government. Yet this has not occurred in countries that get rich by selling petroleum. The benefits of oil booms usually go to men.

This effect has been strongest in the Middle East, where there are fewer women in both the workforce and parliaments than in any other region in the world. The low status of Middle Eastern women is often blamed on the region's Islamic, or Arab, heritage. But this explanation is faulty, or at least incomplete.

Almost all societies have had strong patriarchal traditions in their recent past. One hundred years ago, many traditional cultures in Latin America, East Asia, and South Asia were as patriarchal—probably even more so—than the traditional cultures of the Middle East. Yet in Latin America, East Asia, and South Asia, economic growth led to rapid improvements in the status of women, while similar or higher growth rates in the Middle East have produced relatively few gains. Why has economic growth diluted the strength of patriarchal culture in other regions but not in the Middle East?

This chapter explains why growth that is based on industrialization tends to draw women into the workforce and ultimately lead to female empowerment. Growth that is based on the sale of oil and gas, however, does not produce more jobs for women, and can even block the path toward gender rights.

Empowering Women: Background

When poor countries become richer, the lives of women often change dramatically: women enroll in school in greater numbers, bear fewer children, and become more active in national politics. Arguably the most important change—one that helps trigger the others—is their entry into the job market.

Social theorists have long suggested that joining the workforce has a transformative effect on women and the societies in which they live.[1] Many studies support this claim. When parents believe that their daughters will eventually contribute to family income, they are more likely to keep them in school and invest in their health. As a result, when more jobs become available for women, it usually leads to an increase in the number of girls enrolled in school.[2] Having jobs also encourages women to marry later, which in turn causes them to have fewer children—producing the smaller, nuclear families that are characteristic of modern, high-income societies.[3]

The availability of jobs for women can also have broader effects on gender relations. Studies of female garment workers in Bangladesh—who typically come from poor rural areas, and are hired when they are young and single—have found that factory work helps them gain self-confidence, develop new social networks, gain exposure to new information about health and contraception, and learn how to negotiate with men.[4] When married women in Indonesia have an independent source of income, they acquire greater influence over family decisions about prenatal and child health.[5]

Entering the workforce also sets women on a path toward greater political influence. An influential decade-long study in the United States by Nancy Burns, Kay Schlozman, and Sidney Verba found that when women take jobs outside their homes, they begin to have conversations with their coworkers that kindle their interest in politics; they join informal networks of women that enable them to act collectively; and they come face-to-face with gender discrimination, which motivates them to take action.[6]

---

[1] See, for example, Engels [1884] 1978. For an excellent review of the links between female labor force participation and female political representation, see Iversen and Rosenbluth 2008.

[2] Michael 1985.

[3] Brewster and Rindfuss 2000.

[4] Amin et al. 1998; Kabeer and Mahmud 2004.

[5] Thomas, Contreras, and Frankenberg 2002.

[6] Burns, Schlozman, and Verba 2001. See also Sapiro 1983.

Other studies find a similar pattern in many developing countries. According to Pradeep Chhibber, Indian women who work outside the home develop a new sense of identity, which makes them more likely to participate in politics and vote for female candidates.[7] Valentine Moghadam shows that in many countries where women are widely employed in factory jobs—including Guatemala, Taiwan, Hong Kong, India, Indonesia, Tunisia, and Morocco—they have formed organizations to protect their interests; often these organizations lobby for broader reforms in the status of women.[8]

These and other studies suggest that joining the labor force can boost female political influence through at least three channels: at an individual level, by affecting women's political views and identities; at a social level, by bringing women together in the workplace and allowing them to form political networks; and at an economic level, by amplifying their role in the economy, which causes political leaders to pay more attention to their interests.

While all work is important, not all jobs have the same effects on women's status. Jobs outside agriculture and in the formal sector seem to be more critical. Many women in developing states work in agriculture, but frequently these jobs are on family-owned or family-operated farms, and give them neither economic independence nor a political voice.[9] Jobs in commercial agriculture seem to be more consequential, if they provide women with their own paychecks.[10] But jobs outside agriculture and in the formal sector seem to have the most powerful consequences for gender equality.

Why Not Work?

Why do women join the labor force in some countries but not in others?

One factor is discrimination—sometimes rooted in a country's culture, sometimes in its laws, and sometimes in both. Where it is most severe, women are discouraged from working by both their relatives, who do not want them to interact with strangers, and laws that sharply restrict their economic opportunities.

In theory, these obstacles could be removed by government reforms—for example, by well-enforced laws that would allow women to travel freely without the consent of a male relative, prohibit employers from discriminating against women, and provide for generous

---

[7] Chhibber 2003.
[8] Moghadam 1999.
[9] Oakes and Almquist 1993; Matland 1998.
[10] Anderson and Eswaran 2005.

maternity leave. But this raises a second obstacle: women often have little political influence, and hence cannot persuade lawmakers to enact and enforce reforms. Unfortunately, economic and political marginalization frequently go hand in hand: without jobs, women have less political influence; without political influence, women find it harder to get jobs.

How do women get out of this trap, where they lack both economic and political power?

Sometimes enlightened leadership helps. There is growing evidence that electoral quotas—laws that set aside a certain number of seats in local or national legislatures for women—can have powerful effects on female political influence.[11] Political institutions also matter: women are more likely to hold office in countries with proportional representation systems rather than plurality-majority ones.[12]

Finally, the organization of the economy can sometimes make a difference—especially the presence of sweatshops. Since the early days of the Industrial Revolution, millions of women have entered the workforce by taking low-paying jobs in factories that produce textiles, garments, and countless other inexpensive goods for world markets. In 1890, women held over half the jobs in the US textiles industry. Today, over 80 percent of the world's textile and garment workers are women.[13] There are many reasons to denounce sweatshops, and they can be brutal places to work. Yet they can also be a critical first step for women on the ladder to economic, social, and political empowerment.

There are four reasons why these labor-intensive industries are often conduits for new female workers. First, they do not require workers with great physical strength; men have no natural advantage in these positions. Second, they require little training and few specialized skills; this makes them attractive for women, who periodically leave the labor force to raise children or care for relatives.[14] Third, factories that produce goods for export are more likely to be owned or managed by foreign companies that—for legal or cultural reasons—are less prone to discriminate against women in hiring. Finally, these companies are selling their goods in a global market, where competition is fierce and profit margins are slim; this drives them to find the cheapest possible labor force. Because women are typically willing to work for less than men, and are more reliable and flexible workers, they are usually targeted for recruitment.

Factories, by contrast, are more likely to hire men for jobs that require greater physical strength or many years of continuous training, or if the

[11] Baldez 2004; Tripp and Kang 2008; Bhavnani 2009.
[12] Iversen and Rosenbluth 2008.
[13] World Bank 2001.
[14] Iverson and Rosenbluth 2006.

goods they produce are only sold in domestic markets, especially when there is less price competition.[15]

Women, Work, and Politics in South Korea

The case of South Korea—a country with no oil—illustrates how export-oriented factories can draw women into the labor force, and lead to the erosion of patriarchal laws and institutions.

At the turn of the twentieth century, Korea had one of the world's most patriarchal cultures. Girls were separated from boys beginning at age six, women were not given their own names, and in Seoul, women were not allowed to enter the streets during the daytime. In 1930, 90 percent of Korean women were illiterate.[16]

When South Korea industrialized in the 1960s, women began to take jobs in factories that produced goods for export, including textiles, garments, plastics, electronics, shoes, and dishware. Their low wages— less than half of male wages—made them attractive to employers, and helped fuel Korea's economic boom. By 1975, 70 percent of South Korea's export earnings came from female-dominated industries. As exports grew, so did the female share of the labor force—rising by 50 percent between 1960 and 1980.[17]

Although there were women's organizations in Korea in the 1950s and 1960s, they were socially conservative and sponsored by the government. Typically they were headed by men, and focused on charity work, consumer protection, and classes for housewives and brides-to-be.[18] Beginning in the 1970s, however, women working in export industries mobilized for both labor rights and gender equality. The South Korean government, then under authoritarian rule, showed little interest in their concerns.

In 1987, female organizers took advantage of South Korea's democratic opening to found the Korean Women's Associations United. Unlike earlier women's organizations, it worked for improved labor conditions and women's rights, and took a more confrontational stance toward the government.[19] At the same time, more traditional women's groups started to show a stronger interest in women's rights.[20]

In the mid-1990s, women's organizations began to push for greater female representation at all levels of government. Despite Korea's

[15] Özler 2000.

[16] Park 1990.

[17] Park 1993; World Bank 2005.

[18] Yoon 2003.

[19] Moon 2002. Women also played an important role in South Korea's move toward democracy. See Nam 2000.

[20] Palley 1990.

strong patriarchal traditions, they made substantial gains: the number of female representatives in the national assembly rose from eight in 1992–96 to sixteen in 2000–2004; female membership on policy-setting government committees increased from 8.5 percent in 1996 to 17.6 percent in 2001; and the proportion of female judges rose from 3.9 percent in 1985 to 8.5 percent in 2001.[21]

The lobbying strength of the women's movement and the growing number of women in government has led to a series of landmark reforms. These included the Gender Equality Employment Act (1987), revisions to the family laws (1989), the Mother-Child Welfare Act (1989), the Framework Act on Women's Development (1995), and a bill stipulating that political parties must set aside at least 30 percent of their national constituency seats for women (2000).[22] By drawing women into the workforce, export-oriented manufacturing helped South Korean women gain a foothold in government and opened the door to these historic changes.

A Theory of Female Empowerment

Oil production can have a detrimental effect *under certain conditions* on the role of women. To explain this effect, we must add some new elements to the model of politics sketched out in chapter 3. Suppose that our imaginary country has both male and female citizens; instead of acting as individuals, they act as households; and for women, working outside the home is a critical source of economic, social, and political power.

Let us also stipulate that the number of women in the labor force is determined by two factors. The first is the supply of women who want jobs. Not all women want to work outside the home: remember that citizens are now members of households, and so act in the economic interests of their family, not just themselves. In most societies, men are the primary source of income for households, while women only seek jobs when their family needs a second income. In low-income families, women are more likely to look for jobs, even when wages are low. In higher-income families, they are less likely to seek work and will only take jobs that pay relatively well.

The second factor is the demand for female labor. In many countries, employers are reluctant to hire women for all but a handful of occupa-

---

[21] Yoon 2003.
[22] Park 1993; Yoon 2003.

tions.[23] To capture one of the most common patterns, let us also imagine that women are only hired to work in sweatshops—that is, export-oriented factories that use low-wage labor to produce textiles, garments, and other manufactured or processed goods for export.

To summarize, in our revised model women gain economic and political power by taking a job outside the home; they are more inclined to take these jobs when their families need extra income; and the only places that will hire them are factories that produce inexpensive goods for export. While the first two assumptions are probably valid for all countries, the final one is most likely to hold in countries with strong patriarchal cultures that restrict job opportunities for women—like the United States in the nineteenth and early twentieth centuries, East Asia in the 1950s, 1960s, and 1970s, and many Middle Eastern and North African countries today.

How Oil Affects Women

Under these conditions, oil can have the opposite effect as manufacturing: while manufacturing draws women out of the home and into the workforce, oil wealth encourages them to remain at home, erasing a key pathway toward economic and political empowerment.[24]

A rise in oil income will have two effects—one on the supply of female labor, and the other on the demand for it. Figure 4.1 summarizes these links. We know from chapter 2 that the exceptional size of oil revenues leads to exceptionally large government budgets. Chapter 3 explains that rulers distribute much of this revenue to households— through government jobs, welfare programs, subsidies, and tax cuts— to buy political support. These government transfers may make daily life more comfortable, but they also discourage women from seeking work outside the home by diminishing their families' need for a second income. The scale of the government's oil revenues, when transferred to households, reduces the supply of women looking for jobs.

Oil can also reduce the demand for female labor by shrinking the number of jobs in export-oriented factories. Chapter 2 describes how oil wealth can lead to the Dutch Disease, which causes a country's exchange rate to rise, and its agricultural and manufacturing sectors to lose their overseas markets. Factories that produce goods for the domestic market might still survive if they receive government support.

---

[23] Horton 1999.

[24] For a more detailed explanation of this process, see Ross 2008. Elisabeth Hermann Frederikssen (2007) provides a more complete and explicit model of oil, the Dutch Disease, and female employment, which I loosely draw on here.

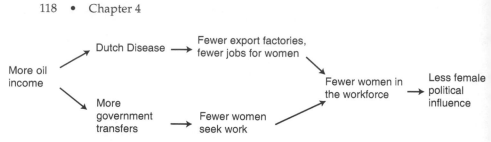

Figure 4.1. How oil production can affect the status of women

But the kinds of factories that are most likely to hire women are export-oriented companies that rely on low-wage labor, and the Dutch Disease will make them unprofitable.

While oil booms create new jobs, they are mostly in the service sector, including construction and retail, and government. If women can find jobs in these sectors, they will be unharmed. If they cannot, a booming oil industry will "push" them out of the labor force, or discourage them from joining it in the first place.

The size of oil revenues, in short, will boost government budgets and hence household transfers, which will discourage women from seeking work, and oil will lead to the loss of a key part of the private sector—low-wage, export-oriented manufacturing—that would otherwise draw women into the workforce. More oil leads to fewer paychecks for women. And because entering the workforce is a critical route to political power, oil wealth can also diminish female influence in government.

Not all oil-rich countries fit this model, so not all of them are susceptible to these problems. In many Western countries, women can readily find work in the service sector and government. In Norway, for example, the oil boom of the 1970s created new jobs in medicine and social services that were often filled by women. Even in some low- and middle-income countries, like Colombia, Syria, Malaysia, and Mexico, many women work in service and government jobs, and have been largely unharmed by their nation's oil wealth. But in countries where women face barriers to working in the service sector, oil wealth is liable to retard their economic, social, and political progress.

Many of these countries are in the Middle East and North Africa. A World Bank study in 2004 found that fourteen of the region's seventeen countries place legal restrictions on the types of jobs that women can take, and the number of hours and time of day they may work. Six of them also restrict women from traveling without permission from their husband or male guardian.[25]

[25] World Bank 2004.

These restrictions have made it unusually hard for women in the Middle East to find work in the service sector.[26] Middle Eastern women are often excluded from jobs that involve public activity and presuppose contact with men.[27] This strongly discourages women from working in retail—one of the largest segments of the service sector—except in shops where all customers are women, and frequently keeps them out of jobs in education and health, except when they are in exclusively female settings.[28] In most Middle Eastern countries, women have also been kept out of jobs in the tourist industry, which in countries like Egypt form a large part of the service sector, due to cultural and legal prohibitions on unsupervised travel as well as contact with men outside the family.[29] And the construction industry in the Middle East—like in most other regions—rarely hires women.

OIL AND WOMEN AROUND THE WORLD

In almost all countries, women have made substantial economic and political progress since the 1960s. Their progress has been slower in some places than others, and petroleum can help explain why, especially since the 1970s.

Figures 4.2 and 4.3 show how women have fared in different regions of the world in terms of joining the workforce and gaining seats in parliament. As the upward-sloping lines suggest, women generally do better in the rich countries (the OECD states) than the poor ones. The Middle East is the great exception: even though it is the world's second-richest region, it has fewer women in the workforce and parliament than anywhere else.

Oil wealth can help explain the Middle Eastern anomaly. Table 4.1 depicts the percentage of the labor force made up of women in both oil- and non-oil-producing countries.[30] Overall, significantly fewer women work in the oil countries—14 percent fewer—than in the non-oil countries. The pattern holds for both rich and poor states, but is stronger

---

[26] Although less well documented, women in sub-Saharan Africa also seem to have special trouble gaining jobs in the service sector. According to a United Nations (1991) study—which unfortunately is the most recent one I could find available—many women in Latin America and the Caribbean work in the service sector; in the Asia Pacific region, their numbers are fewer but still significant; but in sub-Saharan Africa, few women have access to service sector jobs.

[27] Youssef 1971.

[28] Anker 1997; World Bank 2004.

[29] Assaad and Arntz 2005.

[30] This was the most recent year for which data were available for most countries.

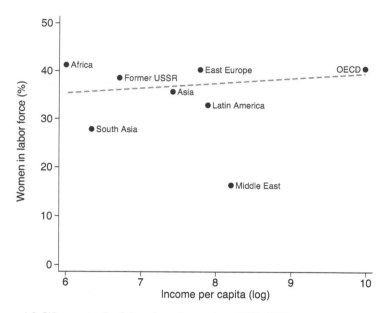

Figure 4.2. Women in the labor force by region, 1993–2002

The vertical axis shows the percentage of the nonagricultural workforce made up of women. The dots show the country average by region.

Source: Calculated from data collected by the International Labor Organization and published in World Bank 2005.

among the rich states, reflecting the large gap between countries that grew wealthy by industrializing (in Europe and North America) and those that grew wealthy by selling off their hydrocarbon assets (in the Middle East).

The gap is largest in the Middle East and North Africa, where the number of working women is about 23 percent lower in the oil states than the non-oil ones. Oil states in the rest of the developing world have fewer working women, although the difference is much smaller.

One reason for this gap is that non-oil states export more manufactured goods, and thus have more factory jobs for women. Consider, for instance, the textiles and clothing industries, which are overwhelmingly staffed by women. As table 4.2 shows, both rich and poor countries without oil export far more textiles and garments than rich and poor countries with oil. Among low-income states, countries without oil export about three times more per capita than countries with oil.[31]

---

[31] When rich and poor states are aggregated together, in the bottom row of table 4.2, oil states appear to export more textiles that non-oil ones. This is only because oil states tend to be rich, and richer countries export more textiles than poorer ones. When countries

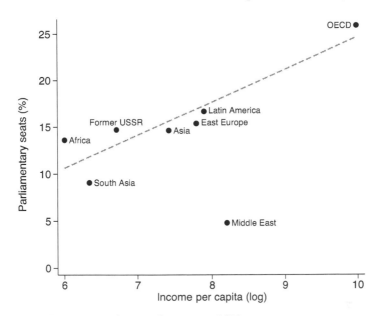

Figure 4.3. Women in parliament by region, 2002

The vertical axis shows the percentage of seats held by women in the lower house of parliament. Each dot shows the country average in a given region.

Source: Calculated from data collected by the Inter-Parliamentary Union, available at http://ipu.org/wmn-e/world.htm.

The oil states also have significantly fewer women in government. Table 4.3 shows the percentage of parliamentary seats held by women—a simple measure of female political strength—in both the oil and non-oil states. Both rich and poor oil producers have fewer female legislators than rich and poor non-oil producers, although the difference is statistically significant only among the poor states. The effects of oil are overwhelmingly concentrated in the Middle East and North Africa, where the non-oil states have more than three times as many female parliamentarians as the oil states. In the rest of the world, the link between petroleum and female legislators is not statistically significant.

I explore these basic patterns more deliberately in appendix 4.1, using regression analysis to control for other factors that might influence the status of women, like a country's income, its level of democracy, and historical, cultural, and regional factors, including the presence of Islam. My analysis suggests that when countries have more oil, they

are separated into income groups, in the first two rows, the effect of oil on textile exports becomes apparent.

TABLE 4.1
Female labor force participation, 2002

These numbers show the percentage of the formal labor force made up by female citizens.

	Non-oil producers	Oil producers	Difference
By income			
Low income (below $5,000)	41.8	38.4	−3.4**
High income (above $5,000)	41.3	33.2	−8.1***
By region			
Middle East and North Africa	30.6	23.5	−7.1**
All other countries	42.0	41.5	−0.6
All other developing countries	42.1	40.1	−2.0*
Overall			
All states	41.6	35.9	−5.8***

*significant at 10%, in a one-tailed t-test
**significant at 5%
***significant at 1%
Source: Calculated from data collected by the International Labor Organization and published in World Bank 2004, 2005.

TABLE 4.2
Textile and clothing exports, 2002

These numbers indicate the value of textile and clothing exports per capita.

	Non-oil producers	Oil producers	Difference
By income			
Low income (below $5,000)	65.6	22.5	−43.1*
High income (above $5,000)	252	210	−41.9
Overall			
All states	115	122	6.5

*significant at 10%, in a one-tailed t-test
**significant at 5%
***significant at 1%
Source: Calculated from data in Freeman and Oostendorp 2009.

TABLE 4.3
Parliamentary seats held by women, 2002

These numbers show the percentage of seats held by women in the lower house of parliament.

	Non-oil producers	Oil producers	Difference
By income			
Low income (below $5,000)	13.9	11.0	−2.9*
High income (above $5,000)	20.1	16.0	−4.0
By region			
Middle East and North Africa	10.4	3.0	−7.5***
All other countries	15.7	17.6	1.9
All other developing countries	14.3	13.9	−0.4
Overall			
All states	15.5	13.3	−2.2

*significant at 10%, in a one-tailed t-test
**significant at 5%
***significant at 1%
Source: Calculated from data collected by the Inter-Parliamentary Union, available at http://ipu.org/wmn-e/world.htm.

tend to have fewer women working outside the home, other things being equal, and more tentatively, that oil wealth reduces the number of women holding seats in parliament. I also demonstrate that oil's impact on women has grown since the 1970s, although this pattern is harder to tease out.[32]

Figures on female parliamentarians are unavailable before 1995, which makes it hard to tell whether oil's effects on the political empowerment of women have also grown. Moreover, in recent years there has been a global trend toward female political empowerment, which has lifted the number of female legislators in more than three-quarters of the world's countries, including some oil-rich countries. But the gains in the oil-rich states have been slower than those in oil-poor states: between 1995 and 2002, oil-poor states had a 5 percent increase

[32] This is partly because of strong global trends in female labor force participation, which must be controlled for, and because of the U-shaped relationship between income and female labor force participation. These problems are explained in the appendix to this chapter.

in the number of female representatives, while oil-rich states had only a 2.9 percent increase. Even though the vast majority of states showed increases in female representation, oil-producing ones like Algeria, Russia, and Kazakhstan—all of which enjoyed a sharp rise in oil revenues—saw a fall in female representation.

Inside the Middle East

How can we be sure that women in the Middle East are impeded by oil, not by Islam, or the region's distinctive culture and history? One way to probe deeper is by looking more closely at the status of women *within* the Middle East. The countries in the region have a common religion, and (broadly speaking) a common culture. If religion or culture were the source of the problem, then women in all Middle Eastern and North African countries should have about the same low economic and political status.

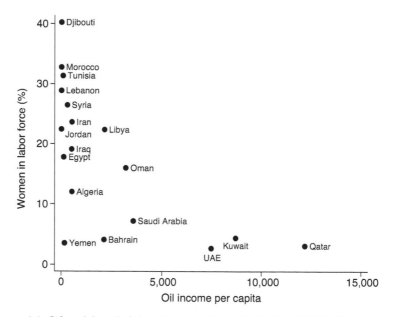

Figure 4.4. Oil and female labor force participation in the Middle East, 1993–2002

Numbers on the vertical axis indicate the percentage of the nonagricultural workforce made up of women, averaged over a ten-year period.

Source: Calculated from data collected by the International Labor Organization and published in World Bank 2004, 2005, n.d.

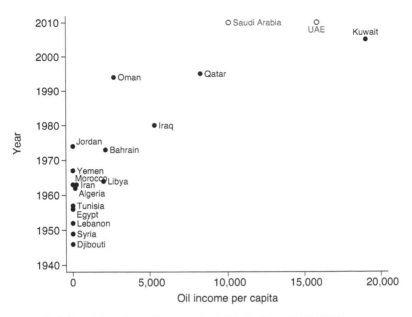

Figure 4.5. Oil and female suffrage in the Middle East, 1940–2010
The year of suffrage is the year that women were first allowed to vote.
Saudi Arabia and the United Arab Emirates do not allow women to vote; they
have been coded as granting suffrage in 2010 so they will not be excluded
from the chart.

But this is not the case. There is striking variation across the region in
the status of women. In some countries they make up more than a quarter of the workforce, and in others less than 5 percent; in some, women
achieved suffrage in the 1940s, while in others they had not achieved it
by 2010; in some governments, women hold over 20 percent of all parliamentary seats, and in others none. What explains these differences?

Unlike religion and culture, oil production varies a lot across the
region—and it is strongly correlated with the status of women. Figures 4.4, 4.5, and 4.6 are scatterplots that show the relationship between
a country's oil wealth and different measures of female status. In general, the states that are richest in oil (Saudi Arabia, Iraq, Libya, Qatar,
Bahrain, the United Arab Emirates, and Oman) have the fewest women
in their nonagricultural workforce, have been the most reluctant to
grant female suffrage, and have the fewest women in their parliaments. States with little or no oil (Morocco, Tunisia, Lebanon, Syria, and
Djibouti) were among the first to grant female suffrage, tend to have
more women in the workplace and parliament, and have more fully
recognized women's rights.

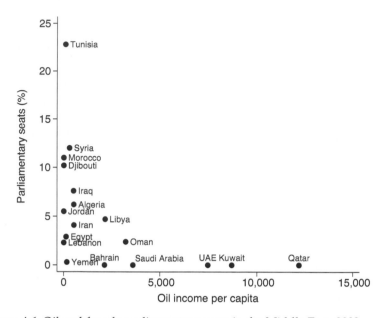

Figure 4.6. Oil and female parliamentary seats in the Middle East, 2002
The vertical axis shows the percentage of seats in the lower house of parliament that are held by women.
Source: Calculated from data collected by the Inter-Parliamentary Union, available at http://ipu.org/wmn-e/world.htm.

The region's oil wealth also helps explain some of the outliers. Even though Yemen, Egypt, and Jordan have little or no oil, they have fewer women in the labor force (see figure 4.4) and parliament (see figure 4.6) than we might expect. These anomalies may be partly the result of labor remittances. From the 1970s to the 1990s, these countries were the largest exporters of labor to the oil-rich countries of the Persian Gulf, and received large remittances from them in turn.[33] Like oil, labor remittances can trigger the Dutch Disease, making it harder for countries to develop the kinds of industries that typically employ women. Yemen is farther below the trend lines for female labor and female representation than any other Middle Eastern country; it has also received more remittances (as a fraction of its GDP) than any other country.

[33] Between 1974 and 1982, official remittances made up between 3 and 13 percent of Egypt's GDP, between 10 and 31 percent of Jordan's GDP, and between 22 and 69 percent of Yemen's GDP. Unofficial remittances were probably much larger. See Choucri 1986.

TABLE 4.4
Comparing Algeria, Morocco, and Tunisia

The numbers are for 2003, except where indicated. Income, oil income, and
textile and clothing exports are in constant 2000 dollars.

	Algeria	Morocco	Tunisia
Background			
Population (million)	31.8	30.1	9.9
Muslim population (%)	97	98	99
Income per capita	$1,915	$1,278	$2,214
Oil versus manufacturing			
Oil income per capita	$1,037	$0	$121
Textile/clothing exports per capita	$0.09	$94	$287*
Female status			
Female labor force participation (%)	12**	26**	25**
Female-held parliamentary seats (%)*	6.2*	10.8*	22.8*
Gender rights index	2.8	3.1	3.2

*2002 figures
**nonagricultural work only; figures are for 2000. See Livani 2007.

Comparing Algeria, Morocco, and Tunisia

Admittedly these patterns could simply reflect the conditions in a handful of countries on the Arabian Peninsula, which by sheer coincidence
have both extraordinary oil wealth and extraordinary discrimination
against women. How can we know that oil is really at fault?

One way to address this question is by looking at Middle Eastern
countries outside the Persian Gulf, to see if oil can be causally linked
to poor conditions for women. We would ideally like to compare
countries with similar histories and cultures, but different levels of
oil wealth. Three adjoining North African countries may be the best
match: Algeria, Morocco, and Tunisia. All three were French colonies,
gained independence in the late 1950s or early 1960s, granted suffrage
to women soon after independence, and are overwhelmingly Muslim.
Yet in Algeria, both female labor force participation and female political representation are relatively low; in Morocco and Tunisia, they are
relatively high (see table 4.4).

Most of these differences can be traced to oil: Morocco and Tunisia
have relatively little, but Algeria has a lot. With little or no oil, labor in

Morocco and Tunisia is cheap by international standards. Beginning around 1970, both countries took advantage of their inexpensive labor to develop export-oriented textile industries.

In both Morocco and Tunisia, these industries played a major role in drawing women into the workforce. In Morocco, for example, the government began to promote textile and garment exports to Europe in 1969, hoping that this would reduce the high unemployment rate for men. Although the textile industry grew quickly, companies deliberately sought out and hired unmarried women, since they could be paid lower wages; by keeping their labor costs low, these firms were able to compete in the European market. By 1980, Morocco's textile workforce was 75 percent female, even though men continued to outnumber women in factories that produced textiles for the domestic market.[34]

The Moroccan textile industry hit a slump in the late 1970s when Europe closed its markets. But after the government carried out structural reforms in the late 1980s and early 1990s, the industry once again grew quickly. By 2004, it was Morocco's main source of exports. It also accounted for three-quarters of the growth in female employment in the 1990s.[35]

The Tunisian textile industry has followed a largely similar path—expanding since about 1970 through exports, relying on low-wage female labor, and weathering changes in European trade policies.[36] Morocco and Tunisia now have the two highest rates of female labor force participation in the Middle East.

The high rates of female labor participation in Morocco and Tunisia have contributed to each country's unusually large and vigorous gender rights movement. Unlike other Middle Eastern countries, Morocco and Tunisia have women's organizations that focus on female labor issues, including the right to maternity leave, raising the minimum work age, sexual harassment, and gaining rights for domestic workers.[37]

In Tunisia, the women's movement began with an important advantage: shortly after independence, President Habib Bourguiba adopted a national family law that gave women greater equality in marriage, and opened the door to major improvements in female education and employment. But Moroccan family laws were much more conservative, and women's groups had little success in reforming them in the 1960s, 1970s, and 1980s.[38]

[34] Joekes 1982.
[35] Assaad 2004.
[36] Baud 1977; White 2001.
[37] Moghadam 1999.
[38] Charrad 2001.

Although Morocco had a small number of women's organizations in the 1950s and 1960s, these groups were headed by men, and concentrated on social and charitable work. From 1970 to 1984, however, the number of women's organizations jumped from five to thirty-two, and many started to focus on women's rights.

Between 1990 and 1992, a coalition of women's groups (including labor unions) gathered more than one million signatures on a petition calling for reform of the family laws to give women new rights in marriage, divorce, child custody, and inheritance. Conservative Islamists rallied their own supporters to block any new laws. Morocco's political parties—even secular opposition ones—declined to support the petition campaign. Still, the movement placed strong pressures on King Hassan II, and he eventually backed a more modest package of reforms.[39]

In the late 1990s and early 2000s, Moroccan women's groups continued to face strong opposition and even death threats. Nevertheless, their lobbying led to further reforms, including a new labor code that recognizes gender equality in the workplace and criminalizes sexual harassment; a more complete reform of the family laws; and an informal 20 percent female quota for political parties in parliament. These new measures, coupled with the grassroots strength of the women's movement, led to a tripling in the number of women running for local office from 1997 to 2002, and an increase in the fraction of parliamentary seats held by women from 0.6 percent in 1995 to 10.8 percent in 2003.[40]

In Tunisia, women's groups have been even more successful, raising the fraction of female-held parliamentary seats from 6.7 percent in 1995 to 22.8 percent in 2002—the highest in the Middle East, and higher than in Western countries like the United States, the United Kingdom, and Canada.[41]

Oil-rich Algeria provides a telling contrast to oil-poor Morocco. A naive observer might expect Algeria to have *more* women in the labor force and parliament than Morocco: Moroccans hold more conservative religious views than Algerians; Algerian incomes are considerably higher; and Algeria has had a series of socialist governments, while Morocco has been ruled by a monarchy with strong tribal roots.[42]

Yet Algeria has fewer women in its nonagricultural labor force, fewer women in its parliament, and fewer protections for gender rights than does either Morocco or Tunisia.

---

[39] Brand 1998; Wuerth 2005.
[40] World Bank 2004.
[41] Moghadam 1999; World Bank 2004.
[42] Blaydes and Linzer 2008.

The lower status of Algerian women is at least partly caused by economic forces, especially Algeria's oil industry. The Algerian economy has long been based on the extraction of hydrocarbons: between 1970 and 2003, about half of its GDP came from oil. It has also suffered from the Dutch Disease: since at least the early 1970s, its tradable sector (agriculture and manufacturing) has been unusually small, and its non-tradable sector (construction and services) has been unusually large, for a country of Algeria's size and income.

In the 1990s, the Algerian government launched an initiative to diversify its export sector, in hopes of competing with Tunisia and Morocco. But thanks to the Dutch Disease, its labor costs were too high. In the textiles industry, wages for Algerian sewing machine operators, thread and yarn spinners, cloth weavers, and loom fixers were two to three times higher than those of their Tunisian counterparts (see figure 4.7).[43] Unable to compete in international markets, Algeria's manufacturing sector remained highly protected, capital intensive, oriented toward domestic needs, and small.[44] Consequently, there was relatively little demand for low-wage labor in the manufacturing sector.

If Morocco and Tunisia had large oil sectors like Algeria, they would not have become major textiles exporters, since the Dutch Disease would have made their labor costs too high. Without large, export-oriented manufacturing sectors, women in Morocco and Tunisia would have been slower to enter the labor force, had fewer opportunities to organize, and major reforms—especially in Morocco, which lacked Tunisia's enlightened leadership—would have been less likely.

Under certain conditions, the extraction of oil and gas can reduce the role of women in the workforce along with the likelihood that they will accumulate political influence. Without large numbers of women participating in the economic and political life of a country, traditional patriarchal institutions will go unchallenged. Petroleum, in short, can perpetuate patriarchy. This dynamic can help explain the surprisingly low influence of women in oil-, gas-, and mineral-rich states in the Middle East (Saudi Arabia, Kuwait, Oman, Algeria, and Libya)—and perhaps also in Latin America (Chile), sub-Saharan Africa (Botswana, Gabon, Mauritania, and Nigeria), and the former Soviet Union (Azerbaijan and Russia).[45]

---

[43] Based on data in Freeman and Oostendorp 2009. This study does not report figures for Morocco.

[44] Auty 2003.

[45] For a series of critiques of my earlier study of oil and women, along with my reply, see the December 2009 issue of the journal *Politics and Gender*.

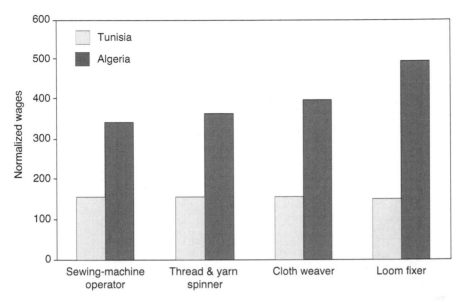

Figure 4.7. Wages for textile workers in Tunisia and Algeria, 1987–1991
These numbers represent the normalized wage rate for each occupation, in Algeria (dark bars) and Tunisia (light bars). Data on the wage rates of loom fixers was only available for 1987–89.
Source: Freeman and Oostendorp 2009.

Oil wealth does not *necessarily* harm the status of women. It depends on whether women have opportunities to work in the service sector, which typically grows in tandem with oil revenues. Seven countries have produced significant quantities of oil and gas, but still made faster progress on gender equality than we would expect based on their income: Norway, New Zealand, Australia, Uzbekistan, Turkmenistan, Syria, and Mexico. In the first three countries, women are able to work in all parts of the economy—not just manufacturing—so rising oil exports did not reduce jobs for women. The two Central Asian states were strongly affected by many years of Soviet rule, which promoted the role of women through administrative fiat. This may have inoculated them against oil-induced patriarchy.

Perhaps the most interesting exceptions are Syria and Mexico: women in both states may have benefited from many years of rule by secular, left-of-center parties that showed an interest in women's rights. Mexico also gained from its proximity to the US market, which allowed it to develop a large, low-wage export-oriented manufacturing sector along the border—pulling women into the labor market despite the flow of

oil rents. Both good fortune and a committed government can sometimes counteract the perverse effects of oil on the status of women.

Appendix 4.1: A Statistical Analysis of Oil and the Status of Women

This appendix describes some of the conditions under which oil income
is statistically correlated with female labor force participation and female representation in government. The key ideas in chapter 4 can be
encapsulated in two hypotheses:

> *Hypothesis 4.1*: When women are excluded from jobs in the service
> sector and government, a rise in the value of oil production will
> reduce female participation in the labor force.
> *Hypothesis 4.2*: When women are excluded from jobs in the service
> sector and government, a rise in the value of oil production will
> reduce female political influence.

If this model is combined with the argument in chapter 2—that the political effects of oil have grown stronger since the 1970s—I can formulate
a third hypothesis:

> *Hypothesis 4.3*: The effects of oil income on women will be larger after
> 1980 than before 1980.

Data and Methods

To illustrate these patterns, I carry out two sets of estimations: the first
uses pooled time-series cross-sectional data for all states between 1960
and 2002, and focuses on changes within countries over time; the second uses only cross-national data and concentrates on differences between states. I use both methods to look at the relationship between
a country's oil income and female labor force participation. I also use
cross-national data to look at the relationship between oil and female
political representation. Since data on female political representation
is only available for recent years, I cannot look at the changes within
countries over time but only the differences across countries.

With the pooled time-series cross-sectional data, I am principally in-
terested in variations within countries over time. I also wish to see how
changes in my independent variables affect changes in my dependent
variable. Hence, I use a first-differences model with country fixed effects, which can be written as:

$$Y_{i,t} - Y_{i,t-1} = \alpha_i + \beta(x_{i,t-1} - x_{i,t-2}) + (\varepsilon_{i,t} - \varepsilon_{i,t-1})$$

where i is the country, t is the year, x is a series of explanatory variables, and the right-hand-side variables are lagged by one year.

The first-differences model with fixed effects has some useful properties. Standard OLS models look at whether the level of the explanatory variable is correlated with the level of the dependent variable. The first-differences model looks at whether changes in the explanatory variable are associated with those in the dependent variable. Because it focuses on changes, not levels, the model helps control for country heterogeneity. It also helps correct for trending in the dependent variable: the steady rise of female labor force participation between 1960 and 2002, if not accounted for, could produce biased estimates of the explanatory variables. The model includes country fixed effects to allow any trends in female labor force participation to vary from country to country. I use an AR1 process to help offset any remaining autocorrelation.

The disadvantage of the first-differences model with fixed effects is that it does not say anything about the influence of factors that vary a lot from country to country, but change little within countries over time, such as a country's religious traditions or its presence in a larger region. I use cross-national tests to capture the role of these fixed and "sluggish" variables.

For the cross-national estimations, I use a between estimator to compare the mean values of the explanatory variables with those of the dependent variable, over some period of time. It may be written as:

$$\bar{Y}_i = \alpha + \beta \, \bar{x}_i + \varepsilon_i$$

where i is the country, x is a series of explanatory variables, and values are averaged over several years. Using the mean value of each variable over a period of time also helps reduce measurement error. I take the mean values of the variables over the most recent ten-year period for which I have data on female empowerment (1993–2002).

Dependent Variables

There are two dependent variables. One is *female labor force participation*, which denotes the fraction of the formal labor force that is made up of female citizens. It is based on data collected by the International Labor Organization from national surveys and censuses, and released by the World Bank in its World Development Indicators. The variable has three notable shortcomings: countries differ in the way they define and measure labor force participation; some countries count foreign workers as part of the labor force, and others do not; and the measure does not distinguish between work in the nonagricultural and agricultural sectors, which is problematic because work in the agricultural sector may include work in the home unit.

The first problem can be addressed by using the first-differences model with fixed effects, since it measures changes over time within countries, not differences between them. As long as countries define "female labor force participation" consistently over time, country-to-country differences in measurement should not bias the estimations in any obvious way. Still, this issue causes problems for the cross-national estimations, and should make us cautious when interpreting them.

The other two problems can be addressed by subtracting the number of female agricultural and foreign workers from *female labor force participation*.[46] Since adjustments can only be done for recent years—there is little data before 1990—the corrected measures can only be used in the cross-national estimations, not the first-differences ones.

The other dependent variable is female political influence, which I measure as the fraction of seats in each country's parliament (or in bicameral systems, the lower house) held by women in 2002. I call this variable *female seats*.[47]

Although *female seats* is a crude measure of female political influence, there is evidence that when more women hold legislative office, it boosts the political knowledge, interest, and participation of other women.[48] There is also evidence that female legislators favor different policies than their male counterparts.[49] Other global studies of female political influence use the same measure.[50] Although the percentage of parliamentary seats held by women is influenced by gender quotas, this does not lessen the value of *female seats* as an indicator of female political influence, since the decision to enact gender quotas is usually itself a sign of female influence.[51] Because the measure is only available for recent years, I can only use it for cross-national analyses.

Independent Variable

In the other chapters, my independent variable is the natural log of oil income per capita. Here I use oil income per capita, but without the log

---

[46] For data on female agricultural workers, see World Bank 2005. For data on female foreign workers, see World Bank 2004, 2005.

[47] The data are collected by the Inter-Parliamentary Union, available at http://www.ipu.org/wmn-e/world-arc.htm.

[48] Hansen 1997; Burns, Schlozman, and Verba 2001.

[49] Chattopadhyay and Duflo 2004.

[50] See, for example, Reynolds 1999; Inglehart and Norris 2003.

[51] Caul 2001; Baldez 2004.

transformation. My reason is not theoretical but rather pragmatic: oil income is robustly correlated with the status of women, yet the log of oil income is not. The theoretical model in chapter 4 offers little guidance about which measure of oil income should be more salient. Conceivably the relationships between oil income and measures of female status are approximately linear. If so, oil income is the more appropriate measure. Since the distribution of oil income is highly skewed, there is a danger that any correlations might be unduly influenced by a small number of observations with large values. To see if this is a problem, I use several robustness tests described below. In the cross-national estimations, both oil income and the log of oil income are correlated with *female labor force participation*, but only oil income is correlated with *female seats*.

The amount of petroleum that a country produces could be correlated with the status of women for reasons beyond those explained in the chapter. Appendix 1.1 notes that oil production rises when more money is invested in exploration and extraction, and these investments are larger in countries that are richer, more stable, and have better-quality governments. But these links probably bias the *oil income* variable toward disconfirming the hypotheses, since countries with better conditions for women (i.e., wealthier and more Westernized countries) attract more investment, and thus tend to produce more oil.

Control Variables

The core *female labor force participation* model includes controls for two other factors. The first is a country's income, which should have a U-shaped relationship with *female labor force participation*, produced by the opposing effects of rising income on female wages (which encourages female labor participation) and unearned household income (which discourages female labor participation).[52] I model this effect by including both the log of per capita income and the square of the log of income in the regressions for *female labor force participation*. The second is *working age*, which is the fraction of the population between the ages of fifteen and sixty-four, and should directly affect the number of women in the workforce.

I check the robustness of the first-differences model in several ways described below. I also look at the robustness of the cross-national model to the inclusion of three other relatively fixed factors that might affect *female labor force participation*:

---

[52] Mammen and Paxson 2000.

- *Middle East*, which is a dummy variable for the seventeen states of the Middle East and North Africa.
- *Muslim population*, a variable that measures the Muslim fraction of each country's population.
- *Communist*, which is a dummy variable for the thirty-four states that had Communist legal systems at some point since 1960. It is included to capture the lasting influence of Communist policies on female employment.

The core model explaining *female seats* includes controls for both *income* and *Middle East*. I also consider the model's robustness to the inclusion of *Muslim population*, and two measures of a state's political institutions: *polity*, which is a measure of a country's regime type and was employed in appendix 3.1; and *proportional representation*, which is a dummy variable for states whose parliaments are chosen through proportional representation. Earlier studies suggest that women are more likely to be elected to parliament in electoral systems with proportional representation.[53]

RESULTS

To simplify the displays, I do not show the constants or the year dummies (when used). I also calibrate *oil income* in thousands of constant (year 2000) dollars per capita.

Female Labor Force Participation

Table 4.5 displays the results of the first-differences estimations. The dependent variable is the annual change in female labor force participation. The first column shows that the control variables—*income, income squared*, and *working age*—are significantly correlated with *female labor force participation* in the expected directions. In column 2, I add *oil income* to the model; it is negatively correlated with *female labor force participation* and statistically significant at the 0.01 level. This is consistent with hypothesis 4.1, which suggests that increases in oil income lead to decreases in female labor force participation.

The remaining columns in table 4.5 show the results of six robustness tests. In column three, I drop the country fixed effects, out of concern that the combination of the AR1 process and fixed effects may lead to

[53] See Reynolds 1999; Tripp and Kang 2008; Iverson and Rosenbluth 2008.

TABLE 4.5
Female labor force participation, 1960–2002

This table shows OLS regression coefficients. All the explanatory variables are in first differences and lagged for a single year. In column four, I use year dummies (not shown) instead of the AR1 process. The robust standard errors are in parentheses.

	(1)	(2)	(3)	(4)	(5)	(6)	(7)	(8)
Income (log)	-0.154** (0.105)	-0.250*** (0.106)	-0.266*** (0.105)	-0.244* (0.170)	-0.033 (0.0860)	-0.0027 (0.107)	-0.476 (0.738)	-0.154** (0.105)
Income (log) squared	0.0135* (0.00760)	0.0215*** (0.00776)	0.0225*** (0.00766)	0.0113* (0.0122)	0.0034 (0.00633)	0.00038 (0.00835)	0.0397 (0.0438)	0.0134*** (0.00762)
Working age	0.0822*** (0.0184)	0.0806*** (0.0184)	0.0823*** (0.0161)	0.134*** (0.00976)	0.0468*** (0.0178)	0.0371** (0.0199)	0.190*** (0.0424)	0.0822*** (0.0184)
Oil income	—	-0.00512*** (0.00105)	-0.00545*** (0.00102)	-0.00968*** (0.00190)	-0.00395*** (0.00999)	0.0072 (0.00297)	-0.00556** (0.00246)	—
Oil income (log)	—	—	—	—	—	—	—	-0.000393 (0.00453)
Fixed effects	Yes	Yes	No	Yes	Yes	Yes	Yes	Yes
Countries included	All	All	All	All	All but Saudi Arabia and Kuwait	Non–Middle East	Middle East only	All
Number of countries	168	168	168	168	166	151	17	168
Observations	5,369	5,569	5,737	5,737	5,502	5,028	541	5,569
Missing observations	11.9%	11.9%	9.3%	9.3%	11.9%	10.3%	24.4%	11.9%
R-squared	0.067	0.072	0.071	0.091	0.071	0.058	0.061	0.067

*significant at 10%
**significant at 5%
***significant at 1%

biased estimates.[54] *Oil income* remains highly significant, and the size of the coefficient changes little. I use an alternative procedure to control for autocorrelation in the model shown in column four, employing a series of year dummies in place of the AR1 process; the results are substantially unchanged.

A leverage-versus-residual-squared plot suggests that observations from two countries, Saudi Arabia and Kuwait, have a strong influence on these results. In column five, I drop all observations of these two countries from the sample. Although the absolute value of the *oil income* coefficient drops almost 25 percent compared to the core model in column two, *oil income* remains significantly correlated with *female labor force participation*.

I carry out a more drastic test of the model in column six, dropping all countries in the Middle East and North Africa from the sample. *Oil income* loses statistical significance. In column seven, I include only observations from the seventeen countries in the Middle East and North Africa; here *oil income* regains its significance. Finally, in column eight I replace *oil income* with the log of oil income. As I note above, it is negatively correlated with *female labor force participation* but not statistically significant.

In table 4.6, I divide the sample temporally to explore the claim in hypothesis 4.3 that oil's effects increased after the 1970s. *Oil income* is not significantly correlated with *female labor force participation* from 1960 to 1979 (column one), but is strongly correlated from 1980 to 2002 (column two). In columns three and four, I again look at these two periods, but include only the countries in the Middle East and North Africa. While *oil income* is significantly correlated with *female labor force participation* in both periods, the *oil income* coefficient is about nine times larger in the latter period (1980–2002) than the former one (1960–79). In the rest of the world, *oil income* is positively associated with *female labor force participation* from 1960 to 1979, but negatively associated with it from 1980 to 2002. These estimates are consistent with hypothesis 4.3: oil strongly reduced female participation in the workforce after 1980 in both the Middle East and the rest of the world.

Oil income is also linked to lower *female labor force participation* in the cross-national estimations (table 4.7). The first column shows only the control variables. In column two, I add the *oil income* variable, which is negatively correlated with *female labor force participation*. I place three further control variables in the model in column three. Their inclusion causes the *oil income* coefficient to fall by about 50 percent, but it remains significantly associated with *female labor force participation*.

---

[54] See, for example, Arellano and Bond 1991.

TABLE 4.6
Female labor force participation, before and after 1980

This table shows OLS regression coefficients. All the explanatory variables are in first differences, and lagged for a single year. The robust standard errors are in parentheses.

	(1)	(2)	(3)	(4)	(5)	(6)
Income (log)	0.0459	−0.406***	0.116	0.607	0.167	−0.0124
	(0.121)	(0.153)	(0.270)	(1.373)	(0.141)	(0.151)
Income (log) squared	−0.00407	0.035***	−0.00699	−0.00549	−0.0150	0.00132
	(0.00894)	(0.0111)	(0.0178)	(0.0770)	(0.0110)	(0.0119)
Working age	0.0202	0.108***	−0.103***	0.286***	0.0575**	0.0339
	(0.0230)	(0.0208)	(0.0373)	(0.0554)	(0.0264)	(0.0228)
Oil income	−0.00071	−0.0132***	−0.00147**	−0.0136**	0.0283***	−0.0191***
	(0.00097)	(0.00245)	(0.000707)	(0.00670)	(0.00747)	(0.00522)
Years	1960–79	1980–2003	1960–79	1980–2003	1960–79	1980–2003
Countries included	All	All	Middle East only	Middle East only	Non–Middle East	Non–Middle East
Number of countries	122	168	14	17	108	151
Observations	1,938	3,505	178	349	1,760	3,156
Missing observations	18.5%	8.3%	34.6%	18.8%	17.5%	6.9%
R-squared	0.060	0.093	0.036	0.098	0.075	0.060

*significant at 10%
**significant at 5%
***significant at 1%

In column four, I consider whether *oil income* has a special impact in the Middle East by adding a variable that interacts *oil income* with the *Middle East* dummy. It is highly significant, and causes the *oil income* variable to change signs and lose statistical significance.

The results in tables 4.5, 4.6, and 4.7 are broadly consistent with hypothesis 4.1, which suggests that in some types of countries—which are arguably prevalent in the Middle East and North Africa—a rise in oil income will lead to a drop in female labor force participation. The pattern holds both across countries in recent years and within countries over time, in both the Middle East and (since 1980) the rest of the world. The robustness checks show that the core model is unaffected by alternative ways to mitigate autocorrelation. While the correlation does

TABLE 4.7
Female labor force participation, 1993–2002

This table shows OLS regression coefficients. All the variables are averaged over the 1993–2002 period. The robust standard errors are in parentheses.

	(1)	(2)	(3)	(4)
Income (log)	−15.04**	−18.50***	−13.02**	−14.22**
	(6.550)	(6.293)	(6.118)	(6.196)
Income (log) squared	0.926**	1.210***	0.973**	1.020***
	(0.402)	(0.383)	(0.374)	(0.376)
Working age	−0.0264	0.000144	−0.636***	−0.529**
	(0.218)	(0.196)	(0.236)	(0.240)
Oil income	—	−3.04***	−1.41***	0.193
		(0.605)	(0.421)	(0.357)
Communist	—	—	8.248***	7.731***
			(2.902)	(2.901)
Middle East	—	—	−11.80***	−8.974**
			(4.262)	(4.519)
Islam	—	—	−4.580	−5.127
			(3.604)	(3.621)
Oil income*Middle East	—	—	—	−2.42***
				(0.683)
Number of countries	168	168	168	168
Observations	168	168	168	168
Missing observations	1.2%	1.2%	1.2%	1.2%
R-squared	0.060	0.21	0.42	0.44

*significant at 10%
**significant at 5%
***significant at 1%

not hold when using the log of oil income, this could indicate a linear relationship between oil and female employment.

There is also support for hypothesis 4.3, suggesting that the effects of oil on women have grown sharply since the 1970s in both the Mideast and other regions.

Female Representation

Table 4.8 shows the results of the cross-national regressions on *female seats*. Column one demonstrates that the control variables—*income* and *Middle East*—are si7gnificantly linked to *female seats* in the expected directions. I add *oil income* to the model in column two. It is significantly associated with lower levels of *female seats*, and its inclusion causes the *Middle East* coefficient to drop by about 20 percent. In column three, I include *Muslim population* as a control variable. It is not significantly correlated with *female seats*, and its inclusion causes little change in the *oil income* coefficient.

The model in column four includes *female labor force participation*, which exhibits a strong and positive correlation with *female seats*. Adding it to the model causes the *oil income* coefficient to fall by almost 30 percent and lose statistical significance. This is consistent with the argument in chapter 4 that oil reduces female political influence because it reduces the number of women in the workforce. Columns five and six show that the *oil income* variable is robust to the inclusion of two controls for political institutions that may affect female political representation: *polity* and *proportional representation*.

Some additional results are not displayed but are useful to note. A variable that measures district magnitude was not statistically significant, nor was a variable that measured migration, which conceivably might be affecting female representation. Another factor that might affect female political representation—the presence of closed lists—was only available for eighty-eight states, and *oil income* was not correlated with *female seats* in the truncated sample. When the sample was split between the Middle East and non–Middle East countries, *oil income* was uncorrelated with *female seats* in both groups, and a term interacting *oil income* and the *Middle East* dummy failed to reach statistical significance, although its inclusion caused *oil income* to lose statistical significance, perhaps due to collinearity.

These results are generally consistent with hypothesis 4.2, which suggests that petroleum income will reduce female political influence under certain conditions. They are also consistent with a key part of the model in chapter 4: that petroleum reduces the number of women in legislatures *because* it reduces their presence in the workforce.

Robustness

I have already shown the results of several robustness tests for the first-differences model in table 4.5. Table 4.9 reports the results of some additional tests for the cross-national models, noting the *oil income* coefficients and their statistical significance under the following conditions:

TABLE 4.8
Parliamentary seats held by women, 2002

This table shows OLS regression coefficients. The robust standard errors are in parentheses.

	(1)	(2)	(3)	(4)	(5)	(6)
Income (log)	1.916***	2.246***	1.955***	2.012***	2.349***	2.195***
	(0.504)	(0.513)	(0.578)	(0.543)	(0.582)	(0.549)
Middle East	−12.22***	−9.817***	−6.904***	−2.786	−8.132***	−8.712***
	(1.913)	(2.111)	(2.654)	(2.967)	(2.689)	(2.538)
Oil income	—	−1.242**	−1.139**	−0.801	−1.373**	−1.229**
		(0.554)	(0.538)	(0.537)	(0.617)	(0.574)
Islam	—	—	−4.071	−2.959	−5.084*	−4.070
			(2.494)	(2.447)	(2.711)	(2.669)
Female labor force part.	—	—	—	0.284***	—	—
				(0.0736)		
Polity	—	—	—	—	−0.216	−0.430***
					(0.163)	(0.159)
Proportional representation	—	—	—	—	—	6.269***
						(1.467)
Number of countries	162	162	162	162	162	162
Observations	162	162	162	162	162	162
Missing observations	4.7%	4.7%	4.7%	4.7%	4.7%	4.7%
R-squared	0.22	0.25	0.26	0.33	0.27	0.34

*significant at 10%
**significant at 5%
***significant at 1%

TABLE 4.9
Female empowerment: Robustness tests

These numbers are the coefficients of the *oil income* variable in each of the models described. See the text for details.

	Female labor force participation	Female seats
Core model	−3.04***	−1.24**
Dichotomous oil	−6.45***	−1.44
Log of oil income	−1.29***	−0.310
Drop key countries	−2.66**	−1.41
Drop Middle East	0.102	−0.883
Regional dummies	−2.57***	−0.917*

*significant at 10%
**significant at 5%
***significant at 1%

1. In the core models, which are displayed in table 4.7, column two, and table 4.8, column two
2. When the continuous measure of *oil income* is replaced by a dichotomous measure, indicating countries that generated at least a hundred dollars per capita in *oil income* (using constant 2000 dollars)
3. When *oil income* is replaced by the log of *oil income*
4. When the two countries that appear to have the largest influence on the cross-national correlations—which according to a leverage-versus-residual-squared plot are Kuwait and Qatar—are dropped from the sample
5. When all Middle Eastern countries are dropped from the sample
6. When regional dummies for Latin America, sub-Saharan Africa, South Asia, East Asia, the former Soviet Union, and the OECD states are added to the core models

Oil income remains correlated with *female labor force participation* in four of these five tests. The correlation loses statistical significance only when all countries in the Middle East and North Africa are dropped from the sample. This could indicate that the conditions under which *oil income* affects *female labor force participation*—in societies where women face strong discrimination in the nontraded sector—are mostly found in the Middle East and North Africa.

The relationship between *oil income* and *female seats* appears to be more fragile. It is robust to the inclusion of controls for *Muslim population*, political institutions (table 4.8, columns five and six), and regional effects. But it loses statistical significance when Kuwait and Qatar are excluded from the sample, when all Middle Eastern countries are dropped, or when *oil income* is replaced by either a dichotomous measure or the log of *oil income*.

Perhaps it should not be surprising that the correlation between *oil income* and *female seats* is less robust than the correlation between *oil income* and *female labor force participation*. The model suggests that *oil income* is linked to the number of women in the labor force directly, but to female political influence only indirectly, through its effect on *female labor force participation*. Still, the limited robustness of this link is an important weakness in my argument about the impact of oil production on female political representation.

These regressions illustrate some of the conditions under which a country's oil income is correlated with the economic and political status of its female citizens. In some ways these correlations are robust. The link between *oil income* and *female labor force participation* is evident both within countries over time and across countries. It also survives the exclusion of the two most influential countries from the sample, and the inclusion of controls for regional effects and the impact of Muslim populations. Consistent with hypothesis 4.3, oil's effect has been much stronger since about 1980. The link between oil and female empowerment is more robust in the Middle Eastern region than the rest of the world.

The correlation between *oil income* and *female seats* is less resilient. Although it is robust to the inclusion of controls for Islamic populations, political institutions, and regional effects, it does not survive the exclusion of the two most influential countries or changes in the way that *oil income* is measured. Here, the harmful effects of oil are only observed in the Middle East. This may be consistent with the model in chapter 4, if the countries where women are excluded from the service sector are concentrated in the Middle East and North Africa. Still, these results place crucial limitations on the generality of my contention about oil wealth and opportunities for women.

CHAPTER FIVE

Oil-Based Violence

> The first and most imperative necessity in war is money, for
> money means everything else—men, guns, ammunition.
> —Ida Tarbell, *The Tariff in Our Times*

CIVIL WAR is the greatest catastrophe that can beset a country. Between 1945 and 1999, over sixteen million people died in civil wars.[1] Economist Paul Collier describes civil war as "development in reverse."[2]

Since the early 1990s, oil-producing countries have been about 50 percent more likely than other countries to have civil wars. Among low- and middle-income countries, oil producers are more than twice as likely to have civil wars. Most oil-related conflicts are small, although a handful—such as the recent wars in Iraq, Angola, and Sudan—have been much bloodier. As oil is extracted from ever-poorer countries, the danger of petroleum-fueled civil wars will almost certainly rise.

It is critical to keep oil's role in perspective. Civil wars are thankfully rare, even among oil producers. When oil-producing states fall prey to civil war, oil is never the only factor; it is sometimes not even the most important factor. Nevertheless, civil war is the fastest and most calamitous way for a country to transform its oil wealth from a blessing into a curse.

CIVIL WAR: BACKGROUND

Since the late 1990s, there has been a flood of new research on the causes and consequences of civil war. Most scholars now agree on some key facts.[3]

---

[1] Fearon and Laitin 2003.

[2] Collier 2007, 27.

[3] For reviews of earlier research on natural resources and civil war, see Ross 2004b, 2006a. For more comprehensive reviews of the study of civil war, see Walter 2002; Kalyvas 2007; Blattman and Miguel 2008. I use the terms "civil war," "violent conflict," and "armed conflict" interchangeably. They refer to both minor conflicts (defined as those that cause from twenty-five to a thousand battle-related deaths in a given calendar year) and major conflicts (defined as conflicts that cause at least a thousand battle-related deaths in a single year). To qualify as a civil war, one of the contesting parties must be the

First, the vast majority of the world's wars now take place *within* states, not *between* them. From 1989 to 2006, 122 armed conflicts were recorded around the world; 115 were civil wars, and just 7 were international wars. In 2009, for example, there were no international wars but 36 civil wars.

Second, civil wars fall into two broad categories: separatist wars, which are fought over regional independence, and governmental wars, which are fought over control of the central government. Between 1960 and 2006, about 30 percent of the civil wars in the world were separatist wars, and 70 percent were governmental wars.

There are important differences between the two. Separatist wars tend to last longer than governmental ones, although they typically lead to fewer casualties.[4] While governmental wars are found in all parts of the world, separatist wars are common in some regions (like South Asia and sub-Saharan Africa) but virtually nonexistent in others (such as Latin America).

Third, since the end of the cold war, the world has become a more peaceful place. From 1992 to 2007, the total number of civil conflicts fell from fifty-two to thirty-four, and the number of major conflicts dropped from eighteen to just five. There were sharp declines in both separatist wars, which fell from twenty-eight to eighteen, and governmental conflicts, which fell from twenty-four to sixteen. Those conflicts that remain can still be horrific—like the carnage in the Democratic Republic of Congo—but on the whole, the world is more peaceful today than it was in the early 1990s.

Finally, scholars have identified a number of factors besides oil that seem to increase the likelihood that a civil war will begin. These include:

- Low income per capita, which may indicate that people have less to lose by taking up arms[5]
- Slow economic growth, including negative "shocks" to the economy[6]
- A large population, which makes the territory more difficult to govern and increases the likelihood of separatist movements[7]

---

government. On the definition of civil wars, see Sambanis 2004. The civil war data for this section is drawn from the "Armed Conflict Dataset." See Gleditsch et al. 2002; Harbom, Högbladh, and Wallensteen 2007. For more on this data set, including more detailed definitions of conflict, see http://www.ucdp.uu.se.

[4] Fearon 2004.

[5] Fearon and Laitin 2003; Collier and Hoeffler 2004.

[6] Miguel, Satyanath, and Sergenti 2004.

[7] Fearon and Laitin 2003; Hegre and Sambanis 2006.

- War-prone and undemocratic neighbors, whose problems can spill over borders and spark unrest[8]
- Mountainous terrain, which makes it easier for rebels to evade capture[9]
- The presence of diamonds, which rebels can sometimes use to fund their operations[10]

Civil wars are also more common in states that have just achieved their independence, perhaps because their governments cannot yet establish order and deter challengers. Armed conflicts also have a high recurrence rate. According to one study, there is a one in five chance that a conflict, once it has ended, will restart within five years.[11] Scholars have looked at many other factors, including ethnic and religious diversity, inequality, democracy, and political instability, but their effects have been harder to sort out.[12]

A Theory of Civil War

Why would oil trigger violent conflict?

Let me once again sketch out a broader theory and then show how oil might fit in. Like before, I begin with citizens who want more income, and an incumbent ruler who wants to remain in power. I have so far focused on the ways that oil revenues affect governments, by making them larger (chapter 2), less accountable (chapter 3), and more dominated by men (chapter 4). Yet none of these features makes countries more conflict prone. Oil triggers civil wars primarily by affecting citizens, not the state.

Civil wars occur when the government fights a rebel army. My model already has one of these elements—a government—and it's safe to

---

[8] Sambanis 2001; Gleditsch 2002.

[9] Fearon and Laitin 2003.

[10] Le Billon 2001; Ross 2003, 2006a; Humphreys 2005; Lujala, Gleditsch, and Gilmore 2005.

[11] Collier et al. 2003.

[12] These factors help explain why civil wars begin. But less is known about why these conflicts vary in their duration and lethality. Some conflicts, like the Karen rebellion in Burma, have a long duration but cause few casualties. Others, like the 1994 Rwandan civil war, are brief but horrendously lethal. Different factors might be influencing each dimension of these conflicts. The things that cause a conflict to begin can be different from those that cause it to continue, and these factors, in turn, might be different from the factors that influence its lethality. On the duration and intensity of civil wars, see Collier, Hoeffler, and Söderbom 2004; Fearon 2004; Kalyvas 2007; Humphreys and Weinstein 2006; Weinstein 2007; Lujala 2009, 2010.

assume that the government will fight back if confronted by a rebellion, since the ruler's goal is to stay in power. But what about the rebel army? To explain a civil war, we must explain why a group of citizens would form an insurgency and challenge the government.[13]

One common explanation is some kind of grievance—like inequality, oppression, or discrimination against an ethnic minority. But remember that our citizens do not care about right and wrong, only about their incomes. They will only join or support a rebellion if the economic benefits of doing so outweigh the costs.

For every potential recruit, the most important economic cost is the opportunity cost of joining the rebel army—meaning the cost of giving up whatever job they would have held in civilian life.[14] In poor countries, where civilian jobs are scarce and pay little, the opportunity cost is small. As countries get wealthier and jobs become more lucrative, the opportunity cost rises. Other things being equal, rebel armies are more likely to form in poor countries, where young people have less to lose.

The money that a soldier can earn represents the benefits. Rebel armies have two ways to raise funds: they can rely on donations (including food and shelter) from citizens who support them; or they can engage in lucrative criminal activities like extortion, kidnapping, and selling contraband.[15] We can think of insurgents who rely on donations as "goal-oriented rebels" who fight for the benefit of a larger community and depend on the goodwill of their fellow citizens; and insurgents who raise money through crime as "greedy rebels" who prey on their fellow citizens, have little popular support, and see rebellion as a way to get rich.[16]

Some scholars argue that rebels might also be motivated by the spoils they hope to earn if they defeat the government and seize its assets—the "honeypot" effect. But the prospect of future spoils after many years of

[13] The main ideas in this model are drawn from the pioneering work of Paul Collier and Anke Hoeffler (2004). Their argument is not without its weaknesses—some of which I have pointed to in earlier studies (Ross 2004b, 2006a)—but a growing body of evidence, including the evidence presented in this chapter, seems to support many of their contentions.

[14] There is good support for this claim from studies on crime: when wages are higher, people are less likely to engage in criminal activities. See Grogger 1998; Gould, Weinberg, and Mustard 2002.

[15] Before the early 1990s, many insurgencies were funded by donations from the superpowers and their allies, as part of the cold war. Outside funding has dropped off sharply since then, and now seems to play little or no role in most rebellions.

[16] These categories are based on ones suggested by Jeremy Weinstein (2007): "activist" rebel organizations whose members are committed to nonmaterial goals, are well disciplined, and use violence selectively; and "opportunistic" rebel organizations, whose soldiers seek short-term profits, are poorly disciplined, and employ indiscriminate violence.

fighting will not help rebels buy the food, equipment, and weapons that they need to survive.

Insurgents might nonetheless get financial support from civilians who believe they will profit from victory themselves: communities may be willing to hire militias whose success would make them richer. Unlike soldiers, civilians have jobs and hence incomes they can draw from to make donations to insurgents. Even if civilians realize that the chances of victory are remote, if the benefits they expect from victory are large enough, they may be willing to make small contributions— much as people buy lottery tickets, in hopes that a small bet against the odds will someday pay off.

This suggests that two conditions must be in place for a rebel army to form: the costs must be sufficiently low, meaning the country must be relatively poor; and the benefits must be sufficiently high, meaning the rebels have funding either from citizens who hope to prosper from a rebel victory or their own criminal activities.

The Role of Oil

For citizens, oil can affect both the costs and benefits of joining a rebellion.

Oil can influence the costs of rebellion by affecting citizens' incomes. If we make the simple assumption that more oil leads to higher incomes—if not through jobs, then through larger government benefits— it should also make it harder for insurgents to recruit soldiers, thus reducing the danger of civil war.[17]

Unfortunately, oil can also raise the benefits of joining a rebel army. To see how this could happen, I must loosen some of the model's assumptions. I have so far assumed that all citizens are alike: they all receive identical benefits from the government, and collectively support or oppose it based on the size of these benefits. Let me keep the assumption that they all get the same benefits, but divide the population into two groups: citizens in the oil-producing region, and those in the rest of the country.

Citizens in the rest of the country should continue to support an oil-rich government, just as they did in chapter 3, since it offers them low taxes and large benefits. But citizens in the oil-producing region would now be better off if they established an independent state, since

---

[17] If oil wealth instead leads to lower incomes, perhaps through calamitous mismanagement, it would boost the danger of armed conflict. But I show in chapter 6 that oil wealth does not typically reduce incomes.

it would provide each resident with a larger share of the oil wealth than they currently receive. By making self-interested donations to a group of insurgents, locals can fund a "goal-oriented rebellion" that would promote their region's independence.[18]

What if the central government anticipates an independence movement? Would giving locals a larger share of their region's petroleum revenues forestall a rebellion? Many governments follow this strategy by allocating a disproportionate share of their region's mineral revenues to local governments.[19] But these arrangements are not always sufficient. Unless the central government is willing to cede all of a region's petroleum revenues to the local government, residents would still be richer if they were independent. And a government that lets locals keep all of their region's oil revenue would lose support in the rest of the country, where citizens still want lower taxes with higher benefits.

Oil can even trigger separatist wars in which locals do not fire the first shot. In any conflict, both sides can act strategically, meaning they act in anticipation of what their adversary may do. Separatists can act strategically by pushing for independence in anticipation of future oil wealth. Governments can act strategically by launching campaigns of repression and terror in anticipation of these independence movements. This preemptive repression could itself ignite a separatist conflict.

Since oil is principally affecting citizens, not the state, it may seem like government revenues have little role in this model, yet the size and secrecy of these revenues are what make oil dangerous. Imagine that a country discovers a new type of oil that has strange economic properties. For people who live in the oil-producing region, it produces the same economic benefits as normal oil, and provides at least a handful of citizens with jobs and boosts local businesses, yet it generates no revenues for the government. Since locals are already enjoying all the benefits that the oil industry has to offer, they have little reason to secede. Their oil wealth might raise the benefits of secession slightly—it could help locals keep out unwanted welfare-seeking migrants from other regions—but it would also raise the costs of rebellion, since the oil industry would lift incomes in the oil-producing region and hence discourage locals from taking up arms. Without large government revenues, locals in the oil region would gain relatively little from independence.

---

[18] Independence could also give locals the power to mitigate the costs of hosting an oil industry, including the environmental and social problems that petroleum industries bring with them. For economic models of secession, see Buchanan and Faith 1987; Bolton and Roland 1997; Alesina and Spolaore 1997.

[19] Ahmad and Mottu 2003; Brosio 2003.

The secrecy of these revenues can also trigger conflict by making it harder for separatists and the government to strike a revenue-sharing bargain. Imagine there is unrest in an oil-producing region, which the central government wants to subdue by offering locals a share of the revenues. The locals would prefer to accept the offer and not fight, but only if they think the government will keep its end of the bargain. Because the true magnitude of the revenues are secret—they are known to the government but not the locals—the locals fear that they will get cheated. Even if the government's plan looks generous, locals will not consider it credible. The only way locals can be confident that they will receive a fair share of the oil revenues is if they become independent; therefore they decide to fight. [20]

So far I have only looked at rebellions that are both goal oriented—motivated by long-term community interests—and secessionist. But the nearby presence of oil facilities may also raise the benefits of launching greed-based rebellions—both separatist and governmental—although for reasons that have little to do with government revenues. In a greedy rebellion, the insurgents profit from crime, and are motivated by the chance to earn money from stolen oil, ransomed oil workers, and extortion paid by oil companies trying to avoid these and other forms of sabotage. Insurgents can also target other types of businesses, but the oil industry is unusually "extortion friendly," for three reasons. [21]

The first is their location: oil firms are more inclined than other large enterprises to work in places where security risks are high. Most large manufacturing firms avoid impoverished regions where the government is unable to provide for their security. But petroleum firms cannot limit their operations to stable, well-governed areas. They must follow the oil, even when it leads them to places that are desperately poor and politically unstable, like the Niger Delta in Nigeria, Colombia's Arauca region, and Yemen's Marib governorate.

Because they must sometimes work in difficult environments, the industry's ability to function in enclaves—described in chapter 2—is

[20] This scenario is drawn from an argument developed (with much greater detail and rigor) by James Fearon (2004) to explain why civil wars in resource-rich regions seemed to last an unusually long time. While Fearon suggests that the volatility of resource revenues will undermine the government's credibility, I place more weight on the secrecy of these revenues: if the rebels could monitor fluctuations in the revenues, volatility would be a much smaller obstacle to peace. Barbara Walter (2002) developed a more general model of credible commitment in separatist rebellions.

[21] Different types of natural resources provide insurgents with different types of economic opportunities. Rebels in poor countries—primarily in sub-Saharan Africa and Southeast Asia—have used gemstones and timber for funding, partly because they are relatively easy to exploit: they can be gathered by unskilled workers with shovels and buckets, or chainsaws and trucks. See Le Billon 2001, 2005; Ross 2003, 2004c.

an advantage, since it allows oil companies to survive under conditions that would ruin most other firms. Yet by enabling them to work in unstable regions, it also raises the likelihood that they will come into contact with insurgents determined to raise money.[22]

Second, oil companies have an unusually strong incentive to stay put—even in the face of danger—thanks to their enormous investments in fixed assets, which cannot be easily sold or moved abroad. Chapter 2 explains that petroleum firms may sink billions of dollars in a project before they extract the first barrel of oil, but once a facility is built, it costs little to send each subsequent barrel through a pipeline to the refinery. This gives petroleum companies a powerful incentive remain in place so they can recoup their initial investments and enjoy the large profits produced by mature facilities. When other types of companies would flee, oil companies have strong incentives to stand their ground. This renders them more willing to strike deals with the military or insurgents to protect their facilities—aggravating grievances that might otherwise dissipate.

Finally, oil companies earn rents. Manufacturing firms, especially those that sell their products in competitive markets, and hence have thin profit margins, are more likely to close before they incur substantial security expenses. Since oil companies can earn rents, they can afford the security costs that come from working in hazardous areas: they can hire special military units to guard their facilities (as they have in Indonesia, Colombia, and Yemen); they can pay large ransoms when their employees are kidnapped (as they have in Nigeria and Colombia); and they can even pay rebels, criminal gangs, and hostile villagers to refrain from attacks (as they have in Nigeria, Iraq, Sudan, and Colombia). Without rents, oil companies would have trouble affording these expenses. Unfortunately, these rents—along with the willingness of oil companies to enter hazardous regions, and then stay put in the face of danger—make hydrocarbon firms excellent targets for extortion.

Overall, the model suggests that rebellions are more likely to break out in poor countries than in rich ones, and when insurgents have enough funding, either from local supporters or lucrative criminal activities. Oil wealth has two contradictory effects: it can deter rebellions by raising incomes, which discourages people from joining insurgencies; and it can induce rebellions by making independence profitable

[22] This means that we must be especially careful about linking oil production to political violence. There is good evidence that oil production tends to cause civil wars. But sometimes the correlation between oil and violence also reflects the unusual willingness of extractive companies to work in politically unstable regions, which places them in the midst of conflicts that they had no role in creating.

in oil-producing regions and making it easier for insurgents to raise money.

Which of these two effects is likely to prevail? The conflict-reducing effects of oil will be diffused across the entire population, as it generates higher incomes for citizens everywhere, but its conflict-inducing effects are concentrated in the oil-producing region. In a low-income country, every dollar of new oil revenue should produce a small increase in civilian incomes everywhere, but a larger increase in potential funding for rebels in oil-rich regions. This implies that oil can raise the potential benefits of rebellion more than it increases the potential costs, but only for people in an oil-producing region.[23]

The model also implies that a given amount of oil will pose a greater danger in poor countries than in rich ones. In a poor country, a well that generates a hundred dollars per capita in oil income will produce a relatively large percentage increase in civilian and rebel incomes, and have a large impact on their incentives. In a rich country, the same amount will produce a much smaller rise in their incomes and thus have a smaller effect.

If we assume that there are diminishing marginal returns to income—that is, beyond a certain point, each additional dollar will bring less and less satisfaction to potential rebels—then as a country gets richer, the costs of rebellion will increasingly outweigh the potential benefits. If a country has enough oil wealth to lift it above some threshold, the danger of conflict will subside. This suggests there is a U-shaped relationship between oil wealth and the danger of civil war: up to a certain point, rising oil wealth will increase the danger of conflict; after that point, it will reduce the conflict danger.[24]

Some of the conditions that lead to petroleum-based rebellions have changed over time. Government oil revenues grew much larger in the 1970s, making it more profitable for the residents of oil-producing regions to acquire their own sovereign governments. The rising oil prices of the 1970s also sent petroleum firms to increasingly remote and unsteady regions—for example, in Indonesia, Colombia, Nigeria, Sudan, and Yemen—thereby setting the stage for a rising incidence of both goal-oriented and greedy rebellions. Other things being equal, oil-fueled insurgencies should be more likely after the 1970s.

---

[23] Pierre Englebert (2009) argues that at a national level, resource wealth can sometimes have conflict-reducing effects. He suggests that Africa's weak states have managed to survive partly because national political elites have been able to translate natural resource revenues and other "sovereignty rents" into incentives that bind local elites to the state.

[24] The argument for a U-shaped relationship between oil and conflict, although for slightly different reasons, was made earlier in Collier and Hoeffler 2004; Basedau and Lay 2009.

Table 5.1
Civil wars, 1960–2006

These numbers show the percentage of countries that had a new civil war in a given year.

	Non-oil producers	Oil producers	Difference
Overall			
All states and periods	2.8	3.9	1.0**
By income			
Low income (below $5,000)	3.8	6.8	3.0***
High income (above $5,000)	1.2	1.4	0.2
By period			
1960–89	2.4	2.7	0.2
1990–2006	3.6	5.3	1.7**

* significant at 10%, in a one-tailed t-test
** significant at 5%
*** significant at 1%
Source: Calculated from data in Gleditsch et al. 2002.

GLOBAL PATTERNS OF CONFLICT

Many statistical studies find that oil production is connected to a country's civil war risk.[25] The simplest way to show this is by calculating the annual rate at which both oil and non-oil states suffer from civil wars. Between 1960 and 2006, countries without petroleum faced a 2.8 percent chance each year that a new conflict would break out; countries with petroleum had a 3.9 percent annual conflict risk, almost 40 percent higher (see table 5.1, row one).

These overall figures conceal some important differences. Having oil has no discernible effect on conflict in relatively rich countries, but boosts the conflict risk of low- and middle-income states by almost 80 percent (see table 5.1, rows two and three).

We can also look at the data with scatterplots. Figure 5.1 displays all low- and middle-income countries, according to their oil income (on the horizontal axis), and the number of conflicts they had between 1960

[25] See, for example, Collier and Hoeffler 2004; Fearon and Laitin 2003; Fearon 2004; de Soysa 2002; de Soysa and Neumeyer 2005; Humphreys 2005; Lujala, Rød, and Thieme 2005; Ross 2006a; Lujala 2010.

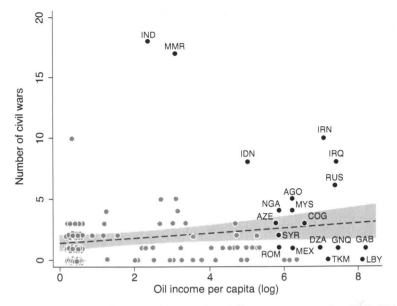

Figure 5.1. Oil and civil wars in low- and middle-income countries, 1960–2006
The vertical axis shows the number of distinct civil wars (both small and large) in each country between 1960 and 2006. Countries are included if their mean incomes, averaged over the whole period, were below five thousand dollars per capita (in 2000 dollars).

Source: Calculated from conflict data in Gleditsch et al. 2002.

and 2006 (on the vertical axis). Remember that if oil is abundant enough to lift a country into the high-income bracket (e.g., Saudi Arabia), it will reduce the danger of civil war. By looking only at low- and middle-income countries, I am excluding these cases—and hence see a fitted line that slopes upward, suggesting that among these countries, more income from petroleum is linked to more frequent conflicts.

Table 5.2 lists the seven oil-producing states that between 1960 and 2006, suffered from the most years of conflict.[26] No single region dominates the list: the problem of oil and conflict is not restricted to Africa, the Middle East, or Eurasia.

Iraq and Iran rank first and third on the list, respectively, and there may be additional reasons—besides those described in the model—why they have been so conflict prone. In the 1920s, Britain and France drew

---

[26] I only count conflicts that occurred in years that a country received at least a hundred dollars per capita in oil and gas income. Nigeria, for example, had six years of armed conflict between 1960 and 2006, but only one since it became a major producer in 1973.

TABLE 5.2
Most conflict-prone oil and gas producers, 1960–2006

These are the oil-producing countries that between 1960 and 2006 had the most years of civil war. In the two right-hand columns, conflicts are counted as separate events if there were two or more intervening years without violence. In the United Kingdom, for example, the Northern Ireland conflict is counted as two discrete wars: one from 1971 to 1991, and a second one in 1998.

	Years of conflict	Years of major conflict	Number of government conflicts	Number of separatist conflicts
Iraq	37	21	5	3
Angola	26	24	2	3
Iran	24	10	5	5
Algeria	16	9	1	0
Russia	14	6	1	5
United Kingdom	13	0	0	2
Congo Republic	6	2	3	0

Source: Calculated from data in Gleditsch et al. 2002.

the boundaries of Iran and Iraq—then under colonial rule—to ensure their own access to the region's oil. This led to the creation of states that were rich in oil and gas, but had sharp ethnic fractures that made them exceptionally prone to civil war. For both countries, the inclusion of territory populated by ethnic Kurds has led to persistent separatist violence. Iran has also faced occasional separatist violence from Azeri and Arab territorial minorities, while Iraq has seen endemic conflict between Shia and Sunni populations. Both have had multiple wars for control of the central government. Oil wealth played a central role in their foundation as states, which may help explain their lamentably frequent violence.[27]

Changes over Time

The incidence of civil war in the oil states rose sharply after 1980. To understand why this took place, it helps to look at three components of this trend.

---

[27] I show in appendix 5.1 that the link between oil and civil war remains strong even when these two countries are excluded from the data.

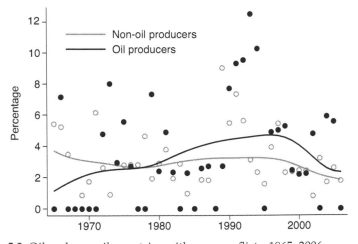

Figure 5.2. Oil and non-oil countries with new conflicts, 1965–2006
These lines show the percentage of countries with oil (solid dots) and without oil (hollow dots) that have a new civil war in a given year. Countries are oil producers if they had at least a hundred dollars per capita in oil income, in constant 2000 dollars. The lines are lowess curves.
Source: Calculated from conflict data in Gleditsch et al. 2002.

First, the *rate* of new conflicts in oil-producing states rose steadily from the mid-1960s to the early 1990s, and then declined (see figure 5.2). In part, this mirrored a broader global trend in the incidence of civil wars: they grew more frequent from the 1960s until the 1990s, and then declined until about 2005. But even after accounting for this global pattern, the conflict rate rose exceptionally fast in the oil-producing world from the mid-1960s to the mid-1990s. Before 1980 or so, oil-producing states had a lower conflict risk than non-oil states; since around 1980 it has been higher.[28]

Another way to see this trend is to divide the period in two. While the conflict rates of the oil and non-oil states began to diverge in 1980, the gap becomes more pronounced after 1990 when the cold war's end led to a drop in violence in the non-oil world.[29] As table 5.1 shows, from 1960 to 1989, there was no appreciable difference in the conflict rates of the oil and non-oil states; since 1990, the conflict rate of the oil states has been about 50 percent higher than that of the non-oil states.

[28] This does not necessarily mean that oil had no conflict-inducing effects before 1980. A closer analysis of this period in appendix 5.1 is inconclusive. While oil may have modestly boosted a country's conflict risk before 1980, this may have been offset by the faster growth and higher incomes of the oil producers at the time.
[29] Kalyvas and Balcells 2010.

How did this trend affect the *actual number* of oil-related conflicts? The number of conflicts in the oil-producing world is the product of two things: the rate of conflict in states with oil, and the number of oil states.

Chapter 1 points out that from 1960 to 2006, the number of oil states rose from twelve to fifty-seven (see figure 1.2, left scale). This was mostly a result of the rise in oil prices, which climbed from less than eight to more than fifty-five dollars a barrel, after accounting for inflation. It was also a consequence of the geographic spread of petroleum production: over the same period, the number of countries that annually produced at least one metric ton of oil per capita (about 7.3 barrels) increased from nineteen to thirty.

The type of states that produced oil and gas also changed over time. Most new producers had lower incomes than the existing ones: as the number of oil states rose, their median income fell from over six thousand dollars per capita in 1970 to just over three thousand dollars per capita by 2004 (see figure 1.2, right scale). The spread of petroleum extraction from more wealthy to less wealthy countries—where oil wealth is more hazardous—has almost certainly boosted the conflict rate in the oil-producing world, above and beyond any other trends.[30]

From the early 1960s to the early 1980s, both the conflict rate in the oil states and the number of oil states rose, causing an increase in the total number of insurgencies in the oil-producing world. From the early 1980s to 2006, though, the number of oil-related conflicts remained more or less the same, as a rise and subsequent fall in the conflict rate was offset by a fall and subsequent rise in the number of oil producers (see figure 5.3). The critical watershed occurred around 1980: from 1960 to 1979, the oil-producing world had about three civil wars under way each year; from 1980 to 2006, it averaged about 7.5 conflicts per year.[31]

The final trend was a sustained increase in the fraction of the world's armed conflict that takes place in oil-producing countries. While the number of conflicts in the oil states has remained steady since the early 1980s, the number of conflicts in the non-oil states has fallen sharply—from twenty-eight in 1992 to just fourteen in 2006.

This pattern is even more striking if we focus on major civil wars—those that cause one thousand or more battle-related deaths a year. From 1992 to 2006, the number of major civil wars among all states

---

[30] This is a further reason to be careful about connecting oil to conflict. Overall, however, the oil states are still relatively rich. The median income of the non-oil states in 2004 was about $1,330, less than half the median income of the oil states.

[31] Note that I am referring here, and in figures 5.4 and 5.5, to the number of ongoing civil wars, while elsewhere I focus on the number of new civil wars. For a pathbreaking study of the link between oil and the duration of conflict, see Lujala 2010.

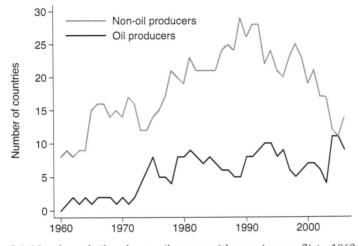

Figure 5.3. Number of oil and non-oil states with ongoing conflicts, 1960–2006
These lines indicate the number of countries with ongoing civil wars each year. Oil-producing countries are represented by the dark line, and non-oil producers are represented by the light line. Countries are classified as oil producers if they received at least a hundred dollars per capita in oil income, in constant 2000 dollars.
Source: Calculated from conflict data in Gleditsch et al. 2002.

dropped from seventeen to five—a fall of more than 70 percent. But all of this change happened in the non-oil world, where the number of major civil wars fell from fourteen to two. The number of large civil wars in the oil states—while fluctuating from year to year—has remained more or less constant, at about three a year.

Collectively, these three trends explain why a growing fraction of the world's armed conflict is taking place in oil-rich states—partly because the oil states have become more conflict prone, partly because the oil states have become more numerous, and partly because the non-oil states have become less conflict prone and less numerous. Figure 5.4 displays the trend: from 1960 to 2006, the fraction of the world's conflicts that broke out in oil-producing states rose from less than 10 percent to almost 40 percent.

How large is oil's impact on the danger of civil war? One simple way to address this question is to once again compare the conflict rates of oil-producing countries with the rest of the world, under different conditions (see figure 5.5). Among countries at all income levels since 1960, the conflict rate in the oil states has been about 40 percent higher; since the cold war ended in 1990, it has been almost 50 percent higher; among lower-income countries since 1960, it has been roughly

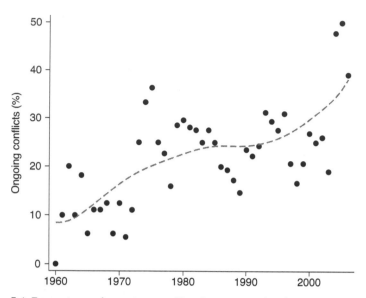

Figure 5.4. Percentage of ongoing conflicts in states with oil, 1960–2006
   These numbers show the percentage of the world's armed conflicts that are taking place in oil-producing countries. The line is a lowess curve.
   Source: Calculated from conflict data in Gleditsch et al. 2002.

75 percent higher; and among lower-income countries since 1990, it has been more than twice as high.

How Does Oil Trigger Conflict?

It is not easy to tell *how* oil leads to conflict. Merely observing that a country is both extracting oil and having a civil war tells us little about the relationship between these two facts. Civil wars are also rare events, making them hard to study systematically, and they usually take place in the poorest countries, where data can be scarce and unreliable. Still, there is convincing evidence from case studies that petroleum has both encouraged separatism and been an important source of rebel funding. And a simple test suggests that many alternative arguments about the causes of oil-based civil wars cannot be true.

Alternative Arguments

One common assertion is that civil wars in oil-producing states are triggered by a honeypot effect: as governments accrue more oil revenues,

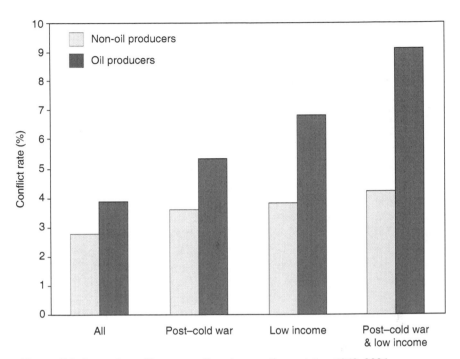

Figure 5.5. Annual conflict rates, oil and non-oil countries, 1960–2006

The bars represent the annual conflict rates among oil-producing states (black bars) and non-oil states (gray bars). The data cover either the full 1960–2006 period, or the "post–cold war" period, which is 1992–2006. Low-income countries are those with incomes below five thousand dollars per capita, in constant 2000 dollars. All of the differences between oil and non-oil states are statistically significant in t-tests.

Source: Calculated from conflict data in Gleditsch et al. 2002.

they become more lucrative targets for insurgents.[32] There are several problems with this claim. For greedy rebels, the lure of a state's oil wealth must be discounted by the small chances of victory and the risk of getting killed in the meantime. And the prospect of future spoils cannot pay the daily costs of supporting a rebel army—costs that are often incurred for many years.[33]

---

[32] According to James Fearon (2005, 487), "Easy riches from oil make the state a more tempting prize relative to working in the regular economy." See also de Soysa 2002; Le Billon 2005; Besley and Persson 2010.

[33] There is a small but crucial set of exceptions, which I discuss below: in the 1997 war in Congo-Brazzaville and the March 2004 coup attempt in Equatorial Guinea, insurgents were backed by foreign investors who hoped to capture a share of the ultimate spoils.

A second widespread argument is that oil wealth weakens the state and makes it more susceptible to violent insurrection. Fearon suggests that

> states with high oil revenues have less incentive to develop administrative competence and control throughout their territory. So while oil revenues help a state against insurgents by providing more financial resources, compared to other countries with the same per capita income they should tend to have markedly less administrative and bureaucratic capacity.[34]

These two theories are closely related: according to the honeypot argument, insurgents will attack oil-rich states because the benefits are larger; according to the "weak state" argument, insurgents will attack because the costs of defeating the government are smaller.

Finally, some observers suggest that oil leads to armed conflict by encouraging foreign military interventions, such as the civil wars that plagued Iraq after both the 1991 and 2003 US-led military campaigns. The major powers have frequently intervened in oil-producing countries—ruling them as colonies, and later, installing and protecting friendly governments. Notwithstanding the interventions in Iraq in 2003 and Libya in 2011, the major powers have grown less likely to intervene in oil-producing countries since the early 1960s, even though the conflict rate in the oil-producing world has grown.[35]

These three arguments have a common feature: they all imply that the location of a country's oil and gas wells is unimportant. If they are right, then both onshore and offshore petroleum wealth should have the same conflict-inducing effects: enlarging the state's honeypot, weakening the government's ability to defend itself, or attracting foreign intervention. By contrast, if oil is harmful because it encourages secession or finances rebels, then it should only lead to conflict when it is found onshore. If it is offshore, it can be neither claimed by local separatists nor attacked by cash-hungry rebels.[36]

---

[34] Fearon 2005, 487. Fearon notes that there is a statistical relationship between fuel exports (measured as a fraction of GDP) and a measure of "government observance of contracts" derived from investor surveys. After controlling for income, he shows that states with more fuel exports are also more likely to repudiate contracts with investors. Contract repudiation may not be a good indicator of state strength or the state's ability to deter civil war. Chapter 2 points out that almost all oil-producing states in the developing world repudiated their contracts with foreign oil companies in the 1960s and 1970s when they nationalized their petroleum industries. Correlations between oil and measures of government institutions, including government observance of contracts, can also be misleading due to problems I describe in chapter 6.

[35] Sarbahi 2005; de Soysa, Gartzke, and Lin 2009.

[36] There are some partial exceptions. A few separatist movements have been inspired by petroleum deposits in nearby waters—like in Aceh, Indonesia—at least if the petro-

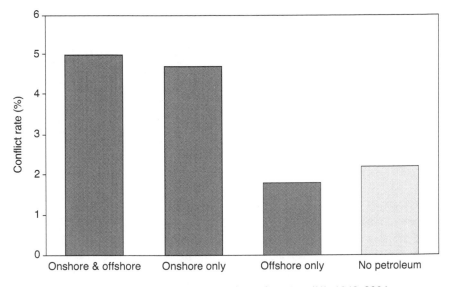

Figure 5.6. Annual conflict rates by petroleum location (%), 1960–2006

These bars show the annual conflict rates, between 1960 and 2006, for countries that produced both offshore and onshore petroleum, only onshore petroleum, only offshore petroleum, or no petroleum at all.

Sources: Calculated from conflict data in Gleditsch et al. 2002, and data on the location of oil production from Lujala, Rød, and Thieme 2007 and US Geological Survey n.d.

It is possible to test these claims, thanks to a data set on the location of oil and gas wells produced by Norwegian scholars Päivi Lujala, Jan Ketil Rød, and Nadja Thieme.[37] Between 1960 and 2006, ninety-five countries at one time or another produced onshore oil or gas, and fifty-eight countries produced offshore oil or gas. Forty-seven countries produced both.

Using these data, figure 5.6 compares the annual conflict rates of four categories of states: those with only onshore oil, those with only offshore oil, those with both, and those with neither. Countries with only onshore oil, or both onshore and offshore oil, had similarly high conflict rates. But countries with only offshore oil had relatively few conflicts—in fact, slightly fewer than countries with no oil at all. A regression analysis in

leum is processed onshore in their region. Recently Nigerian militants have attacked offshore oil rigs. As speedboats and maritime navigation devices become cheaper, offshore oil rigs may become more closely tied to violent conflicts.

[37] Lujala, Rød, and Thieme 2007. I add eight additional countries to their data set, based on information in the US Geological Survey (n.d.) and country reports from the Energy Information Administration, available at http://tonto.eia.doe.gov/country/.

appendix 5.1 confirms this pattern: producing offshore oil has no effect on a country's conflict risk.

These data fit closely with a bounty of new research that finds a strong correlation *within countries* between the location of oil wealth and the location of armed conflict. When oil and gas are found in a conflict zone, conflicts are more likely to flare up, especially if the region is relatively poor.[38] Casualties tend to be higher, and the fighting tends to last longer.[39]

These studies suggest that the location of oil matters—implying that petroleum leads to conflict by affecting the behavior of rebels, not governments.

OIL-BASED SEPARATISM

Table 5.3 lists sixteen separatist conflicts that broke out in petroleum-rich territories between 1960 and 2010.[40] There are two notable patterns. First, the danger of resource-fueled separatism is far greater for poor countries than for rich ones. All sixteen conflicts broke out in countries with incomes below twenty-one hundred dollars per capita, while eleven occurred in countries with less than a thousand dollars per capita. Countries with incomes above twenty-one hundred dollars per capita—about the level of Jordan or El Salvador—seem to face a much smaller danger of petroleum-related separatist wars.

---

[38] Dube and Vargas 2009; Østby, Nordås, and Rød 2009.

[39] Lujala 2009, 2010; Buhaug, Gates, and Lujala 2002.

[40] Eight of these conflicts began in oil states—meaning they produced at least a hundred dollars per capita in oil and gas income in the conflict's first year. In six of these eight cases, petroleum extraction was already under way in the secessionist region (Angola, Iran-Kurdistan, Iran-Arabistan, Iraq, Nigeria-Niger Delta, and Russia). In two cases, extraction was occurring in other parts of the country and about to begin in the region where the rebellion took place (Indonesia and Yemen). The other eight conflicts broke out in petroleum-rich regions of countries that did not cross the hundred dollars per capita threshold—either because oil had been discovered but not yet extracted (in Pakistan-Bangladesh, Bangladesh-Chittagong Hills, Nigeria-Biafra, and Sudan) or because oil was relatively scarce at the national level, even though it was abundant in the secessionist region (in China, India, Pakistan-Baluchistan, and Turkey).

Interestingly, none of these conflicts took place in Latin America. Oil there is statistically associated with governmental conflicts, but not separatist ones. This is not because Latin American petroleum has unusually pacific properties; rather, the region is uniquely secession proof. There have been no separatist conflicts in Latin America for over a century. For more on the Latin American anomaly, see Ross 2010.

Other types of mineral wealth, including copper and gold, have sometimes been linked to secessionist movements in exceptionally poor regions—for example, on the Papua New Guinea island of Bougainville and in Indonesia's West Papua Province (Ross 2004c).

TABLE 5.3
Separatist conflicts in oil-producing regions, 1960–2010

This table shows the separatist conflicts that broke out between 1960 and 2010, in which armed groups in oil-producing regions fought for independence. *Country income* is for the year that the conflict began or the closest year for which data are available. Numbers are in constant 2000 dollars per capita.

Country	Conflict years	Country income	Region
Angola	1975–2007	$1,073	Cabinda
Bangladesh	1974–92	$243	Chittagong Hills
China	1991–	$422	Xinjiang
India	1990–	$317	Assam
Indonesia	1975–2005	$303	Aceh
Iran	1966–	$1,053	Kurdistan
Iran	1979–80	$1,747	Arabistan
Iraq	1961–	$2,961	Kurdistan
Nigeria	1967–1970	$267	Biafra
Nigeria	2004–	$438	Niger Delta
Pakistan	1971	$275	Bangladesh
Pakistan	1974–77	$280	Baluchistan
Russia	1999–2001	$1,613	Chechnya
Sudan	1983–2005	$293	South
Turkey	1984–	$2,091	Kurdistan
Yemen	1994	$443	South

Sources: Calculated from conflict data in Gleditsch et al. 2002; income data in World Bank 2010; missing numbers taken from Maddison 2009.

Second, fifteen of the sixteen conflicts broke out in regions traditionally populated by ethnic or religious minorities.[41] This implies that natural resource wealth alone is insufficient to start a secessionist conflict;

[41] The only exception in this group was the 1994 civil war in Yemen, when the Yemen Socialist Party fought to reestablish independence for South Yemen, which had become part of the unified Republic of Yemen in 1990. The territory claimed by the separatists included recently discovered petroleum reserves in the Hadramout region.

it is much more hazardous when combined with preexisting ethnic or religious grievances. While my model of civil war focuses on the role of oil's economic properties—and purposely leaves ethnic grievances out of the picture—in the real world, ethnic cleavages seem to play a critical role in petroleum-based secessions.

How can we tell if goal-oriented rebels, who were altruistically fighting for independence, or greedy rebels, who were thriving on extortion, were leading these insurgencies? One way is to look at the timing. While most of the conflicts in table 5.3 began after oil production started, the wars in Bangladesh, Nigeria (Biafra), Indonesia, Sudan, and Yemen broke out after the oil was discovered, but before it had been exploited—when looting was still difficult or impossible. An exceptionally careful study by Lujala shows that the mere discovery of hydrocarbon deposits tends to make conflicts in the surrounding region last longer even if production has not begun.[42]

A close look at two of these wars—in Indonesia's Aceh Province and the south of Sudan—illustrates how hydrocarbon wealth can inspire a separatist movement even when there is no looting. The cases highlight two alternative ways that oil can provoke separatism: in the Indonesian case, by triggering the formation of a separatist army; and in the Sudanese one, through the government's preemptive repression.

Separatism in Aceh

Aceh is a province on the northern tip of the island of Sumatra, on Indonesia's northwest frontier. Like the rest of Indonesia, Aceh is overwhelmingly Muslim, although the Acehnese tend to be more devout, and they speak a unique language. Aceh also has a history of political violence. In the nineteenth century, the independent sultanate of Aceh offered the fiercest resistance to Dutch colonial rule in Indonesia and was only subjugated after thirty years of brutal warfare (1873–1903). Although the Acehnese people broadly supported the creation of the Indonesian Republic in the late 1940s, Aceh was the site of a 1953–62 uprising that called for greater local autonomy and a stronger role for Islam in the national government.

Aceh's independence movement—widely known as GAM (Gerakan Aceh Merdeka, or Aceh Freedom Movement)—first emerged in 1976, just a few months before a major new facility began to tap the province's natural gas deposits. The organization's 1976 "Declaration of Independence" railed against the Indonesian government (and the Javanese who dominate it) for "colonizing" Aceh and "stealing" Aceh's

[42] Lujala 2010.

gas revenues—although it did not object to the natural gas project itself. Indeed, the founder of GAM, Hasan di Tiro, was a businessman who just a few years earlier failed in his effort to gain a work contract at the gas facility.[43]

During its first two decades, GAM was small and only sporadically active. Most of GAM'S funding came from Libyan dictator Muammar Qaddafi, who supported radical movements in many pro-Western countries. From 1976 to 1979, most of GAM's work consisted of distributing pamphlets and raising the Acehnese flag.[44] From 1979 to 1989, GAM leaders went into exile in Libya, and had little or no presence in Indonesia.

In 1989, between 150 and 800 Libya-trained fighters slipped into Aceh from Malaysia and Singapore, signaling the start of GAM's second incarnation. GAM was now more aggressive, thanks both to its larger size and better training. It first attacked only Indonesian police and army units, but then expanded its targets to include civil authorities, commercial property, suspected government informers, and non-Acehnese settlers.[45]

The government's response was harsh. In June 1990, President Suharto declared martial law in Aceh and ordered six thousand additional troops to the region. By the end of 1991, many of GAM's field commanders had been captured or killed. But the government's brutality produced a deep-seated antipathy toward Jakarta, ultimately contributing to GAM's revival in 1999.

Between 1991 and 1998 there were few signs of GAM activity in Aceh, and many locals came to believe that GAM no longer existed. Yet in early 1999, GAM reappeared and began to grow more quickly than it ever had before. By mid-2001, GAM had two to three thousand regular fighters and an additional thirteen to twenty-four thousand militia members; at its height, it was reportedly in control of 80 percent of Aceh's villages.[46]

Why did GAM grow so quickly after 1999, following twenty-three years of sporadic low-level activity? One factor in GAM's return was the fall of the dictator, Suharto, in 1998, and Indonesia's subsequent democratic opening. This loosened the military's grip on the region, and enabled Aceh's newly freed media to report on the summary executions, torture, rape, and theft committed by the government over the previous decade. A second factor was the Asian financial crisis, which

[43] Sjamsuddin 1984; Robinson 1998.
[44] Sjamsuddin 1984; Hiorth 1986.
[45] Robinson 1998.
[46] International Crisis Group 2001.

caused the Indonesian economy to contract by 17.8 percent in 1998, and then grow by just 0.4 percent in 1999.

These developments gave new salience to GAM's long-standing arguments about the economic benefits of independence. Soon after GAM's return, speakers and pamphlets appeared arguing that Indonesia's "Javanese" elite were stealing Aceh's natural wealth, and that if it became independent, Aceh would be as wealthy as Brunei, the oil-rich Islamic sultanate on nearby Borneo. This was a highly appealing claim: Brunei's per capita income was almost twenty times higher than Indonesia's. But it was also untrue: even under the most generous assumptions, independence might have made Acehnese incomes at best 50 percent—not 2000 percent—higher.

The final six years of the Acehnese rebellion were the bloodiest, causing perhaps ten thousand deaths. After years of political deadlock, the two sides returned to the negotiating table shortly after Aceh was devastated by the catastrophic tsunami of December 2004. The agreement in August 2005 that brought an end to the war gave Aceh considerable autonomy along with 70 percent of the revenues from all current and future hydrocarbon projects.[47] The settlement was probably made easier by the imminent depletion of Aceh's natural gas reserves, which eased the government's fear that local autonomy would deprive Jakarta of substantial revenues.

Aceh's natural gas wealth was only one of many factors that contributed to the insurgency. The region's distinctive culture, the economic crisis, the cruelty of the military rule, and the fall of Suharto were also important. For the first two decades of gas production, GAM was only a minor annoyance to the government.

Still, Aceh's petroleum industry played a critical role. Indonesia has hundreds of ethnic and religious minorities that were also affected by the military dictatorship, the economic crisis, and Suharto's fall; yet it was the Acehnese who ultimately supported a large, violent independence movement.[48] A key reason was that enough Acehnese people believed that independence would allow them to capture the revenues that went to the central government and the jobs that went to non-Acehnese immigrants. Even though GAM engaged in no resource looting, Aceh's natural gas wealth helped cause the civil war by generating widespread support for independence once other conditions were in place.

---

[47] For more details on the Aceh case, see Kell 1995; Ross 2005b; Aspinall 2007.

[48] Post-1998 Indonesia had two other significant independence movements: one in mineral-rich West Papua, and the other in East Timor—a former Portuguese colony that became independent in 1975, and was invaded by Indonesia shortly thereafter. Following a UN-sponsored referendum in 1999, East Timor became a sovereign state in 2002.

Preemptive Repression in South Sudan

The Acehnese conflict was initiated by an independence movement, which fired the first shot in the thirty-year war. But sometimes resource wealth can lead to secessionist conflicts in which the government makes the first move, such as when the government anticipates separatist pressures in a resource-rich region and preemptively represses the local population.

In 1983, Sudan's President Gaafar Numeiry placed newly discovered oil fields in the country's south under the jurisdiction of the north and decided to build an oil refinery in the north instead of the south. These moves contributed to a breakdown in an eleven-year truce between the predominantly Muslim north and the heavily Christian and Animist south. The main insurgent group, the Sudan People's Liberation Army, charged that the north was stealing the south's resources, including oil; demanded that the government cease working on a pipeline to take oil from the south to the refinery in the north; and in February 1984, attacked an oil exploration base, bringing the project to a halt.[49]

Yet it was not the Sudan People's Liberation Army but rather the government—anticipating that oil would boost proindependence sentiments in the country's south—whose actions sparked the conflict. The government was also responsible for some of the war's greatest brutality, when in 1999 and 2000 it used summary executions, rape, ground attacks, helicopter gunships, and high-altitude bombing to force tens of thousands of people from their homes in regions where oil had been discovered, but not yet exploited.[50]

In April 1999, for example, Lundin Oil (a Swedish firm) discovered a major oil reserve in Thar Jath. Government troops displaced tens of thousands of people from the area a month later, in anticipation of conflicts with the locals. When fighting nonetheless erupted ten months later, Lundin Oil suspended operations while the government used aerial bombing, the burning of villages, and summary executions to depopulate a large area around the oil field. Shortly thereafter, Lundin Oil resumed construction.[51]

After more than two decades of combat, the two sides signed a peace accord in January 2005. Following a popular referendum in January 2011, South Sudan became an independent state. While it received most of the oil fields, South Sudan relies on Sudan's pipelines to export its petroleum; this allows the Khartoum government to collect a

---

[49] O'Ballance 2000; Anderson 1999.
[50] Amnesty International 2000.
[51] Christian Aid 2001.

share of the rents. Like in Aceh, international mediation helped resolve a decades-long conflict that was often aggravated by petroleum wealth.

Oil-Funded Violence

There is also good case study evidence that oil leads to conflict through looting. During the cold war, superpowers and their allies funded many insurgencies; since the end of the cold war, insurgents have increasingly relied on income from natural resources, especially gemstones, timber, and oil.[52]

Insurgents have found three ways to raise money from their local oil facilities: by stealing the oil itself; through extortion and kidnapping; and by selling future oil rights to foreign investors. The rebellions in Nigeria, Colombia, and Congo-Brazzaville, as well as a near rebellion in Equatorial Guinea, illustrate these fund-raising strategies.

Oil Theft in Nigeria

The first method is stealing the oil itself, either by tapping into the pipelines (also known as "bunkering"), or hijacking oil trucks or tankers. The stolen oil can then be sold on the black market.[53] Oil theft can be petty or grand. In 2006 alone, Iraqi insurgents earned between twenty-five and a hundred million dollars from oil smuggling and related activities.[54] Perhaps nowhere has oil theft been grander than in Nigeria.

The Niger Delta has a long and complex history of poverty, state repression, ethnic rivalries, and organized violence.[55] Since the mid-1960s, the region has had three episodes of militancy and rebellion. In the first two, its petroleum wealth gave local minorities an incentive to support groups fighting for autonomy or independence; more recently, it has also helped finance antigovernment militias through both oil theft and extortion.

The Niger Delta is home to twenty million people and covers seventy thousand square kilometers—about the size of Ireland or the US state of West Virginia. Swamps, rivers, and tropical forests cover most of its

---

[52] Keen 1998; Ross 2006a; Kalyvas and Balcells 2010.

[53] In an article on natural resources and civil war, I speculated that oil was "relatively unlootable" compared to resources like timber and alluvial diamonds (Ross 2003). Rebels in Nigeria and Iraq have since proven otherwise. I am grateful to Michael Watts (2007) for pointing this out.

[54] Burns and Semple 2006.

[55] This section is based on the reports of the International Crisis Group 2006a, 2006b; Watts 1997, 2007; Osaghae 1994; Omeje 2006.

land. It has long been one of Nigeria's poorest and most ethnically frag-
mented regions. Between 1650 and 1800, perhaps a quarter of the West
African slaves who were sent to the Americas were shipped from ports
in the delta. The Niger Delta later became a major source of palm oil,
produced under appalling conditions during British rule.

The region's first major episode of violence, following Nigerian independence, was the 1967–70 war for secession. The conflict was caused,
in part, by ethnic tensions between the Igbo and non-Igbo peoples that
had been mounting since independence. But oil wealth contributed to
the conflict: the belief that an independent Igbo state (Biafra) would
prosper was influenced by the growing awareness of the scale of the
region's oil reserves. In 1967, the regional governor instructed his government to collect all oil revenues that originated in the state, instead
of allowing the revenues to pass to the federal government. The federal
government reacted by creating three new states in the delta that offered the prospect of greater wealth and autonomy to the region's minority groups, but deprived the Igbo of the oil revenue it sought. The
governor responded by proclaiming independence for Biafra, marking
the beginning of a catastrophic three-year war.

By the 1990s, the delta had become the source of the overwhelming
majority of Nigeria's oil wealth, which provided the government with
most of its finances and the country with almost all of its exports. Yet it
remained one of Nigeria's poorest regions. According to a government
survey in 1996, the Delta's poverty rate was 58.2 percent, the highest in
the country; literacy rates, access to health services, and access to safe
water were exceptionally low.

The combination of persistent local poverty along with a booming
petroleum industry led to a second bout of political violence between
1990 and 1995. Once again, a dispute over oil revenues played a critical role. Around 1990, the Movement for the Survival of Ogoni People
(MOSOP) and several allied groups began to argue that the region's oil
development had led to environmental degradation, health problems,
the deterioration of fishing grounds, and "genocide" against the Ogoni
people. MOSOP demanded a "fair share" from the federal government
of the economic resources originating in Ogoniland. Allied groups went
further, asserting a right to self-determination and full control over the
oil rights in their traditional lands.

In December 1992, MOSOP leaders demanded ten billion dollars
from oil firms working in Ogoniland as well as environmental res-
toration and other measures. They also threatened to disrupt their
operations if firms failed to meet these demands within thirty days. The
government responded with a military crackdown. Violent clashes
broke out several months later between the Ogonis and the neighboring

Andonis—clashes that the Ogoni believed were instigated by the government. In 1994, MOSOP's leader, Ken Saro-Wiwa, and eight others were arrested; they were placed on trial and executed in 1995.

The death of MOSOP's leaders did little to cure the Niger Delta's ailments. Since 1997, the region has been marked by intermittent conflicts between armed militias and government forces, and among the militias themselves. The aims of these militias vary: some call for complete secession; others demand more oil revenue, but not independence; and others still are largely criminal operations with no obvious political aim.

The militant groups—most prominently, the Movement for the Emancipation of the Niger Delta—have raised remarkable sums of money, partly through extortion and partly through oil theft. The extortion is made possible by sweeping attacks on the delta's petroleum infrastructure. The state-owned National Nigerian Petroleum Company estimated that between 1998 and 2003, its facilities were vandalized four hundred times; its losses totaled over one billion dollars annually. Around the 2003 elections, Chevron reported five hundred million dollars in infrastructure damage.

To avert further sabotage, many companies now make direct or indirect payments to militants. Western companies often have rules forbidding these types of payments; they are hence disguised as "surveillance contracts," given to groups of youths to protect pipelines, flow stations, wells, and other facilities. Militant leaders sometimes publicly brag about these lucrative contracts. The International Crisis Group reported that

> in March 2005, several months after [militia leader Alhaji Dokubo] Asari and his group had signed an amnesty with Nigerian authorities, his deputy, Alali Horsefall, told a Crisis Group researcher he had earned upward of $7,000 a month from Shell contracts held by his company, Dukoaye Security Services, for security, surveillance, and community development—as well as oil well services such as generator repair which, he admitted, it had no capability to supply. He also said he had contracts with oil service contractors Daewoo, Nissco, Willbros, and others. When asked how a leader of what was then the Delta's most feared militant group had acquired contracts with foreign oil companies, he replied: "If they don't want to, then I will fight them."

Some militias also raise money from the theft and sale of oil. According to another report by the International Crisis Group,

> Industry experts have estimated that Nigeria loses anywhere from 70,000 to 300,000 barrels per day to illegal bunkering, the equivalent output of a small oil producing country. In its latest annual report,

released in late August 2006, Shell Nigeria estimated illegal bunkering losses at 20,000 to 40,000 barrels per day in 2005, down from 40,000 to 60,000 in 2004.[56]

The stolen oil is loaded onto barges and tugboats, which bring it to ships and trucks that sell it to refineries around the world. Government personnel frequently play an important role in these shipments by providing escorts or allowing them to pass through checkpoints.

In early 2006, Nigeria's "Bonny Light" crude sold on world markets for about $60 a barrel. At this price, the daily theft of forty thousand barrels was worth about $2.4 million, which adds up to $876 million a year. A large fraction of these proceeds went to militant groups fighting the government—helping to make this one of the world's most intractable conflicts.

Extortion and Kidnapping in Colombia

The sale of stolen oil can be extraordinarily profitable, but only when insurgents have a sophisticated security and transportation infrastructure at their disposal—one that enables them to gather the oil, transport it over land or water, bypass customs or border officials, and sell it to complicit buyers. In Nigeria and Iraq, these activities depended on the collusion or active participation of government officials. When insurgents are too weak or poor to steal and market the oil themselves, they can still raise money by extorting funds from, or kidnapping and ransoming the employees of, companies in the oil business.

Extortion and kidnapping have played a major role in Colombia's conflict, and helped transform it from a low-level insurgency in the early 1980s into a full-fledged civil war in the early 2000s. Colombia is a modest oil producer. In 2006, it earned about three hundred dollars per capita from oil and gas, accounting for about 12 percent of the GDP. The current conflict began in the mid-1960s, when two major insurgent groups—the Fuerzas Armadas Revolucionarias de Colombia (FARC), and the smaller Ejército de Liberación Nacional (ELN)—were founded with the backing of the Soviet Union and Cuba, respectively.[57]

During the 1960s and 1970s, these and other leftist groups waged a low-level guerrilla war against the Colombian state. Oil played no obvious role in the conflict. This began to change around 1983, when Occidental Petroleum discovered a major oil field in the southern state of Arauca, where the ELN had a modest presence. At the time, the ELN was small: it was almost wiped out by a major military defeat in

---

[56] International Crisis Group 2006a, 2006.

[57] This account of the Colombian conflict is based on Chernick 2005; Pearce 2005; Pax Christi Netherlands 2001.

1973, and by the end of the 1970s had dwindled in size to perhaps forty guerrillas.

In 1984, a German company, Mannesmann AG, began to construct a 184-mile pipeline to transport oil from Arauca to the Caribbean coast. After just three weeks of work, the ELN launched the first of four attacks on the project; the kidnapping of three construction workers and a series of labor strikes followed. According to the former project manager, both the state-owned oil company (Ecopetrol) and Occidental advised Mannesmann to come to terms with the rebels. Mannesmann paid a large sum of money to the ELN—at least several million dollars or perhaps much more—and then completed the pipeline on schedule.

The ELN's tactics, however, were too successful to give up. In late 1986, the ELN began to use the slogan, "Awake Colombia . . . they are stealing the oil," and resumed attacks on the now-completed pipeline. Between 1986 and 2001, the pipeline was blown up 911 times. The ELN's extortion techniques, including the kidnapping of oil workers, were so lucrative that other groups joined in. These groups included both right-wing paramilitaries, which extorted money from oil contractors and local officials, and the FARC, which was already profiting from the drug trade. Once the FARC became the dominant force in Arauca in 2001, the pipeline was bombed a record 170 times.

Thanks to the money it earned from kidnapping and pipeline bombing, the ELN grew in size and influence. In 1983, the ELN had just three active fronts; by 1986, it had eleven. Before the bombing campaign, it had just forty guerrillas; by the late 1990s it had about three thousand.

Extortion by the insurgents only tells part of the story: paramilitary organizations linked to the government also raise money through oil-based extortion. One innovative study of nine hundred Colombian municipalities between 1988 and 2005, carried out by economists Oeindrila Dube and Juan Vargas, found that oil-producing municipalities were more frequently subject to paramilitary violence, especially when oil prices rose.[58] Profits from oil and illicit drugs have fueled both sides in Colombia, and helped turn a low-level insurgency in the 1960s and 1970s into a full-scale civil war today.

Booty Futures in Congo-Brazzaville

Finally, rebels have occasionally used a more financially sophisticated way to raise money from oil: by selling what might be called "booty futures." When insurgent leaders are well connected and have a good

---

[58] Dube and Vargas 2009.

chance of victory, they sometimes sell off the right to extract the oil that they hope to eventually control. The insurgents are neither selling actual oil nor extorting money from their country's oil producers; rather, they are selling off the future rights to an oil concession, which can only be redeemed when the rebels are victorious. Insurgents are effectively selling the future rights to war booty, or booty futures.

The sale of booty futures has a dangerous self-fulfilling quality. If a rebel group is unable to make these sales, it might not have the funds to capture the booty itself. Selling the future right to the resource makes its seizure possible. Without a buyer for the resources the rebel group hopes to capture, the rebel offensive—and perhaps the conflict itself—would be less likely to take place.

Funds raised from booty futures helped trigger the civil war that broke out in Congo-Brazzaville (also known as the Republic of Congo) in early June 1997. Congo-Brazzaville is a former French colony and has been a major oil exporter since 1974. For most of its history, authoritarian governments ruled Congo-Brazzaville. It edged toward democratic rule in the early 1990s. Since then it has suffered from three low-level conflicts (in 1993–94, 1999, and 2002) and a major civil war in 1997–98.

Congo-Brazzaville's 1997–98 civil war began when the Congolese president Pascal Lissouba sent government forces to surround the private compound of his chief rival, Denis Sassou-Nguesso.[59] Sassou had been Congo's president from 1979 to 1992; he hoped to be president once again, and was running in an upcoming election. Sassou had his own private militia, and the civil war was triggered when his militia clashed with government troops outside his compound.

Sassou's private militia was funded, in part, by the sale of future exploitation rights to the Congo's oil reserves. On the eve of the conflict, Sassou received substantial assistance from a French oil company, Elf Aquitaine (now Total). Some reports suggest that he received $150 million in cash; others state that Elf Aquitaine helped him purchase arms.[60]

Elf Aquitaine had good commercial reasons for purchasing oil futures from Sassou. When Sassou was president between 1979 and 1992, he had been exceptionally close to both Elf Aquitaine and the French government, giving Elf Aquitaine almost exclusive control of the Congo's oil industry. When Lissouba took over in 1992, the new president began to open the country's oil industry to other firms, including Oc-

[59] For a more complete account of the role of oil in Congo-Brazzaville's conflicts, including conflicts before and after 1997–98, see Englebert and Ron 2004.

[60] Galloy and Gruénai 1997; see also Johannesburg Mail and Guardian, October 17, 1997.

cidental Petroleum, Exxon, Shell, and Chevron. Lissouba's government had also submitted a proposed law to the parliament that would give new companies even greater access to Congolese oil. Elf Aquitaine supported Sassou's bid to replace Lissouba in order to regain its dominant position in the oil industry.

It turned out to be a shrewd investment for Elf Aquitaine. After a bloody four-month war, Sassou overthrew Lissouba and shelved the pending legislation, once again giving Elf Aquitaine a dominant position.[61] Sassou also profited: after defeating the government in the 1997–98 civil war, he became president once again and ended the Congo's democratic experiment. He was overwhelmingly reelected to office in 2002 and 2009, when leading opposition parties boycotted the vote or were prevented from running.

A Splodge of Wonga in Equatorial Guinea

Booty futures can also lead to other kinds of mayhem. In March 2004, foreign mercenaries attempted to overthrow the government of oil-rich Equatorial Guinea. Because the plotters were caught on the coup's eve, it did not lead to a civil war, but it came close. Since many of the actors were brought to trial, we have an unusually complete picture of the

[61] Longtime observers of francophone Africa might wonder if Elf Aquitaine was really backing Sassou for commercial reasons or was acting on behalf of the French government's political interests. Until 1994, Elf Aquitaine was a state-owned company and worked closely with the government to promote French political interests in Africa. But in 1994 it was privatized, and its new leadership adopted a more commercial stance toward foreign governments. Although Elf Aquitaine's involvement in the Congo war has now been scrutinized in both the media and the French and Belgian courts, no evidence has emerged that Elf Aquitaine supported Sassou on behalf or at the direction of the French government.

Sassou was not the only actor in the Congolese conflict who looked to the booty futures market. Once fighting erupted in June 1997, the incumbent president, Lissouba, desperately needed arms to put down the rebellion. In July 1997, Lissouba's government approached Jack Sigolet, who had long worked as Elf Aquitaine's financier at FIBA, a French bank. According to an interview that Sigolet later gave to a Belgian newspaper,

> In late July [1997], Congolese officials were already questioning me about the possibility of arranging pre-financing involving crude oil. . . . If I remember correctly, they needed $50 million. My concern was to find out how many barrels they had available. They indicated that they had access to 10,000 barrels a day, which could potentially later be increased to 15,000 in October. I prepared a conventional crude contract, not knowing who the buyer would be. (quoted in Lallemand 2001)

Fortunately, Lissouba was unable to find anyone to purchase these futures. He was rapidly losing the war and was perhaps too risky to bet on. Had he succeeded, the war might have been longer and costlier.

financing of this operation—which came from a large pile of cash, or a "splodge of wonga," raised from the sale of booty futures.[62]

Equatorial Guinea is a former Spanish colony that has been ruled since 1979 by Teodoro Obiang Nguema Mbasogo, who overthrew his uncle in a military coup. The country is highly corrupt and undemocratic. Following the discovery of oil in 1996, it has also become one of Africa's largest producers. It has never had a civil war.

The coup attempt in 2004 was not organized by rogue military officers or the political opposition but rather by a team of foreigners led by Simon Mann, a well-known British mercenary based in South Africa. Mann was the founder of two companies—Executive Outcomes and Sandline International—that provided mercenary forces to civil wars in Sierra Leone and Angola in the 1990s.

In March 2004, Mann made arrangements to fly sixty-five foreign mercenaries into Equatorial Guinea from Zimbabwe. Once in Equatorial Guinea, his team was planning to join up with fifteen South African and Armenian mercenaries already in the country, depose Obiang, and replace him with Severo Moto, an exiled opposition politician.

Authorities in Equatorial Guinea and Zimbabwe were tipped off, and the coup was averted at the last moment. The planeload of mercenaries was arrested in Harare, Zimbabwe, and the other plotters were picked up in Equatorial Guinea. Mann was later sentenced to seven years of jail in Zimbabwe, and his fellow mercenaries were sentenced to twelve months. In 2008, Mann was extradited to Equatorial Guinea and sentenced to thirty-four years in jail; he received a presidential pardon a year later and was released.

The coup attempt was logistically complex and would not have taken place without substantial funding. A group of British and South African entrepreneurs had financed the plot, using offshore bank accounts in the British Virgin Islands and Guernsey to conceal their transactions. The investors raised between three and fourteen million dollars—the total amount was never made clear—and expected to be paid back out of Equatorial Guinea's oil revenues. Some were promised a tenfold return on their money in just ten weeks; others were planning to form their own oil companies in order to gain access to Equatorial Guinea's valuable oil concessions. Moto, the would-be president, allegedly offered Mann sixteen million dollars and a lucrative set of government contracts. The mercenaries were promised large bonuses if the operation was successful. Although most of the financiers remained anonymous, Mark Thatcher—the son of the former British prime minister, Margaret Thatcher—pled guilty in 2005 at a trial in South Africa to charges that

---

[62] The following account is based on Roberts 2006; Barnett, Bright, and Smith 2004.

he helped finance the plot; he received a suspended sentence and paid a large fine.

Both Sassou in Congo-Brazzaville and Mann in Equatorial Guinea raised money for their ventures by selling future access to the oil revenues they hoped to capture. If they were targeting governments without these assets, they would have found it harder or perhaps impossible to raise enough money to finance their attacks. The sale of booty futures gave them a way to turn a government's oil wealth against itself.[63]

The link between oil wealth and conflict can be deceptive: oil and other mining companies sometimes work in unstable regions where the conflict risk is already high. But the production of oil tends to further heighten the danger of civil war, especially in low- and middle-income countries, and especially since 1989.

Most oil-related conflicts are relatively small. Some of them—like recent conflicts in Colombia and the Niger Delta—are fought by groups that look more like extortion rackets than liberation movements. Others have been genuine struggles for self-determination, such as like the independence movements in Iraqi Kurdistan, southern Sudan, and Indonesia's Aceh Province.

Petroleum is never the only source of a conflict, and it never makes conflict inevitable. Since 1970, almost half of all oil producers have been conflict free. Unfortunately, many of the world's newest oil producers are low-income countries that already have high conflict risks, particularly in Africa, the Caspian Basin, and Southeast Asia. Many of them have only enough petroleum to last for a decade or two. If they succumb to civil war, they will squander any hope of using their petroleum wealth to escape from poverty.

APPENDIX 5.1: A STATISTICAL ANALYSIS OF OIL AND CIVIL CONFLICT

This appendix describes a series of logistic regressions that explore the correlation between petroleum income and the likelihood of civil war.

Four testable hypotheses might be drawn from the conflict model in chapter 5:

Hypothesis 5.1: The greater a country's oil income per capita is, the greater the likelihood that a civil war will begin.

---

[63] For more on the booty futures trade and examples of these transactions in the diamond sector, see Ross 2005a.

Hypothesis 5.2: The lower a country's income per capita is, the larger the impact of oil on the likelihood of conflict.

Hypothesis 5.3: The rate of civil wars in oil-producing countries should be higher after 1980 than before 1980.

Hypothesis 5.4: If oil is extracted from offshore facilities, it will not increase the danger of conflict.

DATA AND METHODS

Since my dependent variable—the onset of civil war—is dichotomous, I use logistic regressions to estimate my models. While civil war onsets are rare events—between 1960 and 2006, just 193 such conflicts began in about 6,200 country years—the logit results are virtually identical to the those produced with the King-Zeng rare-events logit estimator. Hence I prefer to use logit since it is more familiar to other scholars.

To address the problem of temporal dependence—the fact that for a given country, many observations over time are statistically related—I follow the advice of Nathaniel Beck, Jonathan Katz, and Richard Tucker by adding three cubic splines to each model, and controlling for the number of years since the end of the previous conflict in the same country.[64] I lag all of the explanatory variables by a single period to help mitigate endogeneity, and cluster standard errors by country.

Dependent Variable

The key dependent variable is the onset of conflict. I construct it from the 2007 (version 4) Armed Conflict Dataset, which is the most comprehensive and transparent data set on violent conflict. The data set's authors define conflict as "a contested incompatibility that concerns government and/or territory, where the use of armed force between two parties, at least one of which is a government, results in at least 25 battle-related deaths" in a single calendar year. Since I focus on domestic conflicts, not international ones, I restrict my analysis to what the data set's authors call "Type 3" (intrastate conflict) and "Type 4" (internationalized intrastate conflict) events.[65]

---

[64] Beck, Katz, and Tucker 1998. In an earlier set of estimations (Ross 2006a), I showed that an alternative method of addressing temporal dependence (Fearon and Laitin 2003) produced virtually identical results.

[65] Gleditsch et al. 2002.

I use these data to produce a variable called *civil war onset*, which takes the value "one" during the year that a conflict starts, and "zero" otherwise. I only include conflicts that begin after two or more consecutive years of peace to help avoid double counts of ongoing conflicts that temporarily subside.[66] I also use the "Armed Conflict" data set to create variables to measure three subcomponents of *civil war onset*: the onset of conflicts for control of the national government (*government conflict onset*), the onset of conflicts over territory (*separatist conflict onset*), and the onset of large civil wars (*major conflict onset*). Like other scholars, I define the latter as conflicts that generate at least one thousand battle-related deaths in a given calendar year. I also consider whether my results hold if I use the alternative codings of civil war developed by James Fearon and David Laitin as well as Nicholas Sambanis.[67]

Independent and Control Variables

Like in chapter 3, my independent variable is the log of oil income per capita.

There is no single model of civil wars that scholars agree on, which makes it difficult to identify the proper set of controls. Håvard Hegre and his colleagues, Fearon and Laitin, Collier and Anke Hoeffler, Lars Erik Cederman, Andreas Wimmer, and Brian Min, and other prominent scholars have identified many plausible risk factors.[68] Tests by Fearon, Sambanis, and Hegre and Sambanis show that some widely used variables are not robust to changes in model specification, the period covered by the sample, the duration of each observation (i.e., whether country observations are grouped in single-year or five-year periods), and the definition of civil war.[69]

The most consistently robust predictors of civil war seem to be income level and population size; somewhat less robust have been regime type (with anocracies—states that are partly democratic and partly authoritarian—showing the highest conflict risk), and whether or not a state is newly independent.[70] Other factors that may boost the risk of civil war include recent political instability, less economic growth, ethnic marginalization, the presence of mountainous terrain, noncontiguous territory, and having war-prone and undemocratic neighbors.

---

[66] Including conflicts that begin after just one year of peace has virtually no effect on the results.

[67] Fearon and Laitin 2003, Sambanis 2004.

[68] Hegre et al. 2001; Fearon and Laitin 2003; Collier and Hoeffler 2004; Cederman, Min, and Wimmer 2010.

[69] Fearon 2005; Sambanis 2004; Hegre and Sambanis 2006.

[70] See, however, Cederman, Hug, and Krebs 2010.

I begin by developing a "core model" that includes only *oil income* and the two explanatory variables that appear to be most robustly linked to civil war: income and population. As a robustness check, I later add to the model the other explanatory variables used in Fearon and Laitin's seminal civil war model, including all of the factors mentioned above.

RESULTS

Table 5.4 displays the results of estimations in which *civil war onset* is the dependent variable. The first column shows that the two control variables—*income* and *population*—are each significantly correlated with *civil war onset* in the expected direction: states with lower incomes and larger populations are more prone to civil war.

In column two, *oil income* is positively correlated with *civil war onset* and statistically significant at the p = 0.01 level. This is consistent with hypothesis 5.1, the simplest version of the "oil causes civil war" claim.

I split the sample by income in columns three and four. *Oil income* is significantly linked to *civil war onset* among low- and middle-income states (those with incomes below five thousand dollars per capita in constant 2000 dollars), but not among high-income states (above five thousand dollars per capita).

In column five, I use an interaction term (*income quintile*oil income (log)*) as an alternative way to see if the effects of *oil income* vary by a country's overall income. Rather than use *income* in the interaction term, I use *income quintile* to make the coefficient easier to interpret: it is a one-to-five cardinal variable with "five" indicating the lowest quintile and "one" the highest. This means that a larger interaction term— signifying more oil, lower incomes, or both—should be unambiguously associated with a higher civil war risk if hypothesis 5.2 is valid. The interaction term is positive and highly significant, suggesting that the effects of oil depend on a country's overall income level.[71] The results in columns 3, 4, and 5 are consistent with hypothesis 5.2, which states that oil has a larger effect on civil wars in poor states than in rich ones.

In table 5.5, I divide the sample of countries into two periods: the 1960–89 "cold war" era (column one) and the 1990–2006 "post–cold war" era (column two). The *oil income* variable is significantly linked to *civil war onset* only in the latter period, and its coefficient is

[71] I do not include *oil income* and the interaction term in the same model. When both are entered simultaneously, they both fail to attain statistical significance, perhaps due to collinearity.

TABLE 5.4
Civil war onsets, 1960–2006

This table shows logit estimations of the likelihood that a new civil war will break out in a given year. The dependent variable is the onset of a civil war. Each estimation includes a variable that measures the years since the previous conflict, and three cubic splines to correct for temporal dependence (not shown). All of the explanatory variables are lagged for one year. The robust standard errors are in parentheses

	(1)	(2)	(3)	(4)	(5)
Income (log)	−0.316***	−0.444***	−0.280***	−0.533***	−0.410***
	(0.0610)	(0.0690)	(0.0979)	(0.181)	(0.0653)
Population (log)	0.314***	0.258***	0.255***	0.487***	0.247***
	(0.0725)	(0.0776)	(0.0878)	(0.106)	(0.0778)
Oil income (log)	—	0.133***	0.124***	0.146	—
		(0.0383)	(0.0425)	(0.0910)	
Income*oil income (log)	—	—	—	—	0.108***
					(0.0316)
Income group	All	All	Below $5,000	Above $5,000	All
Countries	169	169	140	169	169
Observations	6,426	6,426	4,554	1,872	6,382
Missing observations	6.7%	6.7%	10.6%	3.9%	6.8%

* significant at 10%
** significant at 5%
*** significant at 1%

more than three times larger than in the earlier period. This is consistent with hypothesis 5.3, which suggests that the conflict-inducing effects of oil income have grown since 1980.[72]

Just because *oil income* is associated with *civil war onset* does not mean that it affects both secessionist and government conflicts. In columns

[72] Although the incidence of conflict in the oil states rose steadily from the 1970s to the mid-1990s (see figure 5.2), it did not become significantly different from the conflict rate in the rest of the world until about 1990.

three and four, I look at each type of conflict separately: *oil income* is significantly linked to both types of conflict, and the *oil income* coefficients are surprisingly similar.

Another ambiguity is that low-level conflicts—those that cause between twenty-five and one thousand battle-related deaths a year—are included in the dependent variable. Maybe oil is only linked to small conflicts but not larger civil wars. To see if this is so, I estimate the core model once again in column five, but use *major conflict onset* as the dependent variable. The *oil income* variable falls just short of statistical significance. In column six, I estimate the same model but only include observations from the post–cold war period. Now *oil income* becomes significant statistically.

In column seven, I look separately at the impact of onshore and offshore oil production by creating two new dummy variables: one for onshore oil producers that generate at least a hundred dollars per capita in oil income, and a second for offshore producers that pass the same threshold.[73]

The *offshore oil* variable is close to zero and not statistically significant. The *onshore oil* coefficient is more than ten times larger and statistically significant. Only onshore oil production seems to be linked to civil war. This is consistent with hypothesis 5.4, which states that offshore oil does not lead to violent conflict.

Robustness

Conceivably these results might be driven by a small number of influential cases, the peculiarities of a single, oil-rich region, the ways that the Armed Conflict Dataset defines "civil war," or by omitted variable bias.

Table 5.6 lists the results of seven robustness tests designed to address these concerns. They are carried out for the three models associated with the first three hypotheses—linking oil income to conflict in all states and periods, countries in the post-1989 period only, and low and middle income countries only.

Each cell displays the *oil income* coefficient and its statistical significance under the following conditions:

---

[73] I use dummy variables because there are no data available on the quantity of offshore and onshore production in countries that have both. Data on the location of oil and gas wells is in Lujala, Rød, and Thieme 2004; missing observations for eight countries are filled in using data from the US Geological Survey (n.d.) and country reports from the Energy Information Administration, available at http://tonto.eia.doe.gov/country/.

TABLE 5.5
Separatist, government, and major civil wars, 1960–2006

This table depicts logit estimations of the likelihood that a new civil war will break out in a given year. Each estimation includes a variable that measures the years since the previous conflict, and three cubic splines to correct for temporal dependence (not shown). All of the explanatory variables are lagged for one year. The robust standard errors are in parentheses.

	(1)	(2)	(3)	(4)	(5)	(6)	(7)
Dependent variable	All conflicts	All conflicts	Separatist conflicts	Government conflicts	Major conflicts	Major conflicts	All conflicts
Income (log)	-0.297***	-0.636***	-0.457***	-0.427***	-0.326***	-0.512***	-0.405***
	(0.0727)	(0.124)	(0.174)	(0.0742)	(0.0974)	(0.155)	(0.0648)
Population (log)	0.259***	0.256***	0.537***	0.0493	0.252***	0.203**	0.276***
	(0.0849)	(0.0848)	(0.109)	(0.0549)	(0.0745)	(0.0970)	(0.0785)
Oil income (log)	0.0595	0.206***	0.135**	0.138***	0.0960	0.160**	—
	(0.0470)	(0.0560)	(0.0665)	(0.0438)	(0.0642)	(0.0744)	
Offshore oil	—	—	—	—	—	—	0.0450
							(0.341)
Onshore oil	—	—	—	—	—	—	0.655**
							(0.266)
Years	1960–89	1990–2006	1960–2006	1960–2006	1960–2006	1990–2006	1960–2006
Countries	144	169	169	169	169	169	169
Observations	3,618	2,808	6,426	6,426	6,426	2,808	6,149
Missing observations	9.0%	2.1%	6.7%	6.7%	6.7%	2.1%	10.2%

* significant at 10%
** significant at 5%
*** significant at 1%

TABLE 5.6
Civil war onsets: Robustness tests

These numbers are the coefficients of the *oil income* variable in each of the models described. See the text for details.

	All states and periods	1990–2006	Low and middle incomes
Core model	0.133***	0.207***	0.124***
Dichotomous oil	0.704***	0.965***	0.657***
Drop Iran and Iraq	0.099**	0.182***	0.097**
Drop all Middle East	0.124***	0.213***	0.117**
Regional dummies	0.118***	0.200***	0.111***
Fearon-Laitin controls	0.109***	0.165***	0.096**
Fearon-Laitin civil wars	0.089*	0.194***	0.075
Sambanis civil wars	0.090*	0.129*	0.087

* significant at 10%
** significant at 5%
*** significant at 1%

1. The core model, including only *income* and *population* as controls.
2. The core model, but with a dichotomous measure of *oil income*—denoting countries generating at least a hundred dollars per capita in *oil income* in constant 2000 dollars—which may help reduce the skewness of the *oil income (log)* measure.
3. The core model after dropping all observations of Iran and Iraq. Among the oil states, these two had the largest number of conflict onsets between 1960 and 2006. As I note in chapter 5, the colonial histories of Iran and Iraq arguably make them special cases and unusually prone to conflict.
4. The core model after all Middle Eastern countries are dropped from the data set.
5. The core model, plus dummy variables for four world regions—the Middle East and North Africa, sub-Saharan Africa, Latin America, and Asia—using the World Bank's definition of these regions.
6. The core model, plus all of the control variables in the Fearon-Laitin model: democracy, democracy squared, ethnic fractionalization, religious fractionalization, mountainous terrain, noncontiguous territory, and political instability.

7. The core model with an alternative measure of civil war onsets, taken from Fearon and Laitin's civil war data set, which uses a narrower definition of civil war and hence excludes some low-level conflicts. Since the original Fearon-Laitin data set ends in 1999 and does not include fifteen countries in the Armed Conflict Dataset, I take observations from the latter for the fifteen missing states and all states for the years 2000–2006, and add them to the Fearon-Laitin data set.[74]

8. The core model with another alternate measure of civil war onsets, taken from Sambanis's civil war data set. Since the original Sambanis data set ends in 1999 and does not include eight countries in the "Armed Conflict" data set, I take observations from the "Armed Conflict" data set for the eight missing states and all states for the years 2000–2006, and use them to augment the Sambanis civil war onsets variable.[75]

The association between oil and conflict is robust to each of these tests in the full 1960–2006 period as well as the post–cold war period. In the latter period, the *oil income* coefficients are consistently larger. The link between oil and conflict is less robust among low- and middle-income states, and loses statistical significance (albeit barely) when using the Fearon-Laitin or Sambanis civil war codings—perhaps because they omit smaller conflicts.

In all three sets of models, *oil income* remains significantly correlated with civil war onsets when Iran and Iraq as well as all Middle Eastern countries are dropped. Adding regional dummies has relatively little effect on *oil income*.

Collectively, these estimations suggest that oil income is associated with conflict onsets under a range of plausible conditions. They are also consistent with three of the chapter's four hypotheses—linking oil income to a greater likelihood of civil war, particularly among countries with lower incomes, and when oil production is onshore. While the conflict-inducing properties of oil seem to have grown over time, the division between the pre-1980 and post-1980 periods is less salient than the division between the pre-1990 and post-1990 periods.

---

[74] The fifteen states that are missing from the original Fearon-Laitin data set and were added to the augmented version are: Bahamas, Belize, Barbados, Brunei, Comoros, Cape Verde, Czech Republic, Equatorial Guinea, Iceland, Luxembourg, Maldives, Malta, Solomon Islands, Surinam, and Yemen.

[75] The eight states that are missing from the original Sambanis data set and were added to the augmented version are: Brunei, Equatorial Guinea, Ethiopia (1995–99 only), Madagascar, Maldives, Serbia, Vietnam, and Yemen.

The correlation between oil income and civil war onsets holds for both separatist and governmental conflicts. It also holds for large conflicts, albeit only in the post–cold war era. A series of robustness checks suggest the correlation is not produced by a small number of influential countries, a single region, the distinctive coding decisions of the Armed Conflict Dataset, or the omission of standard right-hand-side variables.

CHAPTER SIX

Oil, Economic Growth, and Political Institutions

> Hectic prosperity is followed all too swiftly by complete
> collapse.
>   —Paul Frankel, "Essentials of Petroleum, 1946"

IN THE 1950s and 1960s, most social scientists believed that natural resource wealth was good for economic growth: the mineral-rich states of Africa seemed to have a promising future but the mineral-poor states of East Asia would probably face great hardships. Yet by the mid-1990s, the opposite seemed to be true: the resource-poor states of East Asia had enjoyed decades of strong growth, while most of Africa's resource-rich states were development failures. The oil-rich Middle Eastern states—which until the mid-1970s, had enjoyed spectacular growth—spent most of the 1980s and early 1990s losing ground. By 2005, at least half of the OPEC countries were poorer than they had been thirty years earlier. Economists began to argue that natural resource wealth in general, and oil wealth in particular, could paradoxically reduce economic growth in the developing world by triggering "corruption, weak governance, rent-seeking, [and] plunder."[1]

Much of this conventional wisdom is mistaken: oil does not typically lead to slower economic growth, bureaucratic ineffectiveness, unusually high levels of corruption, or unusually low levels of human development. Economic growth in the oil states has been erratic, but neither faster nor slower than economic growth in other states. The real mystery is why the oil states have had normal growth rates, when they should have had faster than normal economic growth, given their enormous natural wealth.

DID THE OIL STATES HAVE SLOW ECONOMIC GROWTH?

Many influential studies contend that oil wealth is an *economic* curse: the more oil that countries extract, the slower their economic growth.[2]

---

[1] Sala-i-Martin and Subramanian 2003, 4.

[2] The seminal paper on this topic was by economists Jeffrey Sachs and Andrew Warner (1995). Building on earlier work by Alan Gelb and his colleagues (1988) and Richard Auty

TABLE 6.1

Annual economic growth per capita, 1960–2006

	Non-oil producers	Oil producers	Difference
All countries			
1960–2006	1.76	1.67	−0.09
1960–73	2.77	4.5	1.72***
1974–89	1.14	0.22	−0.93***
1990–2006	1.45	2.04	0.59**
Developing countries only			
1960–2006	1.56	1.54	−0.02
1960–73	2.34	4.67	2.33***
1974–89	0.97	−0.38	−1.35***
1990–2006	1.42	2.24	0.82***

*significant at 10%, in a one-tailed t-test
**significant at 5%
***significant at 1%
Source: Calculated from data collected in Maddison 2009.

Most studies focus on the period between 1970 and 1990, when the oil-producing states were indeed economically troubled. But if we look over a longer period, we see that economic growth in the oil states has not been unusually slow, although it has been unusually volatile.

Table 6.1 summarizes the per capita growth rates of both the oil and non-oil states between 1960 and 2006. Over the whole period, the oil-producing states grew at about the same rate as other countries; in the developing world, their growth rates were virtually identical—just over 1.5 percent a year.

But if we divide these forty-seven years into three shorter periods, we find a surprising pattern: the oil-producing states had alternating

---

(1990), Sachs and Warner looked at the growth rates of ninety-seven countries, and found that countries that were more dependent on natural resource exports in 1971 had abnormally slow growth rates over the next 18 years. The correlation remained significant even after the authors controlled for a wide range of growth-related variables. For important contributions to this debate, see also Manzano and Rigobon 2007; Sala-i-Martin and Subramanian 2003; Papyrakis and Gerlagh 2004; Robinson, Torvik, and Verdier 2006; Melhum, Moene, and Torvik 2006; Collier and Goderis 2009. Recent skeptics include Brunnschweiler and Bulte 2008; Alexeev and Conrad 2009. For reviews of this literature, see Ross 1999; Stevens and Dietsche 2008; Wick and Bulte 2009; Frankel 2010.

spells of exceptionally fast and exceptionally slow economic growth. From 1960 to 1973, the oil producers grew faster than other countries; from 1974 to 1989, they grew more slowly; and from 1990 to 2006, they once again grew more quickly. If we leave out the advanced industrialized countries, the gap between the oil states and everyone else—in both good times and bad—becomes even wider.

We can also look at the standard deviation of these growth rates, to see how much they typically fluctuated from year to year. Among all countries in the world, the standard deviation of growth was about 40 percent higher for oil producers than for non-oil producers. Among the developing countries, it was more than 60 percent higher for the oil producers.

Another way to explore the economic effects of oil is to track the year-by-year economic fortunes of the developing world's major oil producers—the thirteen countries that produced on average at least a thousand dollars per capita in oil and gas during the 1970s and 1980s, and whose fortunes were hence most closely bound to their petroleum assets (see figure 6.1).[3] In 1950, these states were already about six times richer than other developing countries. Over the next two decades, the gap between these states and the rest of the developing world grew larger, reaching a peak at the time of the first oil shock in 1973–74. Yet from 1974 to 1989, their per capita incomes dropped by an average of 47 percent; by 1990, four of them (Iraq, Kuwait, Qatar, and the United Arab Emirates) were poorer than they had been in 1950, when measured by income per capita.

This was partly because their economies were closely tied to global trends in oil prices. Figure 6.2 once again shows the average per capita incomes of these thirteen countries from 1950 to 2006, but now juxtaposes them with the price of oil (all figures are calibrated in constant 2007 dollars). From 1950 to 1973, while the real price of oil was more or less unchanged, all of them enjoyed strong per capita GDP growth; the fastest-growing country was Libya, where per capita incomes rose 678 percent.

Yet their growth rates began stumble in the 1970s, when the real price of oil increased more than ninefold. Almost all of the leading oil

---

[3] In the 1960s, 1970s, and 1980s, the developing world's thirteen-largest petroleum producers on a per capita basis were: Algeria, Bahrain, Gabon, Iran, Iraq, Kuwait, Libya, Oman, Qatar, Saudi Arabia, Trinidad, the United Arab Emirates, and Venezuela. Brunei produced a comparable amount of oil, but there are no reliable data on its growth record. To understand the trajectory of the oil-rich states in the developing world, this is a better group of countries to look at than OPEC, since OPEC excludes some oil-rich countries (like Bahrain, Oman, and Trinidad), but includes more modestly endowed ones (such as Ecuador, Indonesia, and Nigeria).

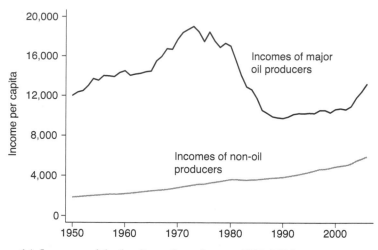

Figure 6.1. Incomes of the leading oil producers, 1950–2006

The dark line shows the mean income per capita of the thirteen-largest oil and gas producers in the 1960s, 1970s, and 1980s, outside of North America and Europe: Algeria, Bahrain, Gabon, Iran, Iraq, Kuwait, Libya, Oman, Qatar, Saudi Arabia, Trinidad, the United Arab Emirates, and Venezuela. Brunei produced a comparable amount of oil, but there are no reliable data on its growth record. The light line includes all other developing states. Incomes are measured in constant 2007 dollars.

Source: Calculated from data in Maddison 2009.

producers had trouble managing the windfalls that they received, although their strategies varied. Some of the biggest producers—including Iran, Venezuela, Kuwait, Qatar, and Bahrain—tried to slow their growth rates to manageable levels by cutting back on oil production. Others maintained or boosted production to fund ambitious development programs.

Between 1980 and 1986, the real price of oil dropped by more than two-thirds, as Western countries reduced their consumption and the Saudi government boosted production. The price collapse led to an abrupt economic decline in almost all of the major producers. Figure 6.3 depicts the change in income per capita among all developing countries between 1974 and 1989 (on the vertical axis), along with their average per capita income from oil and gas (on the horizontal axis). In general, the more petroleum that these countries produced, the greater was the fall in their incomes. Five oil-producing countries—Angola, Gabon, Kuwait, Qatar, and the United Arab Emirates—saw their per capita incomes drop by over 50 percent. During this sixteen-year period, petroleum *was* an economic curse: the more that countries produced, the larger their economic decline.

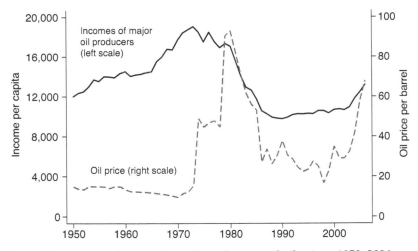

Figure 6.2. Incomes of the leading oil producers and oil prices, 1950–2006
The solid line shows the mean income per capita of the thirteen-largest oil
and gas producers in the 1960s, 1970s, and 1980s outside of North America
and Europe. The broken line shows the price of a barrel of oil in constant 2007
dollars.

Sources: Calculated from data in Maddison 2009; BP 2010.

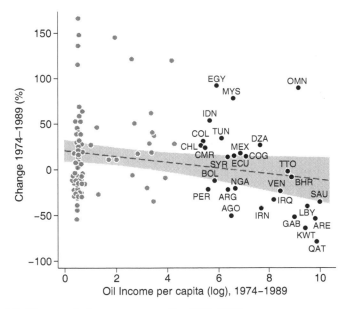

Figure 6.3. Changes in income per capita, 1974–1989
The vertical axis indicates the percentage change in each country's per
capita income from 1974 to 1989. The figure includes all developing countries.

Source: Calculated from data in Maddison 2009.

Not all of the oil states suffered. The two most economically successful oil-producing states during the 1974–89 slump were Oman and Malaysia, whose per capita incomes rose 89 and 78 percent, respectively. In figure 6.3, they are the countries closest to the upper-right corner, combining high oil incomes with high economic growth. Why did Oman and Malaysia do so well?

Government leadership was an important factor. The Malaysian government, in particular, deserves credit for building a well-diversified economy and a strong manufacturing sector, thanks to both skillful industrial policies and an oil endowment that was too small to cause serious problems from the Dutch Disease.[4]

But Oman and Malaysia had another advantage: they were able to compensate for the 1980–86 collapse in oil prices by increasing their production (see figures 6.4 and 6.5). Their strong economic records were at least partly due to good fortune, since new oil reserves gave each nation the capacity to boost production while prices were falling. This was only possible because they were not members of OPEC and thus able to ignore OPEC policies. While OPEC producers tried to limit or restrain their production to reverse the fall in world prices, from 1980 to 1989 Oman and Malaysia were free to increase production by 130 and 110 percent, respectively.

Among the OPEC states, the best performer between 1974 and 1989 was Indonesia, which grew by 54 percent. Several studies have attributed Indonesia's relatively strong record to its wiser policies, including the more deliberate pace of its windfall spending, larger investments in its agricultural sector, and its strict policy of maintaining a balanced budget and convertible currency.[5]

All of these factors mattered. But it is crucial to remember that on a per capita basis, Indonesia produced less oil and gas than any other OPEC state. In 1980, its peak year, it earned $333 per capita in oil and gas income—less than half the oil income of the next-largest producer, Ecuador, and about 1 percent of Saudi Arabia's. Since Indonesia did not enjoy the same windfalls as its OPEC brethren in the 1970s, it suffered less from plummeting oil prices in the 1980s. Indonesia was less cursed because it had less oil.

Despite the strong records of these three states, the 1974–89 period was a disaster for most oil producers, and led many economists to

---

[4] Abidin 2001.

[5] See Bevan, Collier, and Gunning 1999; Lewis 2007. Andrew Rosser (2007) points to broader, structural factors that affected Indonesia's success, including the cold war and Indonesia's position in the global economy.

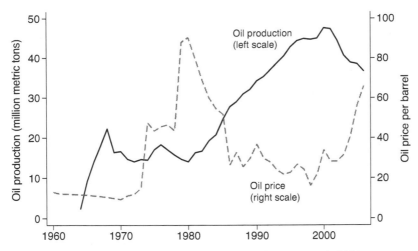

Figure 6.4. Oil production in Oman and world oil prices, 1960–2006
Oil production (solid line) is measured in million metric tons. Oil prices (broken line) are in constant 2007 dollars.
Sources: US Geological Survey n.d.; BP 2010.

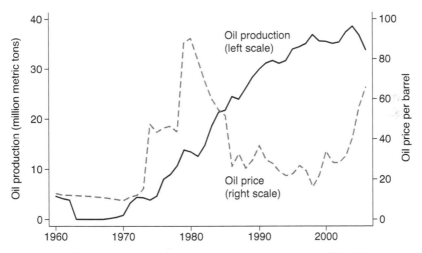

Figure 6.5. Oil production in Malaysia and world oil prices, 1960–2006
Oil production (solid line) is measured in million metric tons. Oil prices (broken) are in constant 2007 dollars.
Sources: US Geological Survey n.d.; BP 2010.

conclude that natural resource wealth in general, and petroleum in particular, was an economic blight. The term resource curse—first used in print by economic geographer Richard Auty in 1993—made its way into popular use to describe to the paradoxical ailments of resource-rich countries.[6] Most of these studies were shortsighted, however. The seminal analysis of Jeffrey Sachs and Andrew Warner, for example, concluded that resource abundance was a curse, but only examined the dismal period from 1971 to 1989. Many later studies of the resource curse covered roughly the same period and came to the same conclusion.

Yet after hitting bottom around 1989, the oil states once again did relatively well. Oil-producing countries grew about 40 percent faster than the rest of the world from 1990 to 2006. Outside of Europe and North America, they grew more than 55 percent faster than other countries. When averaged over the whole 1960–2006 period, the oil and non-oil states had virtually identical growth records.

What has set the oil states apart over the last half century is not less economic growth but more economic volatility. If not for the miserable years between 1974 and 1989, the petroleum states would have significantly outperformed the nonpetroleum ones, especially in the developing world.

This suggests that on average, petroleum has not been an economic curse—even for developing countries—in the strict sense of the term: oil did not make states poorer than they would be otherwise. If oil really was an economic curse, the countries with the greatest per capita oil wealth—like Saudi Arabia, Libya, Venezuela, and Gabon—should be among the world's poorest countries. They are in fact much richer than neighboring countries with little or no oil.

Of course, a country's growth rate may not tell us much about the population's well-being. Perhaps the growth produced by extracting oil does little to alleviate poverty or improve people's lives. A better measure might be a country's child mortality rate, which can explain a lot about the living conditions of people in the lower-income brackets, including their access to clean water, sanitation, maternal and neonatal health care, nutrition, and education. Data on child mortality is available for most countries in the world since about 1970.

Figure 6.6 plots all countries according to how much oil and gas they produced, and how much their child mortality rates changed, between

---

[6] Although Auty may have been the first scholar to use "resource curse" in print, he does not claim to have coined the term. He notes that others used it informally before he placed it in the subtitle of his 1993 book.

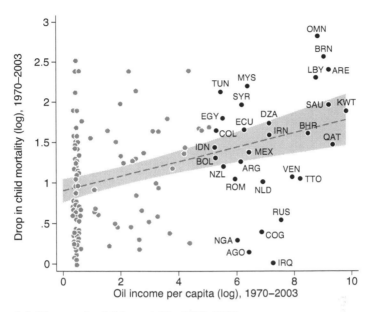

Figure 6.6. Changes in child mortality, 1970–2003
The numbers on the vertical axis indicate how much a country's child mortality rate dropped from 1970 to 2003; higher numbers indicate a larger drop. Rather than measure the absolute change in child mortality rates—since countries with lower initial rates would necessarily show smaller improvements—it measures changes in the natural log of child mortality rates.
Source: Calculated from data in World Bank n.d.

1970 and 2003.[7] There are three notable patterns. First, at a global level more oil is associated with faster improvements in child health. This was not just a product of faster economic growth: even when income growth is controlled for, countries with more oil *on average* made better progress.

Second, there was great variation in the performances of the oil rich states, which was roughly correlated with their region. The global association between oil and improvements in child mortality was driven entirely by the strong records of the Middle Eastern countries in the upper-right-hand corner of figure 6.6—notably Oman, the United Arab Emirates, and Libya, and to a lesser extent, Saudi Arabia, Kuwait,

---

[7]I have reversed the scale on the y-axis so that higher numbers indicate better outcomes—in this case, faster reductions in child mortality.

Bahrain, Algeria, and Iran.[8] If these states are removed from the picture, the salutary effects of petroleum wealth disappear.

The African oil producers—Angola, Nigeria, and Congo-Brazzaville—are at the other extreme, showing almost no gains in human welfare despite their oil wealth. The countries of Latin America fall in the middle, with average (Ecuador, Mexico, Argentina, Bolivia, and Colombia) or slightly below average (Venezuela and Trinidad) records.[9]

Finally, the five-worst performers—Iraq, Nigeria, Russia, Congo-Brazzaville, and Angola, clustered in the bottom-right quadrant—have all suffered from endemic violence. Regardless of how it affects economic growth, oil wealth can hurt social welfare when it leads to large-scale violence.

Taken together, these numbers suggest that oil wealth has not been an economic curse as conventionally defined: in the long run, it has not led to atypically slow economic growth. Moreover, oil-funded growth seems just as likely as other types of growth to improve people's lives—although there has been enormous variation in the welfare gains of the oil-producing states. Most Middle Eastern producers have had remarkably fast gains in child health. But among conflict-ridden oil producers, especially in Africa, there have been few, if any, improvements.

THE PUZZLE OF "NORMAL" GROWTH

Even if oil wealth has not been harmful, many oil producers seem to have a milder form of the resource curse: they are not as well off as they should be, given their geologic wealth. If the oil states grew at the same overall pace as the non-oil ones, it means that they gained no advantage from their remarkable subsoil assets. This implies something went wrong: basic economic theory tells us that countries with more capital—and hence more money to invest in their people and infrastructure—should grow more quickly. Oil windfalls are a kind of capital, and should have produced high levels of investment-fueled growth. Why were the growth rates of the oil-producing countries average, when they should have been above average?

---

[8] The only non–Middle Eastern country to reach the upper-right corner was tiny Brunei. Interestingly, Brunei is similar to oil-rich Persian Gulf countries like Kuwait and Qatar: it is small, overwhelmingly Muslim, and ruled by a traditional monarch.

[9] This variation in outcomes underscores the value of studies that try to explain variations in the trajectories of the oil states. See Melhum, Moene, and Torvik 2006.; Smith 2007; Luong and Weinthal 2010.

Democracy

Many observers tie the disappointing growth records of the oil producers to their lack of democracy. At first the logic seems sound: oil makes governments less accountable, which in turn makes political leaders less inclined to promote the general welfare. Freed from the scrutiny of voters, politicians become shortsighted; according to seminal study of "rentier states" by Hussein Mahdavy, they "devote the greater part of their resources to jealously guarding the status quo," instead of investing in economic development.[10]

One simple way to see if democracy matters is to look at the growth records of countries that have been producing oil over many years—the long-term producers identified in table 1.1 and described in chapter 3. Table 6.2 lists all twenty-eight long-term oil producers outside Europe and North America, ranked by their average annual growth rates between 1960 (or if they became independent after 1960, the first year of their independence) and 2006. It also lists the fraction of this period in which they had democratic governments and ongoing civil wars. These figures range from zero (no years of democracy and no years with civil war) to one (democracy every year and civil war every year). For comparison, it also lists the average numbers for all countries outside the OECD.

Only four of these twenty-eight countries have been democratic for more than half of the time since 1960 (Trinidad, Argentina, Ecuador, and Venezuela). Of these four, one is among the top-ten performers (Trinidad), one is among the bottom ten (Venezuela), and the other two are in the middle. Four other countries had briefer spells of democracy (Mexico, Romania, Nigeria, and the Republic of Congo), but all are clustered in the middle. There is no clear growth advantage to having a democratic government. Some autocrats ruin their country's economies, but others make smart investments in long-term growth.

What is true for the oil states is true more generally for the rest of the world. Most cross-country studies find little evidence that democracy helps economic growth, although there is no consensus.[11] Some analysts argue that whether or not democracy boosts growth, it improves the welfare of the average citizen.[12] Unfortunately, these studies rely on incomplete data sets that overlook the records of well-run autocracies.

[10] Mahdavy 1970, 442.

[11] Barro 1997; Tavares and Wacziarg 2001; Gerring, Thacker, and Alfaro 2005.

[12] Halperin, Siegle, and Weinstein 2005; Bueno de Mesquita et al. 2003; Lake and Baum 2001.

Table 6.2
Economic growth among long-term oil producers, 1960–2006

These are the twenty-eight countries outside North America and Europe that have consistently produced significant quantities of oil or gas since 1960, or if they became independent after 1960, since their first year of independence. They are ranked by their annual per capita growth rate. Also shown is the fraction of this period that they had democratic governments and ongoing civil wars. For comparison, it also lists the average figures for all non-OECD countries.

	Country	Annual growth	Democracy	Civil Wars
1	Oman	5.56	0	0.09
2	Malaysia	4.13	0	0.17
3	Iran	2.85	0	0.51
4	Azerbaijan	2.79	0	0.11
5	Trinidad	2.61	1	0.02
6	Syria	2.36	0	0.11
7	Kazakhstan	2.26	0	0
8	Mexico	2.03	0.15	0.04
9	Saudi Arabia	1.98	0	0.02
10	Bahrain	1.93	0	0
11	Romania	1.89	0.36	0.02
	Non-OECD average	*1.56*	*0.31*	*0.16*
12	Libya	1.54	0	0
13	Nigeria	1.45	0.38	0.13
14	Argentina	1.35	0.68	0.13
15	Algeria	1.34	0	0.34
16	Ecuador	1.17	0.62	0
17	Congo Republic	1.09	0.17	0.13
18	Angola	0.58	0	0.62
19	Uzbekistan	0.51	0	0.04
20	Russia/USSR	0.35	0	0.3
21	Gabon	0.22	0	0.02

TABLE 6.2 (*continued*)

	Country	Annual growth	Democracy	Civil Wars
22	Turkmenistan	0.15	0	0
23	Venezuela	0.11	1	0.04
24	Brunei	−0.48	0	0
25	UAE	−0.64	0	0
26	Kuwait	−0.86	0	0
27	Iraq	−1.03	0	0.79
28	Qatar	−1.51	0	0

Sources: Calculated from economic data in Maddison 2009; democracy data in Cheibub, Gandhi, and Vreeland 2010; conflict data in Gleditsch et al. 2002.

Once these are accounted for, the "democratic advantage" grows weaker or disappears altogether.[13] In theory, democratic governments should be more attentive to the welfare needs of their citizens; in practice, democracies often fail to deliver.

This does not mean democracy is worthless. It provides people with greater opportunities, greater dignity, and greater freedom to live the lives they choose. And the concluding chapter argues that transparency and accountability can help countries escape some of the *political* ailments caused by oil wealth. But historically, democracies have not done much better than nondemocracies at turning their oil wealth into sustainable economic growth.

Civil War

If oil leads to more frequent civil wars, and civil wars are economically damaging, perhaps violent insurgencies explain why oil producers have failed to grow more quickly.

In a handful of countries this is painfully true. Algeria, Angola, Congo-Brazzaville, Iran, Iraq, Nigeria, and Russia have all suffered from devastating conflicts (both civil and international) that drained them of resources that might have otherwise boosted their growth.

[13] Ross 2006b.

Still, civil wars are much rarer than the disappointingly normal growth records of most oil states. Look again at table 6.2. Among the ten countries with the worst records, only two (Russia and Iraq) had significant periods of civil war. Among the ten countries with the best records, four (Malaysia, Iran, Azerbaijan, and Syria) had significant episodes of armed conflict, yet still managed to post higher-than-average growth. Armed conflict can explain a limited number of catastrophes, but it tells us surprisingly little about the economic performance of most oil-rich states.

Women and Population Growth

A more powerful explanation for slower-than-expected growth is that petroleum wealth tends to choke off opportunities for women, as explained in chapter 4. One consequence is that women in oil-rich countries have unusually high fertility rates, which leads to faster population growth and slower per capita economic growth. If their populations grew more slowly, the oil-producing countries would have grown more quickly.

Sociologists have long observed that when women take jobs outside the home, they tend to have fewer children.[14] This is one reason why population growth is slower in rich countries than in poor ones. In more advanced economies, women have more opportunities to earn their own incomes, and the better their opportunities in the workforce, the later they marry and the fewer children they choose to have. Since women in oil-rich states have fewer chances to work outside the home, they typically marry when they are younger and have more children than they otherwise might.

Keeping women out of the labor force also boosts population growth through a second route: by encouraging excessive immigration. When the demand for workers exceeds the number of working-age male citizens, countries have two choices: they can hire more women, or import male workers from abroad. Chapter 4 points out that many oil-rich countries, particularly in the Middle East and North Africa, have taken the second route—bringing in foreign workers instead of employing their own female citizens.

The combination of high fertility and high immigration leads to unusually fast population growth. In countries whose economic growth is fueled by manufacturing, population growth falls quickly. In countries whose growth comes from selling oil, population growth rates fall more slowly or not at all. This is not only true in the Persian Gulf but also in

---

[14] See, for example, Brewster and Rindfuss 2000.

Table 6.3
Annual economic growth, 1960–2006

This table displays the annual growth in the *total* GDP, while table 6.1 shows the annual growth in *per capita* GDP.

	Non-oil producers	Oil producers	Difference
All countries			
1960–2006	3.72	4.05	0.33**
1960–73	5.06	8.21	3.15***
1974–89	3.25	2.83	-0.42*
1990–2006	3.02	3.81	0.79***
Developing countries only			
1960–2006	3.97	4.63	0.66***
1960–73	4.96	9.07	4.11***
1974–89	3.43	2.95	-0.48*
1990–2006	3.58	4.62	1.05***

* significant at 10%, in a one-tailed t-test
** significant at 5%
*** significant at 1%
Source: Calculated from data collected in Maddison 2009.

North Africa (Libya and Algeria), Africa (Gabon and the Republic of Congo), and Latin America (Venezuela and Trinidad).[15]

This pattern has far-reaching economic consequences, since in an economy based on oil exports, the faster a country's population growth is, the slower the growth of its income per capita. Keeping women out of the workforce has led to slower per capita economic growth in the oil states.

Once we control for the effects of population growth, the economic performance of the oil states improves sharply.[16] One simple way to do this is by looking at a country's total GDP growth instead of its per capita

[15] Notice that a country's oil production does not seem to have an *absolute* effect on its fertility rate: more petroleum is not directly correlated with higher fertility and faster population growth. The impact of petroleum only emerges when we control for a country's income. Yet this does not seem to be just a Beverly Hillbillies effect (which I explain below): even after generations of higher incomes, fertility rates in the oil-rich states remain anomalously high. For more on this issue, see Jamal et al. 2010.

[16] Anca Cotet and Kevin Tsui (2010) report a similar finding—that oil rents lead to higher fertility rates, faaster population growth, and hence slower per capita growth.

GDP growth. For example, in Kuwait, the per capita GDP dropped from about $28,900 in 1950 to just $13,200 in 2006—a fall of more than 50 percent—which looks disastrous. But this was only because a 760 percent rise in Kuwait's total GDP was outpaced by an equally astounding 1660 percent leap in its total population. If its population grew at a more normal rate—closer to the rate of non-oil developing countries over the same period—its per capita growth would have been a lot more impressive.

Table 6.3 is similar to table 6.1, but compares countries by the growth of their total GDP, rather than their per capita GDP. There are some striking differences between the two tables. In table 6.1, there is no statistically significant difference between the oil and non-oil states in the growth of their GDP per capita over the full 1960–2006 period. But table 6.3 shows that the oil states recorded significantly higher growth in their total GDP than the non-oil states did over the same period.

When measured by total income growth, the performance of the oil states also improves in each of the three periods: the oil states outpaced the non-oil states by a wider margin when times were good (1960–73

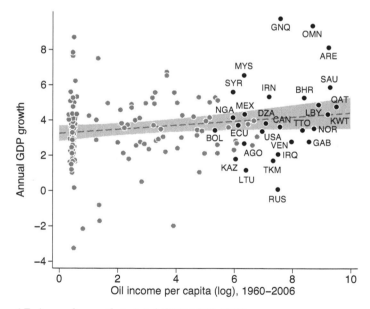

Figure 6.7. Annual growth in total GDP, 1960–2006
These numbers show the average annual GDP growth rate in all countries from 1960 to 2006
Source: Calculated from data in Maddison 2009.

and 1990–2006), and fell behind by a smaller margin when times were bad (1974–89).

We can see the same overall pattern in a scatterplot. Figure 6.7 compares all countries from 1960 to 2006 according to their total GDP growth and oil income: countries with more oil had significantly faster growth. The most obvious outlier is Russia, whose economy was decimated by the Soviet collapse. If not for oil's damaging effects on women's work, the petroleum-rich countries would have outperformed the non-oil states, improving the lives of women and men alike.

The Volatility Problem

The second impediment to faster growth is inappropriate government policies—particularly policies that fail to offset the volatility of oil revenues.

Chapter 2 explains how oil revenues have been volatile, especially since the early 1970s. This volatility can hurt economic growth by creating uncertainty about the future, which in turn discourages private-sector investment.[17] Volatility is more harmful for low-income states than high-income ones, partly because their financial markets are less sophisticated and hence less able to help investors hedge against risks.[18] In commodity-exporting developing states, volatility in the terms of trade has historically kept investors away, causing these countries to fall further behind the United States and Europe.[19] One recent study found that natural resource exports typically have a positive direct effect on growth, but a larger, indirect, negative effect due to the economic volatility that they create.[20]

Yet economic volatility alone cannot be blamed for slow growth: volatility in the oil states is driven by fluctuations in the government's resource revenues, and governments have—at least in theory—the ability to smooth out these fluctuations. If benevolent accountants instead of politicians ran oil-rich governments, their economies would be a lot steadier. The failure of oil-funded governments to stabilize their economies is one of the central puzzles of the resource curse.

The basic method for smoothing out volatility has been known since biblical times, when the Egyptian pharaoh—following Joseph's advice—

[17] Ramey and Ramey 1995; Acemoglu et al. 2003.
[18] Loayza et al. 2007.
[19] Blattman, Hwang, and Williamson 2007.
[20] van der Ploeg and Poelhekke 2009.

saved a fraction of his kingdom's grain during seven years of pros-
perity to carry his people through seven years of famine. In economic
language, the pharaoh had adopted *countercyclical policies*—policies to
set aside a fraction of the surplus during a boom, and draw down this
surplus during a bust.

For countries that depend on exhaustible resources like petroleum,
the careful use of this surplus is unusually important. Chapter 2 notes
that the depletion of oil reserves can lead to a decline in government
revenues. To counteract the economic slowdown that this would
otherwise cause, governments can invest a fraction of their resource
revenues in more sustainable assets, like the nation's physical capital
(infrastructure), human capital (education), or even financial assets
abroad. An oil-producing country that follows this strategy can compensate for the loss of its natural assets by accumulating other types of
assets—in effect, trading wealth below the ground for wealth above the
ground. But if it merely consumes its oil wealth instead of investing it,
future generations will suffer when the oil runs out.

This principle—that when countries rely on nonrenewable resources,
they should invest a certain fraction of their revenues in more sustainable forms of wealth—is known as the Hartwick rule.[21] Countries
that follow the Hartwick rule can grow richer over time, even as they
deplete their natural capital. They should also have more diversified
economies, as their natural capital is transformed into other types of
capital.

Fortunately, these two government tasks—smoothing out volatile
revenues, and investing them in sustainable assets—go hand in hand.[22]
Investment is critical, but it cannot be done all at once. Economies have
a limited ability to absorb new investments, which are typically constrained by diminishing returns. For instance, if a government tries to
build too much infrastructure too quickly, it will lead to poor planning,
lax oversight, and shoddy construction at inflated prices. When governments receive large windfalls, economists advise them to only make
domestic investments that yield a sufficiently high rate of return and
save any remaining funds for countercyclical use.[23]

Virtually all oil-rich governments acknowledge the importance of
countercyclical fiscal policies, yet they rarely have success in imple-
menting them.

---

[21] Hartwick 1977.
[22] Even though these two tasks are distinct, I lump them together for the purposes of
this discussion.
[23] See, for example, Humphreys, Sachs, and Stiglitz 2007; Collier et al. 2009; Gelb and
Grasman 2010.

According to several major studies, many of the largest oil producers in the 1970s and 1980s failed to implement countercyclical fiscal policies, and squandered a large fraction of their windfalls. Alan Gelb's sweeping analysis of Algeria, Ecuador, Iran, Nigeria, Trinidad, and Venezuela found that over the course of the 1973–74 and 1978–79 oil shocks, spending rose faster than revenues in five of the six states—all of them except tiny Trinidad.[24] Auty's study of an overlapping group of oil exporters (Nigeria, Indonesia, Trinidad, and Venezuela) confirmed that all of their governments had performed dismally.[25]

Sometimes politicians acknowledge that managing large revenue windfalls is difficult. In the mid-1970s, Mexican president José López Portillo cautioned his compatriots, "The capacity for monetary digestion is like that of a human body. You can't eat more than you can digest or you become ill. It's the same way with the economy."[26] But governments rarely exercise this restraint; instead, they effectively let the size of their reserves determine the size of their national budgets. Indeed, López Portillo helped boost Mexico's oil production almost fourfold between 1972 and 1980, at the same time that prices were soaring; the result was a sudden glut of revenues that led to Mexico's economic crisis in 1982.

Did the oil states learn from their policy mistakes in the 1970s and 1980s? At first glance, the answer seems to be "yes." Since the early 1990s, many oil producers have established special funds to help them manage their resource revenues for either countercyclical use, investments to offset future depletion, or both. A closer inspection, though, shows that these funds have been surprisingly ineffective. Many governments violate their own rules about depositing money into or withdrawing money from their resource funds; others devise loopholes that undermine their fund's effectiveness. Two recent studies by the IMF—which generally favors the establishment of these funds—found no discernible evidence that they helped governments improve their fiscal performance.[27] A third IMF study of eight African oil producers found that even under highly favorable assumptions, their governments had adopted policies that were fiscally unsustainable.[28]

A recent World Bank study also found that many of the petroleum states have not made large enough investments to satisfy the Hartwick rule. They have used their oil revenues for consumption instead, losing an opportunity to raise incomes and diversify their economies. If

[24] Gelb and Associates 1988.
[25] Auty 1990.
[26] Quoted in Yergin 1991, 667.
[27] IMF 2007; Davis et al. 2003.
[28] York and Zhan 2009.

Nigeria and Gabon had followed the Hartwick rule between 1970 and 2005, they would be about three times wealthier than they are now; Venezuela and Trinidad would be about two and a half times richer.[29]

The overrapid spending of resource windfalls is not a new problem, nor is it confined to oil. One striking historical example is nineteenth-century Peru, which was the world's leading supplier of guano (dried seabird excrement)—at the time, a valuable commercial fertilizer. From 1840 to 1879, a handful of tiny islands off the Peruvian coast provided the world with virtually its only supply of guano. The guano was easy to extract: it was shoveled off cliffs and tossed into wooden chutes, where it slid directly into the holds of waiting ships. Labor costs were low, because the workforce was made up of slaves, prisoners, army deserters, and Chinese "coolies" imported under slavelike conditions.[30]

Thanks to its near monopoly on global supplies and appallingly low labor costs, the guano boom gave the Peruvian government enormous windfalls. Between 1846 and 1873, government revenues jumped fivefold, yet over the same period, government expenditures rose eightfold, producing unsustainable foreign debts. In 1876, with guano supplies close to exhaustion, the Peruvian government declared bankruptcy.[31]

Explaining Failed Policies

If the Old Testament's pharaoh was able to build up resources during the fat years to use during the lean ones, why can't today's oil producers?

One possible answer is that government institutions are themselves damaged by oil revenues. If oil makes governments less effective, it could impair their ability to maintain countercyclical policies—a bit like the doctor who is so weakened by disease, they cannot properly treat their patients.

There are several ways this could occur. Revenue volatility could shorten the government's planning horizon, which would subvert major investment projects. Since revenue fluctuations produce fluctuations in government budgets, projects that take many years to implement—such as major improvements in the country's health, education, or physical infrastructure—stand a high risk of being suspended or

[29] Hamilton, Ruta, and Tajibaeva 2005.

[30] Conditions were so onerous that scarcely a day passed without an attempted suicide among the workers. To solve a labor shortage in 1862, contractors kidnapped about one thousand Easter Island natives—about a third of the island's population. Although the French and British governments eventually forced the Peruvian government to return the Easter Islanders in 1863, only fifteen survived the ordeal and returned home alive.

[31] This account is based on Levin 1960; Hunt 1985.

canceled when revenues drop. Government officials who anticipate this problem may cope by avoiding long-term programs altogether and spending their funds quickly before they disappear.

Another possible culprit is what might be called "bureaucratic overstretch," meaning that a government's revenues expand more quickly than its capacity to efficiently manage them. Most governments worry about having too little money, not too much. But resource-rich countries sometimes receive windfalls that overwhelm their bureaucratic capacity, amplifying the danger that they will be poorly used.[32]

During the early days of his rule, Ibn Saud, the founding monarch of Saudi Arabia, could carry the entire national treasury in his camel's saddlebags. After prospectors discovered oil in 1938, Saud's government was flooded with tens of millions—and soon billions—of dollars in oil revenues, which it had little capacity to manage.[33] The tumultuous expansion of the Saudi state in the 1950s led to administrative chaos. According to Steffen Hertog,

> As far as institutions mattered, their day-to-day operations were often carried out rather autonomously, with ministries run as personal fiefdoms. The administrative sprawl and personalized nature of authority meant that coordination between agencies was largely lacking, with different institutions often producing directly contradictory decisions and jurisdictions remaining unclear. As early as 1952, six different entities were supposed to be in charge of economic planning.[34]

Many scholars make a more ambitious claim: that petroleum wealth leads to "bad institutions," making governments weaker, more corrupt, less competent, and less able to maintain wise fiscal policies. Kiren Aziz

---

[32] Government bodies that manage the booming resource sector are especially vulnerable to bureaucratic overstretch. Since they have authority over resources that have suddenly grown valuable, governments can be plagued by what I called "rent seizing" in an earlier book. Rent seizing occurs when politicians sweep aside institutional constraints to gain control of how a valuable resource is allocated and regulated—giving them the power to use it for patronage or corruption (Ross 2001b).

Madagascar provides a recent example. Until 2005, the government allocated mining rights in an arm's-length manner, through an agency designed to prevent political interference and promote transparency. But the system began to break down in 2006 in the face of rising mineral prices. The power to allocate permits was transferred from the formerly independent Mining Cadastre Office to political appointees who disregarded Madagascar's Mining Code, abandoned measures like competitive bidding that had fostered transparency, and instead distributed licenses through an opaque, discretionary, and almost certainly corrupt process (Kaiser 2010).

[33] Yergin 1991.

[34] Hertog 2007, 546.

Chaudhry asserts that oil rents impair the development of an effective state bureaucracy, which leaves states "weak" and unable to develop sound economic policies.[35] Terry Lynn Karl maintained in her influential book *The Paradox of Plenty* that revenue from petroleum diminishes the state's authority by causing a "rentier psychology," bouts of "petromania," and "multiplying the opportunities for both public authorities and private interests to engage in rent-seeking."[36] Timothy Besley and Torsten Persson develop a formal model in which resource rents discourage politicians from investing in the state's bureaucratic capacity, leaving it weak and unable to foster private-sector growth.[37] Scores of other studies make similar arguments.[38]

These contentions might be right, but they are deceptively hard to verify. Social scientists do a terrible job of defining and measuring "institutions," which makes these claims difficult to falsify. To the extent these arguments can be tested, they do not fit well with the evidence.

If extracting oil were bad for government institutions, we should see a negative correlation between a country's oil income and the quality of its government. Since we typically lack measures of a government's actual performance, social scientists often rely on measures of a government's *perceived* performance. The World Bank has compiled the most carefully assembled measures, based on data from commercial risk-rating agencies, NGOs, and multilateral aid agencies. Higher numbers indicate better outcomes, such as greater "government effectiveness" and better "control of corruption."[39]

In table 6.4, the first row compares the perceived government effectiveness of oil and non-oil states in 2006. The oil-producing states have slightly *better* scores, although the differences are not statistically significant. The second row compares their control of corruption scores. Again, the oil states have better scores, but not significantly so.

We can also look at *changes in* rather than *levels of* government quality. Some theories suggest that a government's quality is harmed by changes in its oil income—that is, by a boom in oil revenues—as opposed

[35] Chaudhry 1989.

[36] Karl 1997, 57, 67, 15.

[37] Besley and Persson 2010.

[38] See also Mahdavy 1970; Leite and Weidemann 1999; Isham et al. 2005; Bulte, Damania, and Deacon 2005. For an excellent review of these arguments, see Wick and Bulte 2009.

[39] Kaufman and Kraay 2008. Unfortunately, expert opinions about corruption seem to be poor predictors of actual corruption. See, for example, Olken 2009; Razafindrakoto and Roubaud 2010.

TABLE 6.4
Perceived government quality, 1996–2006

Higher numbers indicate better government quality—meaning greater effectiveness and better control of corruption. Country scores for government effectiveness range from –2.16 to 2.22; scores for corruption control range from –1.76 to 2.53.

	Non-oil producers	Oil producers	Difference
Level of government effectiveness, 2006	–0.120	0.007	0.0127
Level of corruption control, 2006	–0.132	–0.026	0.107
Change in government effectiveness, 1996–2006	–0.003	–0.077	–0.073
Change in corruption control, 1996–2006	–0.037	0.022	0.059

*significant at 10%, in a one-tailed t-test
**significant at 5%
***significant at 1%
Source: Calculated from data in Kaufman and Kraay 2008.

to its level of oil income.[40] Looking at changes is also a simple way to control for fixed factors that might be also affecting government quality, and masking the true impact of petroleum.

Row 3 shows how government effectiveness scores changed from 1996 to 2006—a time when virtually all hydrocarbon producers were enjoying large revenue increases from surging prices. While government effectiveness declined in the oil states relative to the non-oil ones, the differences were again not statistically significant. Row 4 demonstrates that the corruption scores of the oil states improved slightly more than the non-oil states, but not significantly so.

Figure 6.8 offers a closer look at changes in countries' corruption scores from 1996 to 2006, compared to changes in their oil income. The fitted line slopes slightly upward—countries with more oil became slightly less corrupt—but country performances varied widely. Five states on the Arabian Peninsula improved their ability to control corruption (Saudi Arabia, the United Arab Emirates, Qatar, Oman, and Bahrain), as did some of the African producers (the Republic of Congo and Gabon). Corruption grew worse in other oil-producing states, in

[40] Tornell and Lane 1999.

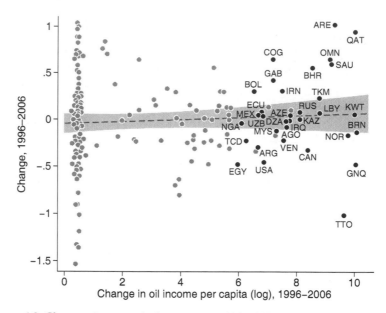

Figure 6.8. Changes in control of corruption, 1996–2006
The numbers show the change in each country's corruption control score from 1996 to 2006. Higher numbers suggest greater improvements in the control of corruption. The horizontal axis shows the absolute change in each country's oil income per capita (log) over the same period.
Source: Calculated from data on corruption control in Kaufman and Kraay 2008.11

both the developing world (Trinidad, Equatorial Guinea, and Venezuela) and the developed one (Norway, Canada, Netherlands, and the United States). There is little prima facie evidence that oil revenues tend to hurt government quality.

Two Fallacies

If having more oil does not damage the quality of government institutions in any clear-cut way, why do so many intelligent studies—often based on data-crunching exercises—claim otherwise?

Many researchers are led astray by two fallacies. The first might be called the Beverly Hillbillies fallacy. In case you missed it, the *Beverly Hillbillies* was a popular television comedy in the 1960s that featured a lovable but unsophisticated family, the Clampetts, from the Ozarks who suddenly become rich when they strike oil. After the Clampetts move into a fancy mansion in Beverly Hills, they clash comically with their snooty, self-absorbed neighbors.

Here is where the fallacy comes in. The Clampetts' sudden windfall made them just as wealthy as their neighbors, but since they were raised in poverty, they lack their neighbors' fancy educations and upper-class manners.[41] A statistical analysis of families in their neighborhood would show that those with oil wealth (i.e., the Clampetts) were less educated than those without; observers might mistakenly infer that oil wealth causes families to become less educated. But oil wealth did not make the Clampetts uneducated or unsophisticated. It made them wealthier—lifting them into a new, more educated peer group—without affecting their education or manners. Comparing the Clampetts to their new Beverly Hills neighbors makes their oil windfall look like a curse. But compared to a more realistic peer group—like their longtime Ozark neighbors—their education and manners are probably quite typical.

Many studies of oil and institutional quality made a similar mistake by implicitly comparing newly enriched oil countries to a new peer group of middle- and high-income states, whose institutions have developed over many years. This makes the nouveau riche oil states look institutionally stunted.

For example, figure 6.9 shows that richer countries tend to have more effective governments. There is a strong correlation between a country's per capita income (on the horizontal axis) and the perceived effectiveness of its government (on the vertical axis). Similar patterns have been found in scores of academic studies that link a country's income and the effectiveness of its government: higher incomes tend to make governments more effective, and more effective governments tend to make their countries richer.[42] This is a bit like the two-way correlation between income and education in Beverly Hills (and everywhere else): richer families can afford higher levels of education, and more educated people tend to earn higher incomes.

Notice the position of countries that produce at least a thousand dollars per person in oil income—marked with three-letter country abbreviations. Most of them lie below the fitted line, suggesting they have unusually ineffective governments for countries at their income levels. If we control for a country's income, we could easily conclude that producing oil tends to diminish the effectiveness of governments.

There is a more benign interpretation, however: perhaps oil raised their incomes, but without influencing the effectiveness of their governments. A spike in global oil prices, or the exploitation of a new oil

---

[41] The Clampetts liked to boast that the most educated member of their family, Jethro Bodine, successfully completed sixth grade.

[42] See, for example, La Porta et al. 1999; Adsera, Boix, and Payne 2003.

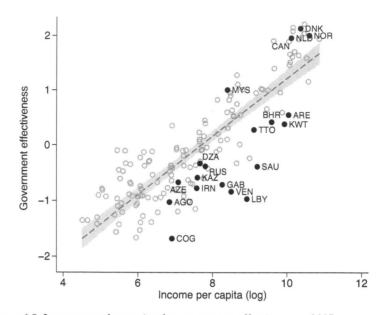

Figure 6.9. Incomes and perceived government effectiveness, 2005
Source: The vertical axis shows government effectiveness scores, with high numbers indicating greater effectiveness. The solid dots are oil-producing countries, and the hollow dots are non-oil countries. Data on perceived government effectiveness are taken from Kaufman and Kraay 2008.

reserve, could make a country richer without either helping or hurting the quality of its government—just as finding oil raised the Clampetts' income without affecting their education levels. If this occurred, we would observe no direct correlation between a country's oil income and the quality of its government—yet oil would still appear to be correlated with low government quality *when we control for a country's income*, since compared to countries with similar incomes, government quality in the oil producers would be anomalously low. Just because oil quickly lifts a country's income without producing an equally fast increase in the effectiveness of its government does not mean that oil has *harmed* the government—only that it has not helped it in the way scholars had naively assumed.[43]

---

[43] The Beverly Hillbillies fallacy could also be seen as a kind of post-treatment bias: oil seems to be negatively correlated with institutional quality once we control for income, but since oil affects income, the inclusion of income in the model produces a biased estimate of oil's true impact. Michael Alexeev and Robert Conrad (2009) make a similar

Scholars might also be misled by the fallacy of unobserved burdens. Imagine a middle-aged professor walking briskly uphill toward a lecture hall, trailed by his much slower teaching assistant. Observers might infer that the professor is in better shape than their teaching assistant. But the teaching assistant's backpack holds the professor's heavy laptop, a projector, and five textbooks. The professor's own backpack is empty except for a piece of chalk. The two individuals are equally fit, but a heavier load slows down the teaching assistant. Yet because people cannot observe the differences in their respective burdens, they erroneously conclude that the professor is more fit.

When looking at government effectiveness, scholars often make the same mistake: we infer that low-performing governments must have "weak institutions," without considering variations in the difficulties of their tasks. We forget to look in the backpack.

When oil-funded governments handle their revenues poorly, observers often blame it on the government's institutional weakness. This assumes that managing volatile resource revenues is no more burdensome than managing a much smoother flow of tax receipts. But maybe enacting consistent countercyclical policies is more onerous than we realize. Perhaps the problem is not that the oil states have exceptionally weak institutions and need normal ones; perhaps they already have normal institutions, but need exceptionally strong ones.

Even countries without resource wealth, whose revenues are much steadier, have trouble maintaining countercyclical fiscal policies. Many studies find that fiscal policies in the developing world, in both oil and non-oil states, tend to be procyclical instead of countercyclical. Having unstable oil revenues makes countercyclical policies even harder to sustain.[44]

---

point in their statistical analysis of oil and institutions, showing that once the impact of oil on income is properly accounted for, oil is no longer correlated with a reduction in institutional quality. Xavier Sala-i-Martin and Arvind Subramanian (2003) also make this argument, but Alexeev and Conrad assert that their econometric remedy is inadequate. Michael Herb (2005) suggests that a similar problem creates the false appearance that oil hinders democracy. Alexeev and Conrad, however, find that oil is still associated with less democracy after accounting for the effect of oil on income.

[44] Catão and Sutton 2002; Manasse 2006; Talvi and Végh 2005; Alesina, Campante, and Tabellini 2008; Ilzetzki and Végh 2008. Some studies of oil and institutions make a third mistake: they argue that oil is detrimental to state strength, but measure state strength as the amount of taxes collected by the government. See, for example, Chaudhry 1997; Thies 2010; Besley and Persson 2010. As chapter 2 shows, oil revenues necessarily reduce a government's reliance on tax revenues by increasing its nontax revenues. Just because an oil-rich country collects less tax revenue does not ipso facto demonstrate that its government is weak or ineffective.

The Mystery of Policy Failure

Why do governments find countercyclical policies so difficult to sustain? Let us return to our basic model of oil politics, which features a ruler who wants to remain in power, citizens who want to improve their welfare, and oil revenues flowing to the government. We know from chapter 3 that the ruler faces constant pressure from citizens to spend more money and improve their welfare. To implement countercyclical fiscal policies, a ruler must make an intertemporal trade-off—displeasing citizens today in order to make them better off in the future.

Scholars recognize four sets of factors that can affect the likelihood of these trade-offs—factors that can affect democracies and dictatorships, wise and foolish leaders, and rich and poor states alike. Unfortunately, these studies underscore how difficult it can be to make these trade-offs, even if they make citizens better off in the long run.

Uncertainty among Rulers

One factor is a ruler's beliefs about how long they will remain in office. Imagine an oil-producing government headed by a wise leader who wants to adopt countercyclical fiscal policies. If these policies are to be effective, they must be maintained in future years, so that any surpluses accrued during a boom are available during a bust. But our leader cannot bind their successors to the course they want to set; policies and institutions established by today's government can be dissolved by future ones. Recognizing that the money they place in reserve might be lost to patronage and corruption by a less responsible successor, a wise ruler might prefer to use it right away on projects that they think have more merit. The more that they believe they will soon lose power, the stronger the ruler's incentive to spend the money quickly.

Similarly, a greedy ruler will also be affected by their expectations about the length of their time in office. Imagine a leader whose fiscal decisions are driven entirely by their desire for power and personal wealth, and who wants to use the windfall solely for patronage and corruption. And assume that there are diminishing marginal returns to patronage and corruption, meaning that the ruler would be better off dispensing favors over several years, rather than all at once. If the ruler believes that they will soon be replaced, they lose any incentive to hold back a budget surplus for future use.

These examples suggest that political leaders who are more secure in office will be more likely to restrain spending during economic booms;

leaders who are less secure will exercise less restraint.[45] This does not necessarily mean that authoritarian governments should have better fiscal policies than democratic ones. Much can be done to give democratic leaders longer time horizons and encourage greater restraint.[46] In *The Federalist*, Alexander Hamilton used this argument to explain the advantages of having a president who could stand for reelection:

> An avaricious man, who might happen to fill the office (of president), looking forward to the time when he must at all events yield up the emoluments he enjoyed, would feel a propensity, not easy to be resisted by such a man, to make the best use of the opportunity he enjoyed while it lasted, and might not scruple to have recourse to the most corrupt expedients to make the harvest as abundant as it was transitory; though the same man, probably, with a different prospect before him, might content himself with the regular perquisites of his situation, and might even be unwilling to risk the consequences of an abuse of his opportunities. . . . But with the prospect before him of approaching an inevitable annihilation, his avarice would be likely to get the victory over his caution, his vanity, or his ambition.[47]

More recently, Macartan Humphreys and Martin Sandbu have shown that when a resource-rich government is subject to more checks and balances, it is less likely to overspend any surpluses.[48] Alberto Alesina, Filipe Campante, and Guido Tabellini maintain that among democracies, the critical factor is corruption: democracies in the developing world with greater corruption have worse fiscal policies than democracies with less corruption.[49]

The Selection of Rulers

The way that leaders are chosen can also make a difference. Suppose that our model country is a democracy, and the government receives a large oil windfall on the eve of an election. Voters must choose between a wise candidate who wants to restrain spending and a greedy candidate who wants to spend the windfall right away. To compete for votes,

---

[45] Herschman 2009. For a discussion of the factors that influence a politician's time horizon and hence their preferred spending rate, see Levi 1988. Macartan Humphreys and Martin Sandbu (2007) use a formal model to explore, in far greater detail, conditions that may affect the likelihood of restraint.

[46] Alesina, Campante, and Tabellini 2008.

[47] Hamilton, Madison, and Jay [1788] 2000, no. 72.

[48] Humphreys and Sandbu 2007.

[49] Alesina, Campante, and Tabellini 2008.

each candidate must raise campaign funds, and the one who raises more money is more likely to win. To raise these funds, each makes promises of future patronage to their supporters.

Under these simple conditions, the candidate who is more willing to spend the government's resources on patronage will gain an advantage over their opponent, since they are able to promise government benefits to a larger number of voting blocs. Even in countries with no patronage, candidates who make more generous promises to the electorate—for new roads, schools, and jobs—can have an edge over opponents who promise less. The same dynamic can occur in authoritarian countries. Michael Herb explains that in some Middle Eastern monarchies, would-be crown princes must bribe other family members with promises of oil money and cabinet appointments to rise toward the throne.[50] Resource-rich countries sometimes face a problem of *adverse selection*: rivals who promise less restraint may end up replacing leaders who favor more fiscal restraint.[51]

The problem of adverse selection can be illustrated by one of the largest corruption scandals in US history—the Teapot Dome scandal, which shook the administration of President Warren Harding in the early 1920s.[52] Among the world's major oil producers, the United States is an anomaly: most of its onshore oil reserves are privately owned and regulated by states, not by the national government. But in 1920, the most valuable untapped oil fields in the country—perhaps in the world—were located on land owned by and under the jurisdiction of the national government. The Teapot Dome field in Wyoming along with several smaller fields in California had been set aside for the exclusive use of the US Navy in times of national emergency. Even though these fields were worth several billion dollars (in today's money), the Wilson administration, in office from 1913 to early 1921, resisted pressure from oil company lobbyists to release them for commercial use.

The Republican Party was heavily favored to win the 1921 general election, and many candidates vied for the nomination. Harding, an obscure senator from Ohio with no special policy agenda beyond "a return to normalcy," was one of the less inspired candidates.[53] A count of party delegates on the eve of the nominating convention showed Hard-

[50] Herb 1999.

[51] For a more carefully developed look at this dynamic, see Collier and Hoeffler 2009.

[52] The following account is drawn from McCartney 2008.

[53] According to William McAdoo, secretary of the treasury under Woodrow Wilson, "[Harding's] speeches left the impression of an army of pompous phrases moving over a landscape in search of an idea. Sometimes these meandering words would actually capture a straggling thought and bear it off triumphantly, a prisoner in their midst, until it died of servitude and overwork." Quoted in McCartney 2008, 43.

ing running a distant sixth. The *Wall Street Journal* gave him an eight-to-one shot at the nomination, while the sportswriter Ring Lardner put his odds at two hundred to one.

As the Republican convention began, several wealthy oil executives approached the leading candidates and offered them large donations in exchange for future access to the navy's oil fields. Most refused, but Harding—whose campaign was desperately short of money—readily agreed to the bargain. With sudden access to several million dollars, Harding was able to purchase the support of enough delegates to capture the nomination. After receiving further infusions of cash from eager oil executives, he won the general election in a landslide. On taking office, Harding appointed Albert Fall, the favored candidate of his oil industry backers, to the post of interior secretary. Fall soon granted extremely valuable no-bid leases for the navy's oil fields to Harding's backers. Harding's willingness to sell off government assets as patronage, instead of saving them for future use in an emergency, helped him triumph in the election.

The Role of Citizens

The preferences of the citizens are also important, especially in democracies. If the citizens are well informed and understand the benefits of countercyclical policies, the ruler should find it easier to exercise fiscal restraint.

But even if the electorate is well informed, under some conditions citizens might nonetheless push for faster spending. If the population is sharply divided into competing factions—perhaps along ethnic, regional, or class lines—supporters of the current government may favor the immediate distribution of any windfalls, out of fear that a future government will favor a rival faction and exclude them from the spoils.[54] Even if they are not divided, voters are also less likely to favor restraint when they perceive the government as corrupt or incompetent, since they fear that an unspent surplus will be squandered or embezzled rather than saved for future use.[55]

Of course, this is not an irrational fear. Many governments *do* squander their windfalls. Inefficient windfall use can hence become a self-fulfilling prophecy: because the public believes any surplus will be misspent, the government may be forced to disburse it right away—even if doing so causes the very misspending that citizens anticipate. But prudent windfall use—accompanied by sufficient transparency—might

[54] Humphreys and Sandbu 2007.
[55] Alesina, Campante, and Tabellini 2008.

also create a positive feedback loop: when citizens believe their government will save and invest a windfall responsibly, they may become more patient about receiving the resulting benefits.

The Role of Credit Markets

Governments bear much of the blame for overrapid spending, yet credit markets also play a role.

There is a common saying that banks will loan you an umbrella when the sun is shining, but ask for it back when it rains. The adage reflects the ironic way that credit markets work: bankers only finance customers who are better off—even though they are less in need—because they are more likely to pay their loans back.

The same pattern holds at a global level when the borrowers are governments: when a government's revenues go up, so does its ability to borrow money. Unfortunately, this means that governments find it easier to borrow money during good economic times and harder to borrow during bad times—fostering procyclical fiscal policies.[56]

The backward logic of credit markets aggravated the economic problems of many oil-producing states in the 1980s. When their oil revenues soared in the 1970s, so did their creditworthiness. Since the value of their exports was growing quickly, international banks believed that these governments would be able to service the debts of large loans, and offered them to the governments on generous terms. A 2008 study by Irfan Nooruddin found that between 1970 and 2000, the more oil that countries produced, the higher their debt burden.

Sometimes it makes economic sense for oil-producing governments to borrow money. Years may pass between the day that a valuable oil field is discovered and the day it begins to yield significant revenues for the government. If the government borrows money against future production, it can expand at a smoother and more manageable pace, and its people can enjoy the benefits of oil wealth sooner. In poor countries, where the need for food, education, and health services is urgent, loans against future revenues can save lives.

But governments should not borrow more than they can pay back, and the ability of oil-dependent governments to repay their loans depends heavily on the future price of oil. In the late 1970s, bankers and government officials believed that the underlying conditions that were producing record oil prices would continue indefinitely, and hence that oil-producing governments would have enough revenues to service large loans.

[56] Catão and Sutton 2002; Kaminsky, Reinhart, and Végh 2004.

When the price of oil collapsed after 1980, the governments of eight major petroleum exporters—Mexico, Venezuela, Nigeria, Gabon, the Republic of Congo, Trinidad, Algeria, and Ecuador—became crippled by debt; all were forced to turn to the IMF for help.[57] The availability of easy credit helped these governments accelerate public spending when prices were high, with loans that had to be repaid when prices were low—making their economies more volatile, not less.

In theory, democracy might help restrain government borrowing, since taxpayers might be more worried than their political leaders about their country's long-term financial health. Nooruddin's study, however, found the reverse: democratic oil producers have had worse debt problems than nondemocratic oil producers.[58] Once again, democracy is less helpful for the economy than we might hope.

The study of oil and economic growth is strewn with misconceptions. Many books and articles claim that oil wealth leads to weak state institutions, slower economic growth, and a decline in human development. Yet these studies typically focus on the troubled 1970–90 period and fall prey to some common fallacies.

A more careful look at the data suggests that the oil states have grown at about the same rate as other countries—indicating that oil has not typically been harmful, but has also not created the economic boost that we might expect. Collier aptly describes the economic troubles of the oil producers as "predominantly a missed opportunity."[59]

One reason for these missed opportunities has been the failure of many oil states to provide good jobs for women, which would slow the growth of their populations. A second reason has been their failure to maintain appropriate fiscal policies—not because the oil producers have abnormally weak institutions, but because offsetting the volatility of oil revenues is abnormally difficult. These policies failures, though, are not caused by atypically bad or weak government institutions. Most oil states seem to have relatively normal institutions. The problem is that the oil states need exceptionally strong ones to cope with the volume and volatility of their revenues.

[57] After the first oil shock in 1975, even Indonesia, which managed its modest windfall more prudently, was troubled by an explosion of debt (Bresnan 1993).

[58] Nooruddin 2008.

[59] Collier 2010, 44.

CHAPTER SEVEN

Good News and Bad News about Oil

> Of all those expensive and uncertain projects, however, which
> bring bankruptcy upon the greater part of the people who
> engage in them, there is none perhaps more ruinous than
> the search after new silver and gold mines. . . . They are the
> projects, therefore, to which of all others a prudent law-giver,
> who desired to increase the capital of his nation, would least
> choose to give any extraordinary encouragement.
> —Adam Smith, *The Wealth of Nations*

THIS BOOK analyzes half a century of data to produce a broad account of the politics and economics of oil wealth. It finds little evidence for some of the more dire claims in the resource curse literature: that extracting oil slows down a country's economic growth, or makes governments weaker or less effective.[1] On some fronts, like reducing child mortality, the typical oil state has outpaced its non-oil neighbors.

Yet this book also shows that since they nationalized their oil industries in the 1970s, oil-producing countries in the developing world have suffered from a series of political ailments: compared to similar states without oil, their governments have been less democratic and more secretive; their economies have provided women with fewer jobs and less political influence; and they have been more frequently marked by violent insurgencies. They suffer from a more subtle kind of economic malady as well. While they have grown at about the same rate as other countries, they should have grown faster, but were slowed down by at least two factors: their failure to provide more economic opportunities for women, which has led to unusually fast population growth; and their failure to prudently manage the volume and volatility of their oil revenues—not because their governments are uncommonly weak, but rather because the task is uncommonly arduous.

Before asking how to reverse these syndromes, let me step back and consider some of their broader implications.

---

[1] As I noted earlier in the book, mea culpa: some of my own previous studies supported several of these claims.

GEOLOGY AND DEVELOPMENT

For centuries, Western philosophers—including Niccolò Machiavelli, Baron Montesquieu, Adam Smith, and John Stuart Mill—have suggested that nations are powerfully shaped by their geography. Often they argue that favorable conditions have unfavorable consequences. According to the sixteenth-century French philosopher Jean Bodin,

> Men of a fat and fertile soil, are most commonly effeminate and cowards; whereas contrariwise a barren country makes men temperate by necessity, and by consequence, careful, vigilant, and industrious.[2]

In recent years, social scientists have taken a new interest in the ways that a country's economic development is affected by its geographic features, including its placement on the continents, location in the tropics, disease environment, access to the sea, and proximity to large markets.[3]

This book shows how another geographic feature—a country's petroleum endowment—can profoundly shape its social, economic, and political evolution. Countries with significant oil wealth will almost certainly have larger and better-funded governments than their oil-poor neighbors, giving them a heightened capacity to alleviate poverty and invest in development. If they use their oil revenues well, they should have faster economic growth and greater improvements in social welfare.

But extracting petroleum will also make their economies more volatile, saddle their governments with revenue-management tasks that are exceptionally onerous, tilt the labor market toward jobs for men and away from jobs for women, trigger relatively fast population growth, and give incumbent politicians the power to entrench themselves in office. If the oil or gas is found onshore, on the territory of marginalized or alienated populations, it will also raise the danger of violent conflict in low- and middle-income countries.

This may sound like geographic determinism, but it is not. While geography can tell us a lot about both the opportunities and obstacles that petroleum-rich countries will face, it tells us little about how well or poorly they will respond. And their response is critical. Governments cannot decide whether their country should reside in the tropics, have access to the sea, or have more prosperous neighbors. But they can de-

---

[2] Bodin [1606] 1967.
[3] See Crosby 1986; Diamond 1997; Landes 1998; Sachs and Malaney 2002; Acemoglu, Johnson, and Robinson 2001; Sachs and Warner 1997; Fujita, Krugman and Venables 2001.

cide whether to drill for oil, how much to extract, and what to do with the revenues.

INCOME FROM OIL IS DIFFERENT

The field of political economy is built on the insight that a country's politics are powerfully shaped by its economy. For example, studies show that an increase in a country's income per capita is tied to improvements in virtually every dimension of its political well-being, including the accountability and effectiveness of its government, the enfranchisement of women, and the incidence of political violence.[4]

Yet social scientists rarely make distinctions between different types of income, assuming that all of them have the same beneficent effects. This book demonstrates that the source of a country's income is critical: while income produced by a country's manufacturing, services, and agriculture sectors has largely beneficial effects, income derived from the sale of state-owned assets, such as oil reserves, has profoundly different political consequences.

It is possible to push this argument too far. Unlike Terry Lynn Karl and D. Michael Shafer, I doubt that each major sector of an economy has a distinctive political imprint—at least I have seen little evidence of this.[5] My claim is more limited: there is a sharp cleavage between the income that flows from a state-owned petroleum sector, which places a large, opaque, and volatile flow of revenues in the hands of the state, and the income generated by most other sources, which is widely diffused through the private sector.[6]

The distinction between oil and non-oil income has two surprising implications. The first might be considered good news: studies that fail to distinguish between oil and non-oil income are underestimating the political benefits of non-oil income. If a country's *total* income has a neutral impact on politics, but its oil income is harmful, it implies that its non-oil income is having a beneficial effect that is masked by the damaging effects of oil.

For example, political scientists disagree about whether richer countries are more likely to transit from authoritarianism to democracy.

[4] La Porta et al. 1999; Adsera, Boix, and Payne 2003; Lipset 1959; Londregan and Poole 1996; Epstein et al. 2006; Inkeles and Smith 1974; Inglehart and Norris 2003; Fearon and Laitin 2003; Hegre and Sambanis 2006.

[5] Karl 1997; Shafer 1995.

[6] Conceivably, other types of nontax revenue, such as foreign aid, might have similar effects, especially when it is comparable to the size, secrecy, and instability of petroleum revenues. See Brautigam, Fjelstad, and Moore 2008; Morrison 2009.

According to the landmark study in 2000 by Adam Przeworski, Michael Alvarez, José Cheibub, and Fernando Limongi, higher incomes have no impact on the likelihood of a democratic transition and only affect the chances that a democracy will remain democratic.[7] But the analysis failed to distinguish between oil and non-oil income, which means that the antidemocratic effects of oil income may have masked the prodemocratic effects of income from everything else.[8]

Statistically minded readers may have noticed this masking effect in the logit estimations in appendix 3.1 (see table 3.7): at first a country's overall income (*income (log)*) appears to be uncorrelated with the likelihood that it will have a democratic transition (column one), in keeping with the argument made by Przeworski and his colleagues; but once we control for the antidemocratic effects of oil income (column two), the *income (log)* variable turns out to have strong prodemocratic effects. Similarly, changes in overall income seem to have little or no influence on female labor force participation (see table 4.5, column one); but after we account for the negative effects of oil income (column two), we see that *income (log)* has a substantial and statistically significant impact on women's work. In chapter 5, the conflict-reducing effects of higher incomes turn out to be more powerful than they initially appear, once we control for the conflict-increasing effects of income from oil (see table 5.4, columns one and two).

This suggests that the bad news about oil income is also good news about income from other sources, like manufacturing, services, and agriculture, and scholars have underappreciated their politically favorable qualities.

The second implication, however, is bad news: the Dutch Disease is more harmful than most observers realize. In spite of its alarming name, many economists argue that there is nothing wrong with having the Dutch Disease.[9] A country's oil wealth might crowd out other enterprises, such as agriculture and manufacturing, but this does not imply that the economy would be better off without oil—only that discovering oil might raise incomes less than we would naively expect, since gains from the sale of oil will be partly offset by a decline in the competitiveness of other "tradable" goods.

---

[7] Przeworski et al. 2000.

[8] To be fair, this study acknowledged the possibility that oil might not be conducive to democracy by dropping seven oil-rich Middle Eastern countries from the data set. Yet it left in many other oil states—like Algeria, Angola, Gabon, Nigeria, Mexico, Venezuela, Trinidad, Iran, Iraq, Indonesia, Malaysia, and the Soviet Union—without controlling for their oil wealth. For important challenges to the work of Przeworski and his colleagues, see Boix and Stokes 2003; Epstein et al. 2006.

[9] Krugman 1987; Matsen and Torvik 2005.

But the Dutch Disease is only benign if the income from oil has the same externalities as the income from agriculture and manufacturing that it is displacing. This appears to be untrue, though: while higher non-oil income is associated with improvements in a country's politics, higher oil income is linked to less democracy, less gender equality, more conflict, and more economic volatility.

The discovery of oil might still make a country better off in other ways—for example, by increasing the stock of public goods. Many Middle Eastern countries have used their oil wealth to fund unusually fast improvements in public health and education. Yet the loss of manufacturing and agriculture is more worrisome than scholars commonly realize, especially for a country's politics. The Dutch Disease might be a disease after all.[10]

The Oil Curse Is New

Social scientists like to believe that they are seeking truths about the world that will transcend time and space. Our achievements, however, are exceedingly modest: we typically do not know if the patterns that we observe in one place at one time will hold in others places at other times.

Past studies have suggested that the resource curse has existed for a long time, plaguing both sixteenth-century Spain and twentieth-century Venezuela.[11] There are obvious similarities between today's oil curse and resource-related maladies in the past—like the Peruvian government's disastrous response to the nineteenth-century guano boom, which I discussed in chapter 6. But as a global phenomenon, the political ailments caused by oil and gas production seem to be limited to both a certain set of countries (described below) and the post-1980 period. Before about 1980, there was little or no global association between oil wealth and either less democracy, less work for women, or more frequent insurgencies, and the oil states had impressively fast economic growth.

There is little to romanticize about the oil-producing world of the 1940s, 1950s, and 1960s, when a handful of international companies controlled the global petroleum supply and kept most of the profits for

---

[10] A famous paper by Paul Krugman (1987) first made a related point: if there are positive economic externalities produced by manufacturing (in his argument, improved productivity through learning by doing) but not mining, the Dutch Disease could have harmful long-term effects on social welfare.

[11] Karl 1997.

themselves. The developing countries that supplied the oil had remarkably little say over its use and received just a fragment of the rents, which ironically made their oil revenues relatively small and stable, easier to manage, and less politically consequential.

The problems that bedevil the oil-rich developing countries today only emerged after the transformative events of the 1960s and 1970s, when host governments seized control of their countries' petroleum industries and prices soared. These events made oil-funded governments larger and richer than ever before; gave authoritarian incumbents the power to resist the democratizing pressures that swept across the rest of the globe in the 1980s and 1990s; created many more opportunities for men than for women; and in lower-income countries, encouraged disenfranchised groups in oil-producing regions to take up arms. At the same time, nationalization destroyed the price-stabilization mechanisms established by the international oil companies, setting off a new era of price volatility that caused unpredictable booms and busts in government finances.

The post-1980 emergence of these ailments helps explain why some of the strongest objections to the idea of a resource curse have come from historians who have studied oil- and mineral-based development in earlier eras.[12] It also fits with an important new study by Pauline Jones Luong and Erika Weinthal of the five petroleum-rich states of the former Soviet Union (Russia, Azerbaijan, Kazakhstan, Turkmenistan, and Uzbekistan), which finds that oil wealth only leads to weakened state institutions when the government has a dominant role in the petroleum industry. Their study argues that when the private sector, especially foreign investors, have a dominant role, governments are likely to have stronger fiscal institutions, including more broadly based tax systems and more stable, transparent budgets.[13] Unfortunately, in the vast majority of oil-producing countries since the 1970s, the government's role has been dominant—which helps account for much of the oil curse described in earlier chapters.

If state ownership is part of the disease, then privatization might seem like part of the cure. But some medicines are worse than the diseases that they are prescribed for, and I explain below why full privatization may not be the right cure for most oil-producing countries in the developing world.

---

[12] Wright and Czelusta 2004; Haber and Menaldo 2009.
[13] Jones Luong and Weinthal 2010.

Differences among Oil States

Oil wealth does not affect all countries equally.[14] While this book underscores the broad differences between oil and non-oil states, it also shows that different types of oil producers are vulnerable to different maladies.

When oil is found in countries already ruled by autocrats, it helps them stay in power, provided they can conceal the size and deployment of the government's oil revenues. This pattern holds in all regions of the world but one: Latin America. Oil and gas wealth did not help autocrats in the Western Hemisphere stay in power, although the reasons are admittedly unclear. Dunning argues that the region's unusually high inequality levels can explain this pattern.[15] Alternatively, it could be due to Latin America's prior experience with democracy and stronger labor unions, which made it harder for governments to keep their oil revenues secret.

When petroleum is found in democracies, its impact depends on the strength of preexisting checks on the executive branch. In low- and middle-income countries that only place feeble constraints on executive power, like Russia, Iraq, or Venezuela, an oil-funded ruler can dismantle checks and balances that would otherwise constrain them, leading to the erosion of democratic institutions. In wealthy, well-established democracies, a rise in oil income may help incumbents get reelected, like in the United States, but without endangering the long-term health of democratic institutions.

Petroleum can curtail economic and political opportunities for women in countries where women cannot easily work in the service and government sectors, which are where most of the new jobs appear in petroleum-rich states. Unfortunately, this is a particularly common condition in the Middle East and North Africa. Countries that enable women to work in their booming service and government sectors, or that find other ways to draw women into the labor force, such as in Mexico, Syria, and Norway, should be immune to this effect. Setting up meaningful gender quotas for elected office can also help countries avoid these problems, as long as women have enough political influence to remove barriers to their participation in the labor force.[16]

---

[14] This is hardly a new insight. Many important studies have shown how "the politics of oil wealth is filtered through local political realities and shaped by historical legacies" (Smith 2007, 7), rendering countries more or less susceptible to a resource curse. See, for example, Yates 1996; Vandewalle 1998; Peluso and Watts 2001; Smith 2007; Omeje 2006; Lowi 2009.

[15] Dunning 2008.

[16] Kang 2009.

Extracting oil and gas can also lead to violent conflict, but again only under certain conditions: when a country is relatively poor; when at least some of the production takes place onshore, or is processed on-shore, in a region populated by either disenfranchised peoples or criminal gangs; or when rebels can sell off future exploitation rights to the oil that they hope to capture in battle—the booty futures effect. Oil can also have a countervailing, conflict-reducing effect: since it only triggers conflicts in countries that are poor, if petroleum is abundant enough to lift a country out of poverty it can also curtail the risk of civil war. Low-income states are most in danger when they have enough oil to make life as a rebel financially attractive, but not enough to make life as a civilian equally attractive.

The impact of oil wealth on economic growth also varies. While the economies of all oil-producing states fluctuate over time in tandem with oil prices, countries that are more dependent on petroleum exports will be more affected by world prices, and have more pronounced booms and busts. The long-run economic success of oil-rich states seems to depend partly on their success in drawing women into the labor force, which reduces fertility rates and the demand for migrant labor, and thus population growth; and partly on the government's capacity to maintain countercyclical policies that smooth out booms and busts. The two most economically successful oil states in the last fifty years—Oman and Malaysia—also had the most successful countercyclical policies when oil prices collapsed in the 1980s and 1990s. Unfortunately, their strategies are not easy for others to emulate. They each offset falling prices by boosting production—a strategy that is only possible for small producers with unexploited reserves who are not OPEC members.

Still, countries that adopt more common types of countercyclical policies, such as paying down their debts, building up their stabilization funds, and fostering growth in nonpetroleum sectors, will be better poised for sustainable growth.

To enact these and other kinds of countercyclical policies, politicians must be able to forgo the short-term political benefits of immediate spending for the long-term ones of sustainable growth. These trade-offs are easier to make when incumbents believe that they or their party is likely to stay in office long enough to profit from future gains; when the government is more constrained by checks and balances; when citizens are both well informed and have confidence in their government; and when they are not sharply divided into competing factions that seek to exclude each other from future benefits.

In one sense, these qualifications should be encouraging: countries are only hurt by oil wealth under certain conditions—some of them fairly restrictive. But it is also discouraging, because of what I termed in chapter 1 "the irony of oil wealth": those countries with the greatest social and economic deficits—countries with low incomes, disenfranchised minorities, few opportunities for women, and relatively fragile institutions—are also the most vulnerable to the oil curse. Where it is most needed, oil wealth is least likely to help. Most countries on the petroleum frontier—states in Africa, the Caspian Basin, and Southeast Asia that have recently begun, or are about to begin, exporting oil and gas—unfortunately are about to confront this vexing dilemma.

Understanding the Middle East

Political scientists who carry out broad, cross-national research often avoid the Middle East. Many landmark studies of political development look at all regions *except* the Middle East.[17] This probably reflects a belief that the Muslim Middle East is *sui generis*, a region that follows a unique historical path and cannot be compared with the rest of the world. Of course, much about the Middle East *is* distinctive. But when social scientists dismiss the region as an oddity, they miss an opportunity to learn more general lessons about the effects that natural resource wealth can have on a country's politics, economy, and social structure.

The Middle Eastern region seems to defy two global patterns: it has become wealthier without becoming democratic; and it has become wealthier without making much progress toward gender equality. Many observers blame both patterns on the region's Islamic traditions.[18]

Can Islam really explain the Middle East's anomalies? It is not easy to disentangle the effects of Islam from those of oil, thanks to a strange geographic accident: most of the world's petroleum is found in countries with Muslim majorities or pluralities, not only in the Middle East and North Africa, but also sub-Saharan Africa (Nigeria, Sudan, and Chad), Southeast Asia (Indonesia, Malaysia, and Brunei), and the Caspian Basin (Azerbaijan, Kazakhstan, and Turkmenistan). True, there are Muslim-majority countries with little or no oil (like Somalia, Turkey, and Afghanistan), and countries with few Muslims and lots of oil (like Angola, Venezuela, and Norway). Still, in 2008, Muslim-majority countries—making up about 23 percent of the world's sovereign states—exported about 51 percent of the world's oil and held 62 percent of its petroleum reserves. Since their share of reserves is greater than their share of current exports, the role of Muslim-majority countries in global petroleum markets will almost certainly grow in the coming decades.

---

[17] See, for example, O'Donnell, Schmitter, and Whitehead 1986; Diamond, Linz, and Lipset 1988; Przeworski et al. 2000; Acemoglu and Robinson 2001, 2002.

[18] See, for example, Midlarsky 1998; Fish 2002; Donno and Russett 2004.

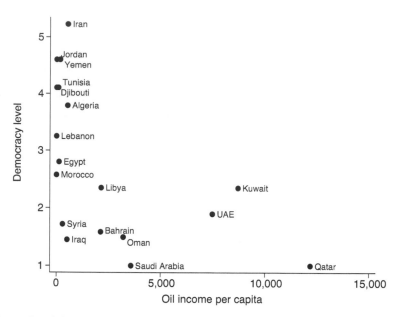

Figure 7.1. Oil and democracy in the Middle East, 1993–2002

A country's democracy level is its mean score on the Polity index, translated to a one-to-ten scale, over the 1993–2002 period. Higher numbers indicate a more democratic government.

Source: Calculated from data in Marshall and Jaggers 2007.

A large fraction of the Middle East's democracy and gender rights deficits can be explained by oil wealth. One way to appreciate the role of oil is to look at variations within the Muslim Middle East. Even though these seventeen countries are commonly lumped together, there are wide differences in both democratic accountability and gender rights across the region. Since all of these countries have large Muslim populations, Islam cannot easily explain these differences.

The Middle Eastern countries have different amounts of petroleum wealth, however, and their petroleum wealth is strongly correlated with both their democratic accountability and gender rights. Figures 7.1 and 7.2 compare their mean oil wealth over a recent ten-year period with their mean democracy scores, and a measure of their gender rights.[19] In general, countries with less oil and gas have more democratic freedoms and gender rights, while countries with more oil and gas have less democracy and worse conditions for women. The pros-

[19] The measure of democracy is from the Polity database, described in chapter 3; Sameena Nazir and Leigh Tomppert (2005) developed the gender rights index.

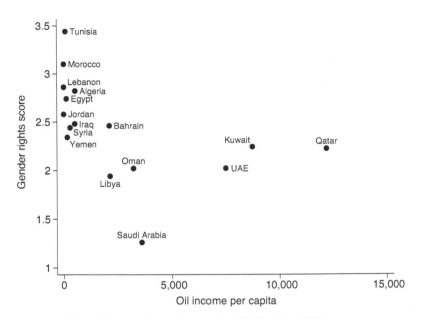

Figure 7.2. Oil and the gender rights in the Middle East, 2004
The gender rights score is a combination of five ordinal measures of
women's rights, including "nondiscrimination and access to justice," "autonomy, security, and freedom," "economic rights and equal opportunities,"
"political rights and civic voice," and "social and cultural rights." Each country
receives a score from one to five for each measure on an ordinal scale, where
higher scores indicate more rights for women. The index takes the mean score
for each country on all five measures.
Source: Tabulated from data in Nazir and Tomppert 2005.

pect of greater democracy in Egypt and Tunisia—two of the region's
oil-poor states—only sharpens these contrasts.

Fewer than half of the world's thirty-nine Muslim-majority states are
in the Middle East and North Africa, yet even in the broader Muslim
world, oil wealth seems to have a democracy-inhibiting effect. At least
six Muslim-majority countries have recently been classified as democracies: Turkey, Mali, Senegal, Bangladesh, Comoros, and Indonesia. The
first five produce little or no oil; only Indonesia has some petroleum
wealth. But Indonesia's petroleum income was quite small—about sixty-
nine dollars per capita—when it transitioned to democracy in 1998.

Income from petroleum helps explain why the Middle East looks so
different than the rest of the world. This does not mean that Islamic traditions are insignificant. Even after accounting for oil, Muslim-majority
countries have been less democratic and provided fewer opportunities

for women than similar non-Muslim countries.[20] Until we take account of their oil-based economies, though—which in turn are based on the world's thirst for their natural resources—we will overestimate the influence of Islamic traditions on the politics of Muslim countries, in both the Middle East and the rest of the world.

This does not mean that democracy movements in the Middle East are doomed to failure, but it underscores the challenges they are confronting. No country with as much oil as Libya, Bahrain, Oman, Algeria, or Iraq has ever made a successful transition from authoritarian to democratic rule. Others have tried: in the 1960s, monarchs in Iraq and Libya were overthrown by military coups, and the 1979 Iranian Revolution led to the fall of the shah. None of these revolutions led to a sustainable democracy. The petrodollars that have empowered Middle Eastern autocrats have also weakened civil society organizations and enfeebled the private sector. We know from other democratic transitions—like in Indonesia, Mexico, and Central Europe—that these groups play a critical role in successful transitions to democracy.

Iraq may still become an exception: it has outspoken political parties, a reasonably free press, and elections that matter. Still, the Iraqi parliament has been unable to pass a new oil law—after four years of trying—and the oil question looms over the volatile and unresolved matter of Kurdish autonomy. Iraqi prime minister al-Maliki managed to remain in office after his party's electoral defeat in March 2010 and has been steadily centralizing power. The Middle East's democracy movements are filled with brave men and women; they will need courage and ingenuity to overcome the challenges posed by their countries' oil wealth.

What Should Be Done?

The oil curse is largely caused by the unusual properties of petroleum revenues. Unless countries are already wealthy and have strong institutions at the time that oil production begins—like Norway or Canada—they can cause profound political and economic problems. Fortunately, much can be done to change these properties, such as limiting the size of these revenues, making them more stable and transparent, and even altering their source. While the most important reforms can only be made by oil-funded governments themselves, international actors such as foreign governments, energy companies, international institutions, and NGOs can play a critical role.

---

[20] See the appendixes to chapters 3 and 4.

To reform their revenues, different countries need different kinds of policies. Measures that are effective in some settings will be useless in others. Rather than suggest a one-size-fits-all solution, I instead offer a menu of ways for countries to change the size, stability, secrecy, and even source of their oil revenues. I also discuss the importance of spending reforms. Some of these ideas are have been around for a long time; others are new and untested. None are panaceas. Still, in appropriate combinations and with local modifications, they might help countries find better ways to harness their natural endowments.

Beyond minimizing the negative political consequences of natural resources, countries should also try to maximize their positive economic consequences. Outstanding recent books by Collier as well as Humphreys, Sachs, and Joseph Stiglitz address this issue with great sophistication, and can be read alongside the discussion below to provide a more complete road map of the challenges and opportunities that confront the oil states.[21]

Reducing the Size of Petroleum Revenues

Large oil revenues help autocrats stay in power, encourage rebellions, and tend to be squandered by overstretched bureaucracies. The first question for reformers should be whether to decrease the size of these revenues. There are at least four ways to do this. The first two are more appropriate for low-income countries with weak bureaucracies; the latter two are more likely to work in middle- and upper-income countries with more sophisticated bureaucracies.

For low-income countries, the first option is to leave the oil in the ground. Countries can also extract their petroleum more slowly, so that revenues do not outmatch the government's capacity to spend them effectively—or civil society's ability to monitor the activities of their rapidly growing government.

Since mineral wealth is a nonrenewable asset, extracting it produces a onetime cash windfall. If wisely invested, it can raise the living standards of future generations, but if squandered it is lost forever. Leaving oil in the ground is like saving it in a bank; it will even earn "interest," since its value will rise over time as the rest of the world's petroleum supplies are depleted.[22]

Deferring the revenues produced by oil extraction admittedly carries a high opportunity cost, especially in low-income countries, where

---

[21] Collier 2010; Humphreys, Sachs, and Stiglitz 2007.

[22] As Harold Hotelling (1931) pointed out, the value of mineral assets in the ground should rise at the same rate as the prevailing discount rate.

people urgently need food, health services, and education. Collier points out that in the world's poorest countries—which are home to the world's "bottom-billion" citizens—the extraction of natural resources can provide a historically unique opportunity for rapid economic growth; the failure of these states to harness their natural assets is "the single most important missed opportunity in economic development."[23]

This highlights the irony of oil wealth: the greater a country's need for additional income—because it is poor and has a weak economy—the more likely its oil wealth will be misused or squandered. For low-income countries, the risks created by oil extraction are great, but so are the costs of leaving it in the ground. Limiting the pace of extraction will help limit the danger of an oil curse, yet it is a decision that cannot be taken lightly.

The second approach is to use barter contracts: instead of selling their oil for cash, low-income countries can trade it directly for the public goods they would ultimately like to acquire. This may sound unorthodox, but several countries, including Angola, Nigeria, Zambia, and Zimbabwe, have already sold petroleum and other mineral rights to Chinese-owned consortia using barter-type deals. Instead of receiving royalties and taxes, these governments got promises of future infrastructure and services.

It has long been common practice for petroleum companies to support their operations in host countries by building ancillary facilities like housing for workers, roads, railways, and even ports. Barter contracts go further, stipulating that companies will pay host governments with *unrelated* projects and services rather than cash. In 2006, Nigeria signed contracts giving Chinese companies exploration licenses to four offshore blocs in exchange for four billion dollars in investment, including promises to build a new hydropower plant, rehabilitate a decrepit railroad, and develop programs to combat malaria and avian flu. Angola has traded oil contracts for new roads, railroads, bridges, schools, hospitals, and a fiber-optic network.[24] Although Chinese companies working in Africa have pioneered barter contracts, companies from India, Malaysia, and South Korea have made similar deals.[25]

Economists are rightly skeptical about contracts like these that entail a process called bundling, in which one transaction (the purchase of exploration or extraction rights) is tied to a second transaction (the construction of roads and bridges). Sometimes companies use bundling to gain an advantage over competitors. In 1998, for example, the US

[23] Collier 2007; 2010, 37.
[24] Vines, Weimer, and Campos 2009.
[25] Chan-Fishel and Lawson 2007.

Department of Justice sued Microsoft for forcing purchasers of its Windows operating system to simultaneously purchase some of its less desirable programs, which were bundled into the same software.

But bundling can sometimes be beneficial if the costs of carrying out the transactions separately are prohibitive. Barter contracts might help low-capacity governments bypass the process of collecting the revenues (when much is lost to corruption), shuffling it among government agencies (where more can be lost), and reallocating the revenues to government projects (where even more is lost to corruption, patronage, and inefficiencies). They can have other advantages, too: barter contracts relieve governments of the need to smooth out revenue fluctuations, since revenue smoothing becomes the company's responsibility; they can help draw foreign infrastructure companies into low-income countries, which the companies might otherwise shun out of fear they would not get paid; and they can help governments make hard-to-reverse commitments to long-term projects that might not otherwise be completed.

The barter contract is a new phenomena in the petroleum world, and so far its record is unimpressive. According to one report on Nigeria's experience,

> It is clear that 2–3 years down the line, there is still nothing on the ground to show for the generous treatment given to the Asian National Oil Companies (in exchange for barter contracts). At the very least, all projects are on hold. There is a strong possibility that the deals in their entirety will be cancelled. . . . [T]he Yar'Adua government has concluded that the whole arrangement was compromised from the start by the absence of transparency and due process compounded by corruption.[26]

It might be possible to find better ways to organize barter contracts. For example, they can be awarded through competitive bidding, in which companies must offer comparable projects so that the best offer is easier to identify; and compliance with the contracts could be more carefully monitored by reliable third-party agents, with strict anticorruption measures, full transparency, and close attention to the quality of the projects. Barter contracts are still experiments, and we do not know how well they can work.

The third strategy is to distribute the oil revenues directly to citizens. Both the US state of Alaska and the Canadian province of Alberta use direct distribution. Of these two programs, the older one—the Alaska Permanent Fund—has been in place since 1977 and is widely considered a success. The fund receives about one-fifth of the state's oil revenues,

---

[26] Wong 2008, 5.

along with other discretionary transfers from the state budget, and annually distributes a share of the accrued interest to all Alaskan citizens. In 2009, the dividend was worth about thirteen hundred dollars. It has grown so popular that politicians "virtually fall over one another to demonstrate to the public their efforts to defend the program."[27]

Some scholars argue that direct distribution funds could help developing countries avoid at least some facets of the oil curse. A fund would keep at least part of the government's petroleum revenues away from politicians, who might otherwise steal or use them for political advantage; it could help hedge against price volatility, if citizens can do a better job than governments of planning ahead; and it might give citizens a powerful incentive to monitor their government's use of resource revenues, creating pressures against corruption and in favor of wise stewardship. True, it would initially reduce the funding available for potentially worthy government programs. But governments could always tax back a portion of the distributed funds, which in turn might induce citizens to demand more government accountability.[28]

Direct distribution might work in Alaska, but would it work in countries with lower incomes and more easily corrupted state institutions? Governments in low-income countries may find it hard to identify and transfer cash to eligible citizens in a fraud-resistant manner—although new biometric and electronic cash transfer technologies hold considerable promise.[29] If the country's financial system is not well developed, citizens could have trouble saving their dividends for future use. It is unclear how a fund would affect regional grievances, since those who live closer to the oil's source might demand a larger dividend. Yet giving larger sums to people in one region could also lead to excessive migration among dividend seekers.[30]

We should also be skeptical about policies that hinge on the creation of specialized funds, including direct distribution funds, since their appeal frequently depends on the belief that they will do a better job than the rest of the government in shielding resource revenues from misuse. But why should a direct distribution fund be better managed and less corrupt than the rest of the government? What if the fund is just as sus-

[27] Goldsmith 2001, 5.

[28] See Birdsall and Subramanian 2004; Sala-i-Martin and Subramanian 2003; Palley 2003; Sandbu 2006; Moss and Young 2009. For skeptical views, see Hjort 2006; Morrison 2007.

[29] On the promise of these new technologies, see Gelb and Decker 2011.

[30] Migration is not a problem in Alaska, partly because the annual dividends are relatively small—they constitute about 6 percent of the average household's total income—and partly because potential immigrants are deterred by Alaska's harsh winters and geographic remoteness. Direct distribution might not work so well in sunny California.

ceptible to fraud and abuse as other government agencies? As chapter 6 points out, specialized resource funds have worked better in theory than in practice—at least, so far.

The fourth way to shrink a government's oil revenues is to directly transfer a portion of the money to regional or local governments. Most of the oil-rich countries in the Middle East are unitary states and have fully centralized revenue systems.[31] Outside the Middle East, however, a growing number of oil and mineral exporters are dividing resource revenues between central and subnational governments, regardless of whether they are unitary states (Colombia, Ecuador, and Kazakhstan) or federal states (Mexico, Nigeria, Russia, Venezuela, and Indonesia).[32]

Subnational governments should be entitled to funds that compensate them for the social, environmental, and infrastructure costs they bear when hosting oil and gas projects.[33] Revenue decentralization, though, goes beyond mitigating *costs*. It entails sharing the financial *benefits* of resource extraction with subnational governments.

There are two broad ways to do this: countries can allow subnational governments to levy taxes directly on the petroleum industry; or they can distribute a fraction of the central government's revenues to subnational governments according to some formula, either before or after smoothing out year-to-year revenue fluctuations.

Revenue decentralization can be an effective way to reduce the size of the national government's discretionary windfall and even may reduce the danger that people in the extractive region will seek independence. Yet there is no a priori reason to expect local governments to make better use of these funds than central governments. Local governments can be just as corrupt, opaque, and incompetent as their national counterparts. They often have less capable bureaucracies, are less able to manage revenue volatility, and have worse fiscal discipline.[34] Oil revenues can have the same antidemocratic effects in local governments that they have in national ones—as suggested in the case of Louisiana's Governor Long, described in chapter 3. Fiscal decentralization has been linked to reduced accountability in both Argentina and Brazil, and less economic reform and less investment in Russia.[35]

---

[31] The United Arab Emirates is a notable exception.

[32] Ahmad and Mottu 2003.

[33] Local and indigenous peoples who live in the extractive region deserve special attention. Their concerns should be addressed before any new project begins.

[34] See Ahmad and Mottu 2003; Brosio 2003; Bahl 2001. Treisman (2007) argues that the alleged benefits of decentralization have been greatly exaggerated.

[35] On Argentina, see Gervasoni 2010. On Brazil, see Brollo et al. 2010. On Russia, see Desai, Freinkman, and Goldberg 2005. Revenue sharing has at best a mixed record in helping to end local conflicts. See Le Billon and Nicholls 2007.

The decentralization of oil revenues is likely to work better in countries with subnational governments that are relatively democratic, transparent, and effective at managing their budgets. The success or failure of decentralization will also depend on how it is done. Policymakers can devise revenue systems that tamp down fluctuations in the volatility of subnational revenues; insist that local governments use any oil revenues to complement, not substitute for, their existing tax base; make sure that new revenues are paired with expenditure responsibilities linked to the provision of public goods; and stipulate that all shared revenue must be fully transparent and regularly audited.[36]

CHANGING THE SOURCE OF PETROLEUM REVENUES

If key elements of the oil curse can be traced back to the nationalizations of the 1960s and 1970s, perhaps they could be reversed by privatization. Privatization would change the source of the government's oil revenues, replacing nontax revenues from national oil companies with tax revenues from private-sector oil companies. Would this make a difference?

Although many other kinds of state-owned enterprises were privatized in the 1980s and 1990s, full privatization has been relatively uncommon in the petroleum world. Only the governments of the United Kingdom (1985), Romania (1992), Poland (1999), and Argentina (1999) have fully divested themselves of any ownership in what were previously national oil companies, and Argentina later renationalized some of its petroleum assets.

Privatization advocates point to a mountain of evidence that state-owned enterprises are economically inefficient.[37] Skeptics suggest that national oil companies are different than other kinds of state-owned enterprises in ways that can make privatization difficult.[38] They also argue that the size and financial sophistication of international oil companies makes them exceptionally tough for governments, especially in low-income countries, to tax and regulate.[39]

When it comes to regulating large oil companies, even the US government has a dismal record. It dismantled its Minerals Management

---

[36] For more specific recommendations, see Brosio 2003; Ahmad and Mottu 2003; Ross 2007.

[37] See, for example, Boardman and Vining 1989; Dewenter and Malatesta 2001; Eller, Hartley, and Medlock 2010. John James Quinn (2002) argues that in Africa, state ownership has also caused governments to adopt self-defeating trade policies.

[38] Aharoni and Ascher 1998.

[39] Stiglitz 2007.

Service in 2010, after a series of sex and drug scandals, and the catastrophic blowout of BP's *Deepwater Horizon* drilling rig in the Gulf of Mexico revealed how poorly it was enforcing basic safety and environmental regulations. Privatization might only replace large, secretive, and unaccountable governments with large, secretive, and unaccountable private companies.

Privatization might have modestly prodemocratic effects, but it is important to first clarify what it would *not* achieve. It would not bring back the pre-1970 era of smaller and steadier oil revenues. Oil revenues were relatively small before the 1970s because world prices were low by historic standards, as the discovery of new reserves outpaced the world's still-modest demands, and because international oil companies were able to keep a large fraction of the profits for themselves. Both conditions have changed, and privatization would not reverse them. If privatization led to a more efficient and hence profitable industry, it could even increase a government's petroleum revenues.

Nor would privatization make oil prices more stable. Oil prices were unusually steady from the end of World War II to the early 1970s, thanks to both the price-setting oligopoly of the Seven Sisters and the Bretton Woods system of fixed exchange rates. Both fell apart in the 1960s and early 1970s, and privatization would not revive them.

Finally, privatization might not cause oil-rich countries to adopt democracy-enhancing forms of taxation. In many low-income oil-producing countries, privatization would only produce a modest shift toward taxes. Most of these countries have national oil companies that work closely with international oil companies through joint ventures or production-sharing contracts, and already collect much of their oil revenue from these companies in taxes, royalties, and other kinds of fees.

Some middle-income countries, like Libya, Mexico, and Saudi Arabia, have national oil companies that manage their own facilities and rely far less on international companies. For them, privatization would lead to a much larger shift toward tax-based revenues. Yet remember that in chapter 3, taxes are only a democratizing force when they increase public recognition of the government's revenues. Privatization in the oil sector might simply replace nontax revenues with levies on a handful of large, often multinational corporations, and therefore provide citizens with little direct information about the size of the government's revenues.

Still, in some cases full or partial privatization could boost government accountability by making it harder for the state to hide its oil revenues. Chapter 2 explains how many governments use their national oil companies to conceal their use (and misuse) of petroleum money. Full or partial privatization can help curtail this *if* the resulting companies are more transparent—for example, if they are publicly listed on stock exchanges that force them to disclose their balance sheets and adhere to internationally recognized accounting standards. Even if the government remains the majority shareholder in partially privatized oil companies, such as in Brazil, Colombia, Malaysia, and Norway, public listings can be a step toward greater revenue transparency.

Some governments will find other ways to hide their oil revenues, but this hardly nullifies the benefits of public listings. Mousetraps are useful even if some mice always escape.

Stabilizing Petroleum Revenues

The instability of petroleum revenues hurts private-sector investment, the government's fiscal policies, and ultimately economic growth in the oil states. Many governments try to fix these problems by setting up stabilization funds to hold surplus revenues when prices are high, so they can be drawn down when prices fall. Chapter 6 notes that these funds have a dismal track record: governments so frequently violate their own rules about moving money in and out of these funds that their benefits seem to be negligible. Are there better ways for governments to stabilize their oil revenues?

Some of the policies already mentioned would affect revenue stability. Extracting oil at a slower pace would limit a government's reliance on oil revenues, which in turn would reduce the impact of fluctuating oil prices on the government's overall budget. Barter contracts, if properly designed, could shift the risk of price fluctuations from governments to companies, which are typically better at managing volatility. Direct distribution could also help by making households responsible for some of the income smoothing. The consequences of decentralization and privatization are less clear; much would depend on how they were structured.

Any stabilization plan needs three elements: a way to reduce government spending when prices are high; a way to increase spending when prices are low; and a mechanism to link the two, so that the money removed from the budget during booms is matched by the money added to the budget during busts.

Stabilization funds combine all three elements in a way that is economically intelligent but politically inept. Their initial funding depends on politically altruistic—even suicidal—behavior by politicians who must cut spending during booms, when the economy is strong and citizens often believe they should not make sacrifices. Even if it receives money during a boom, the fund will only survive if every subsequent ruler exercises the same selfless restraint, leaving the surplus in place until it is needed during a bust. The fund might be managed by a nominally independent government agency that by law adheres to strict guidelines about deposits and withdrawals. But highly motivated politicians typically find ways to siphon off the surplus, either by changing the rules, replacing the people who oversee the fund, or simply borrowing money against the savings.[40] Even farsighted rulers can rarely bind their successors to a course of fiscal restraint.

Under some conditions, stabilization funds are more likely to work: when the government is run by a wise, politically insulated autocrat—or alternatively, by a democratically elected leader whose policies are subject to vigorous checks and balances—when corruption is low; when the public is well informed, and has confidence in the government's policies; and in democracies, when voters are relatively unaffected by campaign spending. None of these conditions are easy to achieve.[41]

Alternatively, we can try to design stabilization mechanisms that are more compatible with the myopic incentives that typically drive politicians. Political leaders benefit when they can increase spending and are hurt when they must decrease it. Stabilization funds fail because the politically painful part of stabilization (diminished spending) is both voluntary and a necessary precondition for the politically beneficial part (increased spending). A better design would place the politically beneficial part first and make the politically painful part mandatory, or at least more costly to avoid. Since increased spending would precede increased savings, the two pieces could not be connected by a stabilization fund—since funds can run surpluses but not deficits—but they could be connected by a loan.

Here is one way it might work: when oil prices were low, oil-producing governments could borrow money from foreign banks, governments, or international financial institutions to stabilize their budgets as well as stimulate their economies. Chapter 6 explains that in the past, oil states have used loans procyclically—borrowing when prices were high instead of low—making their economies more volatile, not less. To encourage countercyclical borrowing, the World Bank or other international financial institutions could have a special credit facility

---

[40] Eifert, Gelb, and Tallroth 2003. For the classic statement on how this happened to Africa's agricultural marketing boards, see Bates 1981.

[41] These conditions are discussed more carefully in chapter 6. The remarkable *Bringing in the Future* by William Ascher (2009) offers an inventory of more detailed strategies to foster long-range policymaking in politically challenging environments. For an insightful treatment of the international dimensions of oil market volatility, see Jaffee and El-Gamal 2010.

for resource-dependent countries, which would only make loans when global prices fell below some benchmark.

The key feature of these loans would be the way that they were repaid, which would depend on the current price of oil. Governments would set aside the proceeds from a fixed number of barrels of oil each month to repay their creditor until the value of the loan was fully paid off. The value of the loan would not fluctuate, only the rate at which it was paid back. If prices stayed low, the loan would be repaid slowly and cost the government relatively little in revenue foregone; if prices rose, so would the value of the repayment barrels sold each month, and hence the rate at which the loan was repaid. An "oil-denominated loan," offered by a special facility only when prices were low, could both increase spending when revenues were scarce and reduce it when revenues were abundant.

Unlike a stabilization fund, which holds a surplus that can be robbed at any time by the government that established it, foreign loans are owned by foreign banks and governments, thereby making defaulting on them costly. In fact, Angola has been using oil-denominated loans for decades with little fanfare.[42] Although it pays a modest premium for these loans—since the lender is assuming the cost of managing oil price volatility—it has found both commercial banks and foreign governments willing to make them.[43]

In a country ruled by benevolent accountants, the problem of stabilization would be easy to solve. In the real world, stabilization plans are commonly rendered ineffective by the self-interested behavior of political leaders. Better institutional design could help make stabilization policies more sustainable politically and ultimately more effective.

Lifting the Secrecy of Petroleum Revenues

Most of the oil world is hidden from public view. In many countries, little is known about the contracts that oil companies sign; the signing bonuses, taxes, royalties, fees, and other payments they make to governments; the operations of national oil companies; the flow of oil revenues within governments; and how these revenues are eventually

---

[42] Vines, Weimer, and Campos 2009.

[43] Governments can use other devices to hedge against volatility. In 2008, the Mexican government paid $1.5 billion to insure itself against falling oil prices; when prices fell in 2009, the treasury earned a $5 billion windfall. Still, buying insurance against falling prices also entails new expenditures during a boom, which can be politically difficult. For a discussion of debt obligations linked to commodity prices, see also Frankel 2010.

spent.[44] This secrecy helps autocrats stay in power, impedes the resolution of oil-based civil wars, and makes it harder to stop corruption. Transparency alone cannot fix all of these problems, but it should help.

Transparency has recently gained attention in policy circles, although democracy advocates have long recognized its importance. In 1822, James Madison wrote in a personal correspondence that

> a popular Government, without popular information, or the means of acquiring it, is but a Prologue to a Farce or a Tragedy; or, perhaps, both. Knowledge will forever govern ignorance: And a people who mean to be their own Governors must arm themselves with the power which knowledge gives.[45]

Recent studies suggest that when governments are more transparent, they are also likely to have less corruption, higher levels of human development, stronger fiscal discipline, and many other desirable qualities.[46] It is hard to know if transparency is causing these outcomes, but most observers believe that on balance, transparency promotes better governance.[47]

Even if the benefits of transparency are hard to measure, it has one great advantage. Most of the other policies discussed above—from barter contracts through the use of oil-denominated loans—have the potential to do good, but may be costly to enact and carry some risk of backfiring. Transparency is cheap to implement and unlikely to do harm.

Transparency begins with the disclosure of information, but does not end there. The information released by governments must be complete and accurate, which means it should be subjected to independent audits that also are made public. It must be made widely available at little or no cost, and it should be presented in a format that ordinary people can understand.

A free press and well-informed civil society groups are essential to turn publicly disclosed information into a meaningful tool for better resource governance. Even these groups may have trouble evaluating government documents and policies. Many technical dimensions of resource management are known to industry insiders, but not to the wider public. This makes public education an essential component of transparency.

---

[44] Gillies 2010.

[45] Quoted in Piotrowski 2010, 31.

[46] Bellver and Kaufmann 2005; Hameed 2005.

[47] Fung, Graham, and Weil 2007; Piotrowski 2010. For a skeptical view, which sensibly argues that transparency needs to be complemented by other measures, see Kolstad and Wiig 2009.

In 2009, an international group of policy experts launched a "Natural Resources Charter," which offers guidelines for citizens and governments that want to maximize the beneficial use of their country's natural resources. It is not a binding document but rather a standard to which all countries—rich and poor—can aspire. The charter includes twelve core precepts that offer guidelines on a wide range of issues, including whether or not to extract resources, how to negotiate contracts, how to mitigate social and environmental costs, and how revenues should be used. By distilling and publicizing the best available knowledge, the charter is designed to both inform policymakers and help citizens figure out if their governments are abiding by internationally recognized principles—and if not, what should be changed.[48]

There has been a lot of progress on oil-sector transparency since 2000, thanks to the remarkable work of NGOs in scores of resource-rich countries. The key groups include Global Witness, a London-based NGO that since the 1990s has called attention to the role of natural resources in conflict and corruption around the world; a global network of NGOs that sponsors a campaign called Publish What You Pay, which encourages companies in the extractive sector to reveal what they pay to governments, and governments to disclose what they receive from these companies; and the Revenue Watch Institute, a nonprofit policy, research, and grant-making institute begun in 2002 that promotes the use of oil, gas, and mineral resources for the public good. In 2002, British prime minister Tony Blair launched the Extractive Industries Transparency Initiative (EITI) to encourage resource-rich countries to make their revenues fully transparent. In 2007 it became an independent, Oslo-based multistakeholder organization; it had thirty member countries by 2010.[49]

Despite these initiatives, much of the petroleum world is still shrouded in secrecy. Of the thirty countries that were EITI members in 2010, only three (Azerbaijan, Timor-Leste, and Liberia) were certified as "fully compliant" with the organization's transparency standards. Six others—including Angola, Bolivia, Chad, Equatorial Guinea, São Tomé, and Trinidad—had dropped out of EITI or were suspended for noncompliance. A Revenue Watch study in 2010 of forty-one oil-, gas-,

---

[48] The charter was drafted by an independent group of academics, lawyers, and practitioners organized by economists Paul Collier, Anthony Venables, and Michael Spence. I was a member of the technical group that drafted the charter. For more on the charter, see http://www.naturalresourcecharter.org.

[49] For more on these groups, see http://www.globalwitness.org; http://www.publish whatyoupay.org; http://www.revenuewatch.org; http://www.eiti.org. As noted in the preface, I received a grant from the Revenue Watch Institute to complete this book and serve on its advisory board.

and mineral-producing countries—some EITI members, and some not—found that three-quarters of them provided only "partial" or "scant" information about their resource revenues.[50]

Despite this progress, the transparency movement has a lot of work ahead. Transparency cannot magically solve the problems of resource-rich countries, but it is probably the safest and simplest way to bring about improvements.

SPENDING REVENUES WISELY

Even if oil revenues become smaller, more stable, and more transparent, countries must still decide how to spend them. If spent wisely, they can contribute to sustainable improvements in social welfare; if not, they can disappear in a cloud of waste and corruption.

All countries, with or without resource wealth, face similar questions about government spending. Much of what has been learned in the non-oil states about appropriate fiscal policies can also be applied to the oil states.[51] Resource-rich countries also have some distinctive challenges: their governments constitute a larger fraction of their economies; their revenues are less stable, which tends to make their expenditures less stable; and the resource revenues they rely on will eventually disappear. All of these factors make it even more important for oil producers to get their spending policies right.

The issue of government spending in resource-rich economies is complex and goes beyond my expertise.[52] Let me simply outline the key decisions that countries face and mention some critical considerations.

Oil-producing countries have to make two broad decisions about how to deploy their revenues. The first is how much money should enter the annual budget, and how much should be set aside for future use—both to stabilize the economy in the short run and offset petroleum depletion in the long run.[53] The decision touches on both practical issues, such as how much money the economy can absorb at any given time without triggering bureaucratic overstretch, waste, and corruption; and moral ones, including how to balance the needs of the current generation with the rights of future ones.

[50] Revenue Watch Institute 2010.

[51] For a thoughtful distillation of these lessons, see Commission on Growth and Development 2008.

[52] For state-of-the-art discussions of the salient issues, see Humphreys, Sachs, and Stiglitz 2007; Collier 2010; Gelb and Grasman 2010; text of the Natural Resource Charter, available at http://www.naturalresourcecharter.org.

[53] How and where the money is saved—domestically or overseas—is also critical.

Experts vary in their recommendations. Gelb's study of oil-exporting states during the 1973–81 boom concluded that countries should have set aside about 80 percent of their incremental revenues; it argued that their failure to save explains their disastrous economic slumps when prices fell after 1980.[54] Others caution that low-income countries can hurt themselves by saving too much, since their best long-term investments are in their own economies—in the health and education of their citizens as well as the infrastructure that can help their non-oil sectors grow.[55]

The second decision is how much of the money that enters the budget should go toward consumption, and how much toward investment in physical and human capital. The poorer the country, the more people can benefit from higher consumption: when people cannot eat, it makes no sense to save for the future. Governments should be careful, though, about how they boost consumption. Two of the most popular methods in oil-producing countries have harmful side effects: reducing taxes will increase household incomes, but also make the government's finances more dependent on oil, and thus more volatile and opaque; and increasing fuel subsidies is disproportionately beneficial for the middle and upper classes, and boosts carbon emissions.

Whether or not countries have oil, high levels of investment are essential for long-term development. According to a report by the Commission on Growth and Development, "No country has sustained rapid growth without also keeping up impressive rates of public investment—in infrastructure, education, and health."[56] If oil-producing countries want future generations to benefit from today's resource extraction, they must invest an even larger fraction of their revenues than other countries.

The government's investment decisions can also have a powerful effect on gender disparities. Chapter 4 explains that oil-rich governments typically invest in their economies by building new infrastructure, whose construction creates jobs for men but not for women; and when the economy is affected by the Dutch Disease, companies that would normally draw women into the labor force—especially export-oriented manufacturing firms—will become unprofitable. If a booming oil economy creates other kinds of jobs for women, none of this will matter: men can get new jobs in construction and petroleum, while women can take new jobs in other sectors.

[54] Gelb and Associates 1988.
[55] Collier 2010.
[56] Commission on Growth and Development 2008, 5. See also Hausmann, Pritchett, and Rodrik 2005.

But as chapter 4 demonstrates, in many countries—especially in the Middle East—women are denied jobs in the booming service sector and hence remain outside the labor force. Governments can readily counteract this problem by placing some of their investments in sectors that draw women into the labor force such as health and education—professions that typically hire a larger proportion of women—and aggressively hiring women in government positions.

A certain level of construction spending is valuable. One early priority should be investments in removing development bottlenecks, so that subsequent investments will be more effective. Collier calls this strategy "investing in investing"—focusing on projects that help reduce the cost and increase the efficiency of future investments. This entails targeting both infrastructure bottlenecks and bureaucratic ones, like weaknesses in the government's capacity to evaluate and oversee new projects, and red tape that discourages private-sector investment. These reforms are hard to implement when revenues are booming, since politicians will be too busy spending the windfall. The wiser strategy is to undertake them before extraction begins, or when prices slump, so that future windfalls will be better used.

I have already described some policies that would help constrain spending. Adopting a slower extraction rate or distributing revenues directly to citizens will remove cash from the government's hands, reducing its capacity to overspend any windfall. Barter contracts can help bind governments to major investment projects they might otherwise lack the financial stability, administrative capacity, or political will to carry out. If governments take out stabilization loans when prices are low, and their repayments are denominated in barrels of oil, it can help curtail overspending when prices rise.

Transparency in government spending can also be useful. Most resource-related transparency initiatives focus on how revenues are collected, not how they are spent. Unfortunately, some countries, like Azerbaijan, have become models of revenue transparency while keeping their expenditures opaque. A 2010 study found that seventy-four of the ninety-four governments surveyed had national budgets that failed to meet basic standards of transparency and accountability. Oil- and gas-producing countries were among the most opaque. Algeria, Cameroon, Chad, Equatorial Guinea, Iraq, and Saudi Arabia published virtually no information about their budgets.[57]

Expenditure transparency may be even more important than revenue transparency: the more citizens know about how their money is

---

[57] International Budget Partnership 2010. See also their report, available at http://www.internationalbudget.org.

allocated, the less likely the funds will be lost to corruption. Thankfully, a growing number of NGOs in the developing world have taken up the cause of budget and spending transparency. According to the International Budget Partnership,

- In India, Mazdoor Kisan Shakarti Sangathan, an organization of small farmers and workers, has pieced together budget information to uncover corruption, such as falsified payrolls and payments for work never done.
- At the urging of the Uganda Debt Network, which monitors local spending, Ugandan officials have identified substandard work in school construction and evidence of corruption by local officials.
- In the Philippines, an NGO called Government Watch has used budget information to monitor the delivery of school textbooks, the construction of new schools and other infrastructure, and the distribution of disaster relief funds. Working with other groups, their efforts have dramatically reduced the cost and improved the quality and delivery of textbooks.[58]

Although the issue of government spending is intrinsically complex, certain simple steps, like gender targeting, investing in investing, and greater transparency, can help improve the quality of government programs.

What Should Oil Importers Do?

The resource curse begins in the oil-consuming countries, since it is their money that inundates the oil producers. There is relatively little they can do to change the nontax nature of these revenues. They are also unlikely to have much impact on revenue stability. Multilateral efforts in the 1960s and 1970s to stabilize world commodity prices, under the auspices of the UN Conference on Trade and Development, failed utterly and are unlikely to be tried again in the foreseeable future. Affecting the way that the oil states spend their revenues is even harder. The World Bank's far-reaching efforts from 2000 to 2008 to compel the government of Chad to manage its oil revenues transparently and spend them on poverty-reducing programs also ended in failure.[59]

Oil-importing countries can nonetheless affect the size and secrecy of the revenues that flow to oil-exporting governments. A priority should be curtailing petroleum consumption and imports. At a global level,

[58] International Budget Partnership 2008. See also Reinikka and Svensson 2004.
[59] Frank and Guesnet 2010.

this will not be easy: if current laws and policies go unchanged, the global market for oil and other liquid fuels will rise from 86.1 million barrels a day in 2007 to 110 million barrels a day in 2035; the market for natural gas will rise from 108 to 156 trillion cubic feet. Eighty-four percent of these increases are expected to come from outside of Europe and North America, especially from China and India.[60] These figures could be sharply altered by changes in policies, changes in technology, and unexpected improvements or declines in the world economy. Still, even the most aggressive push toward alternative energy technologies will take decades to have an effect.

Alternatively, oil consumers could curtail the revenues of the most reprehensible oil states by being more selective in their oil and gas purchases. Philosopher Leif Wenar points out that when oil-exporting countries have high corruption rates and undemocratic governments, political leaders are in effect stealing the resource revenues that belong to their citizens. This implies that when we buy their oil, we are purchasing stolen goods. Wenar argues that

> these goods flow through the system of global commerce under cover of a rule that is little more than a cloak for larceny. . . . The international commercial system breaks the first rule of capitalism in transporting stolen goods, and does so on an enormous scale. The priority in reforming global commerce is not to replace "free trade" with "fair trade." The priority is to create trade where now there is theft.[61]

Would economic sanctions bring about better governance in the oil states? The campaign against conflict diamonds—meaning diamonds used to fund civil wars—has been surprisingly effective. In the mid-1990s, as much as 15 percent of the world diamond trade was made up of conflict diamonds, which were helping fund wars in six African states. By 2006, conflict diamonds made up no more than 1 percent of the diamond trade, and all six conflicts had ended—thanks in part to sanctions imposed by the UN Security Council, and enforced by an unusual coalition of governments, NGOs, and major diamond traders working through an accord known as the "Kimberley Process."

Sanctions against oil-producing states have been less effective. Would-be pariah states with oil wealth, such as Iran, Sudan, Burma, and Libya in the 1980s and 1990s, have been able to sell enough petroleum to keep their regimes in power. Even international sanctions endorsed by the UN Security Council can be insufficient. The severe restrictions placed on Iraq's oil sales between 1990 and 2003 seemed to

[60] Energy Information Administration 2010.
[61] Wenar 2008, 2.

have had little effect on Hussein's policies or grip on power. The strong demand for new sources of petroleum makes targeted sanctions a relatively weak policy tool.[62]

At a minimum, oil importers should stop funding conflicts by making it illegal for their citizens to purchase oil from concessions sold by insurgent groups or their agents. The insurrection in Congo-Brazzaville in 1997 and the 2004 coup attempt in Equatorial Guinea were both financed by investors hoping to win oil contracts from rebel-led governments. Rebels and criminal gangs steal huge quantities of Niger Delta oil every day, and then ship it overseas. A ban on these kinds of purchases could help prevent future violence.

Perhaps oil-importing countries can have a larger impact through transparency. The money that consumers send to the oil states helps empower the governments of these states; disclosing information about this money would help empower their citizens. In most Western countries, consumers can find out where their clothes, cars, and computers come from by looking at the labels. If they are purchasing high-value, internationally traded commodities like coffee or wine, they can often pinpoint the province or hillside where it was grown. Yet they know nothing about the source of the gasoline they purchase. Energy companies could change this by "publishing what they pump"—disclosing the country of origin of the petroleum they sell. This would help make consumers aware of the consequences of their purchases. It would also encourage energy companies to be more selective in their transactions and even help improve conditions in the countries that they work in.

International energy companies should also disclose all of the payments that they make to the governments of oil-producing countries. Until now, companies have been able to avoid these disclosures—making it possible for oil-rich governments to keep their finances secret. In July 2010, the United States took an important step toward transparency when Congress adopted legislation, as part of the Dodd-Frank Wall Street Reform and Consumer Protection Act, to compel companies listed on the New York Stock Exchange to reveal these payments.[63] Other governments should follow suit.

---

[62] Wenar (ibid.) suggests an intriguing way to make sanctions more effective: oil importers could both cease buying resources from highly undemocratic countries and impose tariffs on other states that continue to buy from them. The money raised by these tariffs would be placed in a trust fund, payable to a democratically elected government that replaces the targeted regime. William Kaempfer, Anton Lowenberg, and William Mertens (2004) contend that economic sanctions can backfire, strengthening an autocrat's grip on power.

[63] For a legal analysis of the new law, see Firger 2010.

Oil-producing governments that want to remain opaque can always sell their oil to companies from less transparent countries, like China, Malaysia, and Russia. But even in these countries, reforms are possible. The London-based International Accounting Standards Board sets global accounting standards. Over 120 countries today require or permit companies on their soil to use these standards when they issue financial statements. Currently, the standards allow petroleum and mining companies to avoid disclosing their payments to specific governments. Adopting reforms that bring greater transparency to the oil business could have a far-reaching effect.

Since the oil nationalizations of the 1970s, oil-producing countries have had less democracy, fewer opportunities for women, more frequent civil wars, and more volatile economic growth than the rest of the world, especially in the developing world. But geology is not destiny. Oil has become a curse because the revenues that it generates for governments are abnormally large, do not come from taxing citizens, fluctuate unpredictably, and are easy to conceal from public scrutiny. Most of these qualities can be changed—by citizens, governments, international institutions, and even consumers in oil-importing countries. The consequences of petroleum wealth are different today than they were in the past, and they can change again in the future—perhaps for the better.

References

Abidin, Mahani Zainal. 2001. "Competitive Industrialization with Natural Resource Abundance: Malaysia." In *Resource Abundance and Economic Development*, edited by Richard M. Auty, 147–64. Oxford: Oxford University Press.

Acemoglu, Daron, Simon Johnson, and James A. Robinson. 2001. "The Colonial Origins of Comparative Development: An Empirical Investigation." *American Economic Review* (5): 1369–401.

———. 2002. "Reversal of Fortune: Geography and Institutions in the Making of the Modern World Income Distribution." *Quarterly Journal of Economics* 117 (4): 1231–94.

Acemoglu, Daron, Simon Johnson, James A. Robinson, and Yunyong Thaicharoen. 2003. "Institutional Causes, Macroeconomic Symptoms: Volatility, Crises, and Growth." *Journal of Monetary Economics* 50 (1): 49–123.

Acemoglu, Daron, Simon Johnson, James A. Robinson, and Pierre Yared. 2008. "Income and Democracy." *American Economic Review* 98 (3): 808–42.

Acemoglu, Daron, and James A. Robinson. 2005. *Economic Origins of Dictatorship and Democracy*. New York: Cambridge University Press.

Achen, Christopher H. 2002. "Toward a New Political Methodology: Microfoundations and Art." *Annual Review of Political Science* 5:423–50.

Achen, Christopher H., and Larry Bartels. 2004. "Blind Retrospection: Electoral Responses to Drought, Flu, and Shark Attacks." Unpublished paper, Princeton University, Princeton, NJ.

Adsera, Alicia, Carles Boix, and Mark Payne. 2003. "Are You Being Served? Political Accountability and Quality of Government." *Journal of Law, Economics, and Organization* 19 (2): 445–90.

Aharoni, Yair, and William Ascher. 1998. "Restructuring the Arrangements between Government and State Enterprises in the Oil and Mining Sectors." *Natural Resources Forum* 22 (3): 201–13.

Ahmad, Ehtisham, and Eric Mottu. 2003. "Oil Revenue Assignments: Country Experiences and Issues." In *Fiscal Policy Formulation and Implementation in Oil-Producing Countries*, edited by Jeffrey Davis, Rolando Ossowski, and Annalisa Fedelino, 216–42. Washington, DC: International Monetary Fund.

Alesina, Alberto, Filipe Campante, and Guido Tabellini. 2008. "Why Is Fiscal Policy Often Procyclical?" *Journal of the European Economic Association* 6 (5): 1006–36.

Alesina, Alberto, Nouriel Roubini, and Gerald Cohen. 1997. *Political Cycles and the Macroeconomy*. Cambridge, MA: MIT Press.

Alesina, Alberto, and Enrico Spolaore. 1997. "On the Number and Size of Nations." *Quarterly Journal of Economics* 112 (4): 1027–56.

Alexeev, Michael, and Robert Conrad. 2009. "The Elusive Curse of Oil." *Review of Economics and Statistics* 91 (3): 586–98.

Alnasrawi, Abbas. 1994. *The Economy of Iraq*. Westport, CT: Greenwood Press.

Ames, Barry. 1987. *Political Survival: Politicians and Public Policy in Latin America*. Berkeley: University of California Press.

Amin, Sajeda, Ian Diamond, Ruchira T. Naved, and Margaret Newby. 1998. "Transition to Adulthood of Female Garment-Factory Workers in Bangladesh." *Studies in Family Planning* 29 (2): 185–200.

Amnesty International. 2000. "Oil in Sudan: Deteriorating Human Rights." Report AFR 54/01/00ERR. London: Amnesty International.

Anderson, G. Norman. 1999. *Sudan in Crisis*. Gainesville: University Press of Florida.

Anderson, Lisa. 1995. "Democracy in the Arab World: A Critique of the Political Culture Approach." In *Political Liberalization and Democratization in the Arab World; Volume One, Theoretical Perspectives*, edited by Rex Brynen, Bahgat Korany, and Paul Noble, 77–92. Boulder, CO: Lynne Rienner.

Anderson, Siwan, and Mukesh Eswaran. 2005. "What Determines Female Autonomy? Evidence from Bangladesh." BREAD Working Paper No. 101. Department of Economics, University of British Columbia, Vancouver.

Anker, Richard. 1997. "Theories of Occupational Segregation by Sex: An Overview." *International Labour Review* 136 (3): 315–39.

Arellano, Manuel, and Stephen Bond. 1991. "Some Tests of Specification for Panel Data: Monte Carlo Evidence and an Application to Employment Equations." *Review of Economic Studies* 58 (2): 277–97.

Arezki, Rabah, and Markus Brückner. 2010. "Oil Rents, Corruption, and State Stability: Evidence from Panel Data Regressions." Unpublished paper, International Monetary Fund, Washington, DC.

Ascher, William. 1999. *Why Governments Waste Natural Resources: Policy Failures in Developing Countries*. Baltimore: Johns Hopkins University Press.

———. 2009. *Bringing in the Future: Strategies for Farsightedness and Sustainability in Developing Countries*. Chicago: University of Chicago Press.

Aslaksen, Silje. 2010. "Oil as Sand in the Democratic Machine?" *Journal of Peace Research* 47 (4): 421–31.

Aspinall, Edward. 2007. "The Construction of Grievance: Natural Resources and Identity in a Separatist Conflict." *Journal of Conflict Resolution* 51 (6): 950.

Assaad, Ragui. 2004. "Why Did Economic Liberalization Lead to Feminization of the Labor Force in Morocco and De-Feminization in Egypt?" Unpublished paper, University of Minnesota, Twin Cities.

Assaad, Ragui, and Melanie Arntz. 2005. "Constrained Geographical Mobility and Gendered Labor Market Outcomes under Structural Adjustment: Evidence from Egypt." *World Development* 33 (3): 431–54.

Auty, Richard M. 1990. *Resource-Based Industrialization: Sowing the Oil in Eight Developing Countries*. Oxford: Claredon Press.

———. 2003. "Third Time Lucky for Algeria? Integrating an Industrializing Oil-Rich Country into the Global Economy." *Resources Policy* 29 (1): 37–47.

Bahl, Roy. 2001. "Equitable Vertical Sharing and Decentralizing Government Finance in South Africa." International Studies Program Working Paper Series. Georgia State University, Atlanta.

Bailyn, Bernard. 1967. *The Ideological Origins of the American Revolution*. Cambridge, MA: Harvard University Press.

Baldez, Lisa. 2004. "Elected Bodies: The Adoption of Gender Quota Laws for Legislative Candidates in Mexico." *Legislative Studies Quarterly* 29 (2): 231–58.

Balzer, Harley. 2009. "Vladimir Putin's Academic Writings and Russian Natural Resource Policy." *Problems of Post-Communism* 53 (1): 48–54.

Barma, Naazneen, Kai-Alexander Kaiser, Tuan Min Le, and Lorena Viñuela. 2011. *Rents to Riches? The Political Economy of Natural Resource-Led Development*. Washington, DC: World Bank.

Barnett, Anthony, Martin Bright, and Patrick Smith. 2004. "How Much Did Straw Know and When Did He Know It?" *Observer*, November 28.

Barrett, David B., George Kurian, and Todd Johnson. 2001. *World Christian Encyclopedia: A Comparative Survey of Churches and Religions in the Modern World*. New York: Oxford University Press.

Barro, Robert J. 1997. *Determinants of Economic Growth: A Cross-country Empirical Study*. Cambridge, MA: MIT Press.

Basedau, Matthias, and Jann Lay. 2009. "Resource Curse or Rentier Peace? The Ambiguous Effects of Oil Wealth and Oil Dependence on Violent Conflict." *Journal of Peace Research* 46 (6): 757–76.

Bates, Robert H. 1981. *Markets and States in Tropical Africa*. Berkeley: University of California Press.

Bates, Robert H., and Da-Hsiang Donald Lien. 1985. "A Note on Taxation, Development, and Representative Government." *Politics and Society* 14 (2): 53–70.

Baud, Isa. 1977. "Jobs and Values: Social Effects of Export-Oriented Industrialization in Tunisia." In *Industrial Re-adjustment and the International Division of Labour*. Tilburg, Netherlands: Development Research Institute.

Beblawi, Hazem, and Giacomo Luciani. 1987. *The Rentier State in the Arab World*. Vol. 2, *Nation, State, and Integration in the Arab World*. London: Croom Helm.

Beck, Nathaniel, Jonathan N. Katz, and Richard Tucker. 1998. "Taking Time Seriously in Binary Time-Series Cross Section Analysis." *American Journal of Political Science* 42 (4): 1260–88.

Bellver, Ana, and Daniel Kaufmann. 2005. "Transparenting Transparency." Washington, DC: World Bank.

Besley, Timothy, and Torsten Persson. 2010. "State Capacity, Conflict, and Development." *Econometrica* 78 (1): 1–34.

Bevan, David L., Paul Collier, and Jan Willem Gunning. 1999. *Nigeria and Indonesia*. New York: Oxford University Press.

Bhattacharya, Rina, and Dhaneshwar Ghura. 2006. "Oil and Growth in the Republic of Congo." Washington, DC: International Monetary Fund.

Bhavnani, Rikhil R. 2009. "Do Electoral Quotas Work after They Are Withdrawn? Evidence from a Natural Experiment in India." *American Political Science Review* 103 (1): 23–35.

Birdsall, Nancy, and Arvind Subramanian. 2004. "Saving Iraq from Its Oil." *Foreign Affairs* 83 (4): 77–89.

Blattman, Christopher, Jason Hwang, and Jeffrey Williamson. 2007. "Winners and Losers in the Commodity Lottery: The Impact of Terms of Trade Growth and Volatility in the Periphery, 1870–1939." *Journal of Development Economics* 82 (1): 156–79.

Blattman, Christopher, and Edward Miguel. 2008. "Civil Wars." *Journal of Economic Literature* 48 (1): 3–57.

Blaydes, Lisa. 2006. "Electoral Budget Cycles under Authoritarianism: Economic Opportunism in Mubarak's Egypt." Paper presented at the annual meeting of the Midwest Political Science Association, Chicago.

Blaydes, Lisa, and Drew A Linzer. 2008. "The Political Economy of Women's Support for Fundamentalist Islam." *World Politics* 60 (4): 576–609.

Block, Steven A. 2002. "Political Business Cycles, Democratization, and Economic Reform: The Case of Africa." *Journal of Development Economics* 67 (1): 205–28.

Blundell, Richard, and Stephen Bond. 1998. "Initial Conditions and Moment Restrictions in Dynamic Panel Data Models." *Journal of Econometrics* 87 (1): 115–43.

Boardman, Anthony, and Aidan Vining. 1989. "Ownership and Performance in Competitive Environments: A Comparison of the Performance of Private, Mixed, and State-Owned Enterprises." *Journal of Law and Economics* 32 (1): 1–33.

Bodin, Jean. [1606] 1967. *Six Books of a Commonwealth*. New York: Barnes and Noble.

Boix, Carles. 2003. *Democracy and Redistribution*. New York: Cambridge University Press.

Boix, Carles, and Susan Stokes. 2003. "Endogenous Democracy." *World Politics* 55 (4): 517–49.

Bolton, Patrick, and Gérard Roland. 1997. "The Breakup of Nations: A Political Economy Analysis." *Quarterly Journal of Economics* 112 (4): 1057–90.

Bordo, Michael David. 1975. "John E. Cairnes on the Effects of the Australian Gold Discoveries, 1851–73: An Early Application of the Methodology of Positive Economics." *History of Political Economy* 7 (3): 337–59.

Bornhorst, Fabian, Sanjeev Gupta, and John Thornton. 2009. "Natural Resource Endowments and the Domestic Revenue Effort." *European Journal of Political Economy* 25 (4): 439–46.

BP. 2010. "BP Statistical Review of World Energy." London: British Petroleum.

Brady, Henry, and David Collier, eds. 2004. *Rethinking Social Inquiry*. Lanham, MD: Rowman and Littlefield.

Brand, Laurie A. 1992. "Economic and Political Liberalization in a Rentier Economy: The Case of the Hashemite Kingdom of Jordan." In *Privatization and Liberalization in the Middle East*, edited by Iliya Harik and Denis J. Sullivan, 167–88. Bloomington: Indiana University Press.

———. 1998. *Women, the State, and Political Liberalization*. New York: Columbia University Press.

Brautigam, Deborah, Odd-Helge Fjeldstad, and Mick Moore, eds. 2008. *Taxation and State-Building in Developing Countries: Capacity and Consent*. New York: Cambridge University Press.

Brennan, Geoffrey, and James M. Buchanan. 1980. *The Power to Tax: Analytical Foundations of a Fiscal Constitution*. New York: Cambridge University Press.

Bresnan, John. 1993. *Managing Indonesia: The Modern Political Economy*. New York: Columbia University Press.

Brewster, Karin, and Ronald Rindfuss. 2000. "Fertility and Women's Employment in Industrialized Nations." *Annual Review of Sociology* 26:271–96.

Brollo, Fernanda, Tommaso Nannicini, Roberto Perotti, and Guido Tabellini. 2010. "The Political Resource Curse." London: Centre for Economic Policy Research.

Brosio, Giorgio. 2003. "Oil Revenue and Fiscal Federalism." In *Fiscal Policy Formulation and Implementation in Oil-Producing Countries*, edited by Jeffrey Davis, Rolando Ossowski, and Annalisa Fedelino, 243–72. Washington, DC: International Monetary Fund.

Brumberg, Daniel, and Ariel Ahram. 2007. "The National Iranian Oil Company in Iranian Politics." Unpublished paper, Baker Institute for Public Policy, Rice University, Houston.

Brunnschweiler, Christa, and Erwin Bulte. 2008. "The Resource Curse Revisited and Revised: A Tale of Paradoxes and Red Herrings." *Journal of Environmental Economics and Management* 55 (3): 248–64.

Buchanan, James M., and Roger L. Faith. 1987. "Secession and the Limits of Taxation: Toward a Theory of Internal Exit." *American Economic Review* 77 (5): 1023–31.

Buchanan, James M., Robert Tollison, and Gordon Tullock. 1980. *Toward a Theory of the Rent-Seeking Society*. College Station: Texas A&M University Press.

Bueno de Mesquita, Bruce, Alastair Smith, Randolph M. Siverson, and James D. Morrow. 2003. *The Logic of Political Survival*. Cambridge, MA: MIT Press.

Buhaug, Halvard, Scott Gates, and Päivi Lujala. 2002. "Lootable Natural Resources and the Duration of Armed Civil Conflict, 1946–2001." Paper presented at the thirty-sixth annual Peace Science Society meeting, Tucson, AZ, November.

Bulte, Erwin, Richard Damania, and Robert T. Deacon. 2005. "Resource Intensity, Institutions, and Development." *World Development* 33 (7): 1029–44.

Bunyanunda, Mac. 2005. "A Comparative Study of Mining Laws." Unpublished paper, University of California at Los Angeles.

Burns, John F., and Kirk Semple. 2006. "US Finds Iraq Insurgency Has Funds to Sustain Itself." *New York Times*, November 26.

Burns, Nancy, Kay Lehman Schlozman, and Sidney Verba. 2001. *The Private Roots of Public Action: Gender, Equality, and Political Participation*. Cambridge, CA: Harvard University Press.

Cashin, Paul, and C. John McDermott. 2002. "The Long-run Behavior of Commodity Prices: Small Trends and Big Variability." *IMF Staff Papers* 49 (2): (2002): 175–99.

Catão, Luis, and Bennett Sutton. 2002. "Sovereign Defaults." Washington, DC: International Monetary Fund.

Caul, Miki. 2001. "Political Parties and the Adoption of Candidate Gender Quotas: A Cross-national Analysis." *Journal of Politics* 63 (4): 1214–29.

Cederman, Lars Erik, Simon Hug, and Lutz F Krebs. 2010. "Democratization and Civil War: Empirical Evidence." *Journal of Peace Research* 47 (4): 377–94.

Cederman, Lars Erik, Andreas Wimmer, and Brian Min. 2010. "Why Do Ethnic Groups Rebel?" *World Politics* 62 (1): 87–119.

Chan-Fishel, Michelle, and Roxanne Lawson. 2007. "Quid Pro Quo? China's Investment-for-Resource Swaps in Africa." *Development* 50 (3): 63–68.

Charrad, Mounira. 2001. *States and Women's Rights: The Making of Postcolonial Tunisia, Algeria, and Morocco.* Berkeley: University of California Press.

Chattopadhyay, Raghabendra, and Ester Duflo. 2004. "Women as Policy Makers: Evidence from a Randomized Policy Experiment in India." *Econometrica* 72 (5): 1409–43.

Chaudhry, Kiren Aziz. 1989. "The Price of Wealth: Business and State in Labor Remittance and Oil Economies." *International Organization* 43 (1): 101–45.

———. 1997. *The Price of Wealth: Economies and Institutions in the Middle East.* Ithaca, NY: Cornell University Press.

Cheibub, José Antonio, Jennifer Gandhi, and James R. Vreeland. 2010. "Democracy and Dictatorship Revisited." *Public Choice* 143 (1–2): 1–35.

Chernick, Marc. 2005. "Economic Resources and Internal Armed Conflicts: Lessons from the Colombian Case." In *Rethinking the Economics of War*, edited by Cynthia J. Arnson and I. William Zartman, 178–205. Washington, DC: Woodrow Wilson Center Press.

Chhibber, Pradeep. 2003. "Why Are Some Women Politically Active? The Household, Public Space, and Political Participation in India." In *Islam, Gender, Culture, and Democracy*, edited by Ronald Inglehart, 186–206. Willowdale, ON: de Sitter.

Choucri, Nazli. 1986. "The Hidden Economy: A New View of Remittances in the Arab World." *World Development* 14 (6): 697–712.

Christian Aid. 2001. "The Scorched Earth: Oil and War in Sudan." London: Christian Aid.

Cingranelli, David L., and David L. Richards. 2008. "Cingranelli-Richards (Ciri) Human Rights Dataset." Available at http://www.humanrightsdata.org.

Colander, David C. 1984. *Neoclassical Political Economy: The Analysis of Rent-Seeking and Dup Activities.* Cambridge, MA: Ballinger Publishing Company.

Colgan, Jeffrey. 2010a. "Changing Oil Income, Persistent Authoritarianism." Unpublished paper, American University, Washington, DC.

———. 2010b. "Oil and Revolutionary Governments: Fuel for International Conflicts." *International Organization* 64 (4): 661–94.

Collier, Paul. 2007. *The Bottom Billion.* New York: Oxford University Press.

———. 2010. *The Plundered Planet.* New York: Oxford University Press.

Collier, Paul, V. L. Elliot, Havard Hegre, Anke Hoeffler, Marta Reynal-Querol, and Nicholas Sambanis. 2003. *Breaking the Conflict Trap: Civil War and Development Policy.* Washington, DC: World Bank.

Collier, Paul, and Benedikt Goderis. 2009. "Commodity Prices, Growth, and the Natural Resource Curse: Reconciling a Conundrum." Unpublished paper, Center for the Study of African Economies, Oxford.

Collier, Paul, and Anke Hoeffler. 1998. "On Economic Causes of Civil War." *Oxford Economic Papers* 50:563–73.

———. 2004. "Greed and Grievance in Civil War." *Oxford Economic Papers* 56:663–95.

————. 2009. "Testing the Neocon Agenda: Democracy in Resource-Rich Societies." *European Economic Review* 53 (3): 293–308.

Collier, Paul, Anke Hoeffler, and Mans Söderbom. 2004. "On the Duration of Civil War." *Journal of Peace Research* 41 (3): 253–73.

Collier, Paul, Frederick van der Ploeg, Michael Spence, and Anthony Venables. 2009. "Managing Resource Revenues in Developing Economies." Oxcarre Research Papers. Oxford: Oxford: Department of Economics, Oxford University.

Commission on Growth and Development. 2008. *The Growth Report: Strategies for Sustained Growth and Inclusive Development.* Washington, DC: World Bank.

Corden, W. Max, and J. Peter Neary. 1982. "Booming Sector and De-Industrialization in a Small Open Economy." *Economic Journal* 92:825–48.

Cotet, Anca, and Kevin K. Tsui. 2010. "Resource Curse or Malthusian Trap? Evidence from Oil Discoveries and Extractions." Unpublished paper, Muncie, IN.

Coughlin, Con. 2002. *Saddam: His Rise and Fall.* New York: HarperCollins.

Crosby, Alfred. 1986. *Ecological Imperialism: The Biological Expansion of Europe, 900–1900.* New York: Cambridge University Press.

Crouch, Harold. 1978. *The Army and Politics in Indonesia.* Ithaca, NY: Cornell University Press.

Crystal, Jill. 1990. *Oil and Politics in the Gulf: Rulers and Merchants in Kuwait and Qatar.* New York: Cambridge University Press.

Daude, Christian, and Ernesto Stein. 2007. "The Quality of Institutions and Foreign Direct Investment." *Economics and Politics* 19 (3): 317–44.

Davis, Jeffrey, Rolando Ossowski, James Daniel, and Steven Barnett. 2003. "Stabilization and Savings Funds for Nonrenewable Resources: Experience and Fiscal Policy Implications." In *Fiscal Policy Formulation and Implementation in Oil-Producing Countries*, edited by Jeffrey Davis, Rolando Ossowski, and Annalisa Fedelino, 273–315. Washington, DC: International Monetary Fund.

de Soysa, Indra. 2002. "Ecoviolence: Shrinking Pie or Honey Pot?" *Global Environmental Politics* 2 (4): 1–34.

de Soysa, Indra, Erik Gartzke, and Tove Grete Lin. 2009. "Oil, Blood, and Strategy: How Petroleum Influences Interstate Disputes." Unpublished paper, University of California at San Diego, La Jolla.

de Soysa, Indra, and Eric Neumayer. 2005. "Natural Resources and Civil War: Another Look with New Data." *Conflict Management and Peace Science* 24 (3): 201–18.

Desai, Raj, Lev Freinkman, and Itzhak Goldberg. 2005. "Fiscal Federalism in Rentier Regions: Evidence from Russia." *Journal of Comparative Economics* 33 (4): 814–34.

Dewenter, Kathryn, and Paul Malatesta. 2001. "State-Owned and Privately Owned Firms: An Empirical Analysis of Profitability, Leverage, and Labor Intensity." *American Economic Review* 91 (1): 320–34.

Diamond, Jared. 1997. *Guns, Germs, and Steel.* New York: W. W. Norton.

Diamond, Larry. 2008. *The Spirit of Democracy: The Struggle to Build Free Societies throughout the World.* New York: Times Books.

Diamond, Larry, Juan J. Linz, and Seymour Martin Lipset. 1988. *Democracy in Developing Countries*. Boulder, CO: Lynne Rienner.

Donno, Daniela, and Bruce Russett. 2004. "Islam, Authoritarianism, and Female Empowerment." *World Politics* 56 (4): 582–607.

Dube, Oeindrila, and Juan Vargas. 2009. "Commodity Price Shocks and Civil Conflict: Evidence from Colombia." Unpublished paper, Harvard University, Cambridge, MA.

Duncan, Roderick. 2006. "Price or Politics? An Investigation of the Causes of Expropriation." *Australian Journal of Agricultural and Resource Economics* 50 (1): 85–101.

Dunning, Thad. 2008. *Crude Democracy: Natural Resource Wealth and Political Regimes*. New York: Cambridge University Press.

Egorov, Georgy, Sergei Guriev, and Konstantin Sonin. 2009. "Why Resource-Poor Dictators Allow Freer Media." *American Political Science Review* 103 (4): 645–68.

Eifert, Benn, Alan Gelb, and Nils Borje Tallroth. 2003. "The Political Economy of Fiscal Policy and Economic Management in Oil-Exporting Countries." In *Fiscal Policy Formulation and Implementation in Oil-Producing Countries*, edited by Jeffrey Davis, Rolando Ossowski, and Annalisa Fedelino, 82–122. Washington, DC: International Monetary Fund.

Elian, Gheorghe. 1979. *The Principle of Sovereignty over Natural Resources*. Amsterdam: Sijthoff and Noordhoof International Publishers.

Eller, Stacy, Peter Hartley, and Kenneth Medlock. 2010. "Empirical Evidence on the Operational Efficiency of National Oil Companies." *Empirical Economics* 39 (3).

Energy Information Administration. 2010. "International Energy Outlook." Washington, DC: Energy Information Administration.

Engel, Eduardo, and Rodrigo Valdés. 2000. "Optimal Fiscal Strategy for Oil-Exporting Countries." IMF Working Paper. Washington, DC: International Monetary Fund.

Engels, Friedrich. [1884] 1978. "The Origin of the Family, Private Property, and the State." In *The Marx-Engels Reader*, edited by Robert C. Tucker. New York: W. W. Norton.

Englebert, Pierre. 2009. *Africa: Unity, Sovereignty, and Sorrow*. Boulder, CO: Lynne Rienner.

Englebert, Pierre, and James Ron. 2004. "Primary Commodities and War: Congo-Brazzaville's Ambivalent Resource Curse." *Comparative Politics* 37 (1): 61–81.

Entelis, John P. 1976. "Oil Wealth and the Prospects for Democratization in the Arabian Peninsula: The Case of Saudi Arabia." In *Arab Oil: Impact on the Arab Countries and Global Implications*, edited by Naiem A. Sherbiny and Mark A. Tessler, 77–111. New York: Praeger Publishers.

Epstein, David L., Robert Bates, Jack Goldstone, Ida Kristensen, and Sharyn O'Halloran. 2006. "Democratic Transitions." *American Journal of Political Science* 50 (3): 551–69.

Fearon, James D. 2004. "Why Do Some Civil Wars Last So Much Longer Than Others?" *Journal of Peace Research* 41 (3): 275–303.

———. 2005. "Primary Commodity Exports and Civil War." *Journal of Conflict Resolution* 49 (4): 483–507.

Fearon, James D., and David D. Laitin. 2003. "Ethnicity, Insurgency, and Civil War." *American Political Science Review* 97 (1): 75–90.

Firger, Daniel. 2010. "Transparency and the Natural Resource Curse: Examining the New Extraterritorial Information Forcing Rules in the Dodd-Frank Wall Street Reform Act of 2010." *Georgetown Journal of International Law* 41 (4): 1043–95.

First, Ruth. 1980. "Libya: Class and State in an Oil Economy." In *Oil and Class Struggle*, edited by Petter Nore and Terisa Turner, 119–42. London: Zed Press.

Fish, M. Stephen. 2002. "Islam and Authoritarianism." *World Politics* 55:4–37.

———. 2005. *Democracy Derailed in Russia*. New York: Cambridge University Press.

Frank, Claudia, and Lena Guesnet. 2010. "We Were Promised Development and All We Got Is Misery: The Influence of Petroleum on Conflict Dynamics in Chad." Bonn: Bonn International Center for Conversion.

Frankel, Jeffrey A. 2010. "The Natural Resource Curse: A Survey." NBER Working Paper. Cambridge, MA: National Bureau of Economic Research.

Frankel, Paul. 1989. "Essentials of Petroleum: A Key to Oil Economics." In *Paul Frankel: Common Carrier of Common Sense*, edited by Ian Skeet, 1–71. Oxford: Oxford University Press.

Frederikssen, Elisabeth Hermann. 2007. "Labor Mobility, Household Production, and the Dutch Disease." Unpublished paper, University of Copenhagen.

Freedom House. 2007. "Freedom of the Press." Available at http://www.freedom house.org/template.cfm?page=16.

Freeman, Richard B., and Remco H. Oostendorp. 2009. "Occupational Wages around the World Database." Available at http://www.nber.org/oww/.

Friedman, Thomas. 2006. "The First Law of Petropolitics." *Foreign Policy* 154: 28–39.

Fujita, Masahisa, Paul Krugman, and Anthony Venables. 2001. *The Spatial Economy: Cities, Regions, and International Trade*. Cambridge, MA: MIT Press.

Fung, Archon, Mary Graham, and David Weil. 2007. *Full Disclosure: The Perils and Promise of Transparency*. New York: Cambridge University Press.

Gaddy, Clifford G., and Barry W. Ickes. 2005. "Resource Rents and the Russian Economy." *Eurasian Geography and Economics* 46 (8): 559–83.

Gaidar, Yegor. 2008. *Collapse of an Empire: Lessons for Modern Russia*. Translated by Antonina W. Bouis. Washington, DC: Brookings Institution Press.

Galloy, Martine-Renée, and Marc-Éric Gruénai. 1997. "Fighting for Power in the Congo." *Le Monde Diplomatique*, November.

Gandhi, Jennifer, and Ellen Lust-Okar. 2009. "Elections under Authoritarianism." *Annual Review of Political Science* 12:403–22.

Gassebner, Martin, Michael J. Lamla, and James R Vreeland. 2008. "Extreme Bounds of Democracy." Unpublished paper.

Gause, F. Gregory, III. 1995. "Regional Influences on Experiments in Political Liberalization in the Arab World." In *Political Liberalization in the Arab World*, edited by Rex Brynen, Bahgat Korany, and Paul Noble, 283–306. Boulder, CO: Lynne Rienner.

Gauthier, Bernard, and Albert Zeufack. 2009. "Governance and Oil Revenues in Cameroon." Oxcarre Research Papers. Oxford: Oxford: Department of Economics, Oxford University.

Gelb, Alan, and Associates. 1988. *Oil Windfalls Blessing or Curse?* New York: Oxford University Press.

Gelb, Alan, and Caroline Decker. 2011. "Cash at Your Fingertips: Technology for Transfers in Resource-Rich Countries." Center for Global Development, Washington, DC.

Gelb, Alan, and Sina Grasman. 2010. "How Should Oil Exporters Spend Their Rents?" Working Paper. Washington, DC: Center for Global Development.

Gerring, John, Strom C. Thacker, and Rodrigo Alfaro. 2005. "Democracy and Human Development." Unpublished paper, Boston University.

Gervasoni, Carlos. 2010. "A Rentier Theory of Subnational Regimes." *World Politics* 62 (2): 302–40.

Gesellschaft für Technische Zusammenarbeit. 2007. "International Fuel Prices 2007." Eschborn, Germany: Federal Ministry for Economic Cooperation and Development.

Gillies, Alexandra. 2010. "Reputational Concerns and the Emergence of Oil Sector Transparency as an International Norm." *International Studies Quarterly* 54 (1): 103–26.

Gleditsch, Kristian Skrede. 2002. *All International Politics Is Local: The Diffusion of Conflict, Integration, and Democratization.* Ann Arbor: University of Michigan Press.

Gleditsch, Kristian Skrede, and Michael D Ward. 2006. "Diffusion and the International Context of Democratization." *International Organization* 60: 911–33.

Gleditsch, Nils Petter, Peter Wallensteen, Mikael Eriksson, Margareta Sollenberg, and Harvard Strand. 2002. "Armed Conflict, 1946–2001: A New Dataset." *Journal of Peace Research* 39 (5): 615–37.

Goldberg, Ellis, Erik Wibbels, and Eric Mvukiyehe. 2009. "Lessons from Strange Cases: Democracy, Development, and the Resource Curse in the U.S. States." *Comparative Political Studies* 41 (4–5): 477–514.

Goldman, Marshall I. 2004. "Putin and the Oligarchs." *Foreign Affairs* 83 (6): 33–44.

———. 2008. *Petrostate: Putin, Power, and the New Russia.* New York: Oxford University Press.

Goldsmith, Scott. 2001. "The Alaska Permanent Fund Dividend Program." Unpublished paper, Anchorage.

Gould, Eric D., Bruce A. Weinberg, and David B. Mustard. 2002. "Crime Rates and Local Labor Market Opportunities in the United States: 1979–1997." *Review of Economics and Statistics* 84 (1): 45–61.

Greene, Kenneth. 2010. "The Political Economy of Authoritarian Single-Party Dominance." *Comparative Political Studies* 43 (7): 807–34.

Grogger, Jeff. 1998. "Market Wages and Youth Crime." *Journal of Labor Economics* 16 (4): 756–91.

Guriev, Sergei, Anton Kolotilin, and Konstantin Sonin. 2010. "Determinants of Nationalization in the Oil Sector: A Theory and Evidence from Panel Data." *Journal of Law, Economics, and Organization.*

Guriev, Sergei, and William Megginson. 2007. "Privatization: What Have We Learned." In *Annual World Bank Conference on Development Economics: Beyond Transition*, edited by Francois Bourguignon and Boris Pleskovic, 249–96. Washington, DC: World Bank.

Haber, Stephen, and Victor Menaldo. 2009. "Do Natural Resources Fuel Authoritarianism?" Unpublished paper, Stanford University, Palo Alto, CA.

Haggard, Stephan, and Robert R. Kaufman. 1995. *The Political Economy of Democratic Transitions*. Princeton, NJ: Princeton University Press.

Halperin, Morton H., Joseph T. Siegle, and Michael W. Weinstein. 2005. *The Democracy Advantage*. New York: Routledge.

Hameed, Farhan. 2005. "Fiscal Transparency and Economic Outcomes." IMF Working Paper. Washington, DC: International Monetary Fund.

Hamilton, Alexander, James Madison, and John Jay. [1788] 2000. *The Federalist Papers*. New York: Signet.

Hamilton, James. "Understanding Crude Oil Prices." 2008. *Energy Journal* 30 (2): 179–206.

Hamilton, Kirk, and Michael Clemens. 1999. "Genuine Savings Rates in Developing Countries." *World Bank Economic Review* 13 (2): 333–56.

Hamilton, Kirk, Giovanni Ruta, and Liaila Tajibaeva. 2005. "Capital Accumulation and Resource Depletion: A Hartwick Rule Counterfactual." World Bank Policy Research Working Papers. Washington, DC: World Bank.

Hansen, Susan B. 1997. "Talking about Politics: Gender and Contextual Effects on Political Proselytizing." *Journal of Politics* 59 (1): 73–103.

Harbom, Lotta, Stina Högbladh, and Peter Wallensteen. 2006. "Armed Conflict and Peace Agreements." *Journal of Peace Research* 43 (5): 617–31.

Hartshorn, Jack E. 1962. *Oil Companies and Governments*. London: Faber and Faber.

Hartwick, John M. 1977. "Intergenerational Equity and the Investing of Rents from Exhaustible Resources." *American Economic Review* 67 (5): 972–74.

Hassmann, Heinrich. 1953. *Oil in the Soviet Union: History, Geography, Problems*. Princeton, NJ: Princeton University Press.

Hausmann, Ricardo, Lant Pritchett, and Dani Rodrik. 2005. "Growth Accelerations." *Journal of Economic Growth* 10 (4): 303–29.

Heal, Geoffrey. 2007. "Are Oil Producers Rich?" In *Escaping the Resource Curse*, edited by Macartan Humphreys, Jeffrey Sachs, and Joseph E. Stiglitz, 155–72. New York: Columbia University Press.

Hegre, Håvard, Tanja Ellingsen, Scott Gates, and Nils Peter Gleditsch. 2001. "Toward a Democratic Civil Peace? Democracy, Political Change, and Civil War, 1816–1992." *American Political Science Review* 95 (1): 33–48.

Hegre, Håvard, and Nicholas Sambanis. 2006. "Sensitivity Analysis of Empirical Results on Civil War Onset." *Journal of Conflict Resolution* 50 (4): 508–33.

Heilbrunn, John. 2005. "Oil and Water? Elite Politicians and Corruption in France." *Comparative Politics* 37 (3): 277–96.

Herb, Michael. 1999. *All in the Family: Absolutism, Revolution, and Democracy in the Middle East*. Albany: State University of New York Press.

———. 2005. "No Representation without Taxation? Rents, Development, and Democracy." *Comparative Politics* 37 (3): 297–317.

Herschman, Andrea. 2009. "The Politics of Oil Wealth Management: Lessons from the Caspian and Beyond." Unpublished paper, University of California at Los Angeles.

Hertog, Steffen. 2007. "Shaping the Saudi State: Human Agency's Shifting Role in Rentier-State Formation." *International Journal of Middle East Studies* 39:539–63.

———. 2010. *Princes, Brokers, and Bureaucrats: Oil and the State in Saudi Arabia.* Ithaca, NY: Cornell University Press.

Heston, Alan, Robert Summers, and Bettina Aten. n.d. "Penn World Table Version 6.1." Philadelphia: Center for International Comparisons, University of Pennsylvania.

Heuty, Antoine, and Ruth Carlitz. "Resource Dependence and Budget Transparency." New York: Revenue Watch Institute.

Hibbs, Douglas. 1987. *The American Political Economy.* Cambridge, MA: Harvard University Press.

Hiorth, Finngeir. 1986. "Free Aceh: An Impossible Dream?" *Kabar Seberang* 17:182–94.

Hirschman, Albert O. 1958. *The Strategy of Economic Development.* New Haven, CT: Yale University Press.

Hjort, Jonas. 2006. "Citizen Funds and Dutch Disease in Developing Countries." *Resources Policy* 31 (3): 183–91.

Hoffman, Philip T., and Kathryn Norberg, eds. 1994. *Fiscal Crises, Liberty, and Representative Government, 1450–1789.* Stanford, CA: Stanford University Press.

Horton, Susan. 1999. "Marginalization Revisited: Women's Market Work and Pay, and Economic Development." *World Development* 27 (3): 571–82.

Hotelling, Harold. 1931. "The Economics of Exhaustible Resources." *Journal of Political Economy* 39 (2): 137–75.

Hudson, Michael. 1995. "The Political Culture Approach to Arab Democratization: The Case for Bringing It Back in, Carefully." In *Political Liberalization and Democratization in the Arab World; Volume One, Theoretical Perspectives,* edited by Rex Brynen, Bahgat Korany, and Paul Noble, 61–76. Boulder, CO: Lynne Rienner.

Human Rights Watch. 2004. "Some Transparency, No Accountability: The Use of Oil Revenue in Angola and Its Impact on Human Rights." Human Rights Watch, New York.

Humphreys, Macartan. 2005. "Natural Resources, Conflict, and Conflict Resolution: Uncovering the Mechanisms." *Journal of Conflict Resolution* 49 (4): 508–37.

Humphreys, Macartan, Jeffrey Sachs, and Joseph E. Stiglitz. 2007. *Escaping the Resource Curse.* New York: Columbia University Press.

Humphreys, Macartan, and Martin E. Sandbu. 2007. "The Political Economy of Natural Resource Funds." In *Escaping the Resource Curse,* edited by Macartan Humphreys, Jeffrey Sachs and Joseph E. Stiglitz, 194–234. New York: Columbia University Press, 2007.

Humphreys, Macartan, and Jeremy Weinstein. 2006. "Handling and Manhandling Civilians in Civil War." *American Political Science Review* 100 (93): 429–77.

Hunt, Shane J. 1985. "Growth and Guano in Nineteenth-Century Peru." In *The Latin American Economies*, edited by Roberto Cortes Conde and Shane J. Hunt, 255–318. New York: Holmes and Meier.

Huntington, Samuel P. 1991. *The Third Wave: Democratization in the Late Twentieth Century*. Norman: University of Oklahoma Press.

Ilzetzki, Ethan, and Carlos A. Végh. 2008. "Procyclical Fiscal Policy in Developing Countries: Truth or Fiction?" Unpublished paper.

Inglehart, Ronald. 1997. *Modernization and Postmodernization*. Princeton, NJ: Princeton University Press.

Inglehart, Ronald, and Pippa Norris. 2003. *Rising Tide*. New York: Cambridge University Press.

Inkeles, Alex, and David H. Smith. 1974. *Becoming Modern*. Cambridge, MA: Harvard University Press.

International Budget Partnership. 2008. "Open Budget Survey 2008." Washington, DC: International Budget Partnership.

International Budget Partnership. 2010. "Open Budget Survey 2010." Washington, DC: International Budget Partnership.

International Crisis Group. 2001. "Aceh: Why Military Force Won't Bring Lasting Peace." Brussels: International Crisis Group.

———. 2006a. "Fuelling the Niger Delta Crisis." Brussels: International Crisis Group.

———. 2006b. "The Swamps of Insurgency: Nigeria's Delta Unrest." Brussels: International Crisis Group.

———. 2007. "Venezuela: Hugo Chavez's Revolution." Brussels: International Crisis Group.

International Labor Organization. 2007. "Data on Saudi Arabian Labor Force." Available at http://laborsta.ilo.org/.

International Monetary Fund. 2007. "Russian Federation: 2007 Article IV Consultation." Washington, DC: International Monetary Fund.

———. 2008. "Islamic Republic of Iran: Selected Issues." IMF Country Report. Washington, DC: International Monetary Fund.

Isham, Jonathan, Michael Woolcock, Lant Pritchett, and Gwen Busby. 2005. "The Varieties of the Rentier Experience: How Natural Resource Export Structures Affect the Political Economy of Growth." *World Bank Economic Review* 19 (2): 141–74.

Iversen, Torben, and Frances Rosenbluth. 2006. "The Political Economy of Gender: Explaining Cross-national Variation in the Gender Division of Labor and the Gender Voting Gap." *American Journal of Political Science* 50 (1): 1–19.

———. 2008. "Work and Power: The Connection between Female Labor Force Participation and Female Political Representation." *Annual Review of Political Science* 11:479–95.

Jaffee, Amy Myers, and Robert Manning. 2000. "The Shocks of a World of Cheap Oil." *Foreign Affairs* 79 (1): 16–29.

Jaffee, Amy Myers, and Mahmoud El-Gamal. 2010. *Oil, Dollars, Debt, and Crises: The Global Curse of Black Gold*. New York: Cambridge University Press.

Jamal, Amaney, Irfan Nooruddin, Michael L. Ross, and Michael Hoffman. 2010. "Fertility and Economic Development in the Muslim World." Unpublished paper, Princeton University, Princeton, NJ.

Javorcik, Beata Smarzynska. 2004. "Does Foreign Direct Investment Increase the Productivity of Domestic Firms? In Search of Spillovers through Backward Linkages." *American Economic Review* 94 (3): 605–27.

Jensen, Nathan, and Leonard Wantchekon. 2004. "Resource Wealth and Political Regimes in Africa." *Comparative Political Studies* 37 (9): 816–41.

Jodice, David A. 1980. "Sources of Change in Third World Regimes for Foreign Direct Investment, 1968–1976." *International Organization* 34 (2): 177–206.

Joekes, Susan P. 1982. "Female-Led Industrialization: Women's Jobs in Third World Export Manufacturing—the Case of the Moroccan Clothing Industry." Unpublished paper, Institute for Development Studies, Sussex, UK.

Johnston, David. 2007. "How to Evaluate Fiscal Terms." In *Escaping the Resource Curse*, edited by Macartan Humphreys, Jeffrey Sachs, and Joseph E. Stiglitz, 56–95. New York: Columbia University Press.

Jones, Bryan, and Walter Williams. 2008. *The Politics of Bad Ideas: The Great Tax Delusion and the Decline of Good Government in America.* New York: Pearson Longman.

Jones Luong, Pauline, and Erika Weinthal. 2010. *Oil Is Not a Curse: Ownership Structure and Institutions in Soviet Successor States.* New York: Cambridge University Press.

Kabeer, Naila, and Simeen Mahmud. 2004. "Globalization, Gender, and Poverty: Bangladeshi Women Workers in Export and Local Markets." *Journal of International Development* 16:93–109.

Kaempfer, William, Anton Lowenberg, and William Mertens. 2004. "International Economic Sanctions against a Dictator." *Economics and Politics* 16 (1): 29–51.

Kaiser, Kai. 2010. *Rents to Riches.* Washington, DC: World Bank.Kalyvas, Stathis. 2007. "Civil Wars." In *Handbook of Political Science*, edited by Susan Stokes and Carles Boix, 416–34. New York: Oxford University Press.

Kalyvas, Stathis, and Laia Balcells. 2010. "International System and Technologies of Rebellion: How the End of the Cold War Shaped Internal Conflict." *American Political Science Review* 104 (3): 415–29.

Kaminsky, Graciela, Carmen Reinhart, and Carlos A. Végh. 2004. "When It Rains, It Pours: Procyclical Capital Flows and Macroeconomic Policies." *NBER Macroeconomics Annual* 19:11–53.

Kang, Alice. 2009. "Studying Oil, Islam, and Women as If Political Institutions Mattered." *Politics and Gender* 5 (4): 560–68.

Karl, Terry Lynn. 1997. *The Paradox of Plenty: Oil Booms and Petro-States.* Berkeley: University of California Press.

Kaufmann, Daniel, and Aart Kraay. 2008. "Governance Indicators: Where Are We, Where Should We Be Going?" *World Bank Research Observer* 23 (1): 1–30.

Keen, David. 1998. "The Economic Functions of Violence in Civil Wars." Adelphi Paper. London: International Institute of Strategic Studies.

Kell, Tim. 1995. *The Roots of Acehnese Rebellion, 1989–1992.* Ithaca, NY: Cornell Modern Indonesia Project.

Key, Valdimer O. 1949. *Southern Politics in State and Nation.* New York: Knopf.

Kilian, Lutz. 2008. "The Economic Effects of Energy Price Shocks." *Journal of Economic Literature* 46 (4): 871–909.

King, Gary, and Langche Zeng. 2001. "Logistic Regression in Rare Events Data." *Political Analysis* 9 (2): 137–63.

———. 2006. "The Danger of Extreme Counterfactuals." *Political Analysis* 14 (2): 131–59.

Klare, Michael. 2006. "America, China, and the Scramble for Africa's Oil." *Review of African Political Economy* 33 (108): 297–309.

Kobrin, Stephen J. 1980. "Foreign Enterprise and Forced Divestment in LDCs." *International Organization* 34 (1): 65–88.

Kolstad, Ivar, and Arne Wiig. 2009. "Is Transparency the Key to Reducing Corruption in Resource-Rich Countries?" *World Development* 37 (3): 521–32.

Kotkin, Stephen. 2001. *Armageddon Averted: The Soviet Collapse, 1970–2000*. New York: Oxford University Press.

Krasner, Stephen D. 1978. *Defending the National Interest: Raw Materials Investments and U.S. Foreign Policy*. Princeton, NJ: Princeton University Press.

Kretzschmar, Gavin, Axel Kirchner, and Liliya Sharifzyanova. 2010. "Resource Nationalism: Limits to Foreign Direct Investment." *Energy Journal* 31 (2): 27–52.

Krueger, Anne O. 1974. "The Political Economy of the Rent-Seeking Society." *American Economic Review* 64:291–303.

Krugman, Paul. 1987. "The Narrow Moving Band, the Dutch Disease, and the Competitive Consequences of Mrs. Thatcher: Notes on Trade in the Presence of Dynamic Scale Economies." *Journal of Development Economics* 27:41–55.

La Porta, Rafael, Florencio Lopez-de-Silanes, Andrei Shleifer, and Robert W. Vishny. 1999. "The Quality of Government." *Journal of Law, Economics, and Organization* 15 (1): 222–79.

Lake, David A., and Matthew Baum. 2001. "The Invisible Hand of Democracy: Political Control and the Provision of Public Services." *Comparative Political Studies* 34 (6): 587–621.

Lallemand, Alain. 2001. "June 1997 Civil War: Lissouba Needs Weapons and Money." *Le Soir*, July 7.

Landes, David S. 1998. *The Wealth and Poverty of Nations*. New York: W. W. Norton.

Le Billon, Philippe. 2001. "The Political Ecology of War: Natural Resources and Armed Conflicts." *Political Geography* 20:561–84.

———. 2005. *Fuelling War: Natural Resources and Armed Conflicts*. New York: Routledge, 2005.

Le Billon, Philippe, and Eric Nicholls. 2007. "Ending 'Resource Wars': Revenue Sharing, Economic Sanctions, or Military Intervention?" *International Peacekeeping* 14 (5): 613–32.

Leite, Carlos, and Jens Weidmann. 1999. "Does Mother Nature Corrupt? Natural Resources, Corruption, and Economic Growth." IMF Working Paper. Washington, DC: International Monetary Fund.

Lerner, Daniel. 1958. *The Passing of Traditional Society*. New York: Free Press.

Levi, Margaret. 1988. *Of Rule and Revenue*. Berkeley: University of California Press.

Levin, Jonathan V. 1960. *The Export Economies: Their Pattern of Development in Historical Perspective*. Cambridge, MA: Harvard University Press.

Levy, Brian. 1982. "World Oil Marketing in Transition." *International Organization* 36 (1): 113–33.

Lewis, John P. 1974. "Oil, Other Scarcities, and the Poor Countries." *World Politics* 27 (1): 63–86.

Lewis, Peter. 2007. *Growing Apart: Oil, Politics, and Economic Change in Indonesia and Nigeria.* Ann Arbor: University of Michigan Press.

Lewis, W. Arthur. 1955. *The Theory of Economic Growth.* Homewood, IL: R. D. Irwin.

Libecap, Gary D. 1989. *Contracting for Property Rights.* New York: Cambridge University Press.

Lipset, Seymour Martin. 1959. "Some Social Requisites of Democracy: Economic Development and Political Legitimacy." *American Political Science Review* 53 (1): 69–105.

Livani, Talajeh. 2007. "Middle East and North Africa: Gender Overview." Washington, DC: World Bank.

Loayza, Norman V., Romain Ranciere, Luis Serven, and Jaume Ventura. 2007. "Macroeconomic Volatility and Welfare in Developing Countries: An Introduction." *World Bank Economic Review* 21 (3): 343–57.

Londregan, John B., and Keith T. Poole. 1996. "Does High Income Promote Democracy?" *World Politics* 49:1–30.

Lowi, Miriam R. 2009. *Oil Wealth and the Poverty of Politics: Algeria Compared.* New York: Cambridge University Press.

Lubeck, Paul, Michael Watts, and Ronnie Lipschutz. 2007. "Convergent Interests: U.S. Energy Security and the 'Securing' of Nigerian Democracy." International Policy Report. Washington, DC: Center for International Policy.

Lujala, Päivi. 2009. "Deadly Combat over Natural Resources: Gems, Petroleum, Drugs, and the Severity of Armed Civil Conflict." *Journal of Conflict Resolution* 53 (1): 50.

———. 2010. "The Spoils of Nature: Armed Civil Conflict and Rebel Access to Natural Resources." *Journal of Peace Research* 47 (1): 15–28.

Lujala, Päivi, Nils Petter Gleditsch, and Elisabeth Gilmore. 2005. "A Diamond Curse? Civil War and a Lootable Resource." *Journal of Conflict Resolution* 49 (4): 538–62.

Lujala, Päivi, Jan Ketil Rød, and Nadja Thieme. 2007. "Fighting over Oil: Introducing a New Dataset." *Conflict Management and Peace Science* 24 (3): 239–56.

Maass, Peter. 2009. *Crude World: The Violent Twilight of Oil.* New York: Knopf.

Maddison, Angus. 2009. "Historical Statistics of the World Economy, 1–2008." Unpublished paper, Groeningen, Netherlands.

Magaloni, Beatriz. 2006. *Voting for Autocracy: Hegemonic Party Survival and Its Demise in Mexico.* New York: Cambridge University Press.

Mahdavi, Paasha. 2011. "Oil, Monarchy, Revolution, and Theocracy: A Study on the National Iranian Oil Company." In *Oil and Governance: State-Owned Enterprises and the World Energy Supply*, edited by David G. Victor, David Hults, and Mark Thurber. New York: Cambridge University Press.

Mahdavy, Hussein. 1970. "The Patterns and Problems of Economic Development in Rentier States: The Case of Iran." In *Studies in Economic History of the Middle East*, edited by M. A. Cook, 428–67. London: Oxford University Press.

Mammen, Kristin, and Christina Paxson. 2000. "Women's Work and Economic Development." *Journal of Economic Perspectives* 14 (4): 141–64.

Manasse, Paolo. 2006. "Procyclical Fiscal Policy: Shocks, Rules, and Institutions—a View from Mars." Washington, DC: International Monetary Fund.

Manzano, Osmel, and Roberto Rigobon. 2007. "Resource Curse or Debt Overhang?" In *Natural Resources: Neither Curse nor Destiny*, edited by Daniel Lederman and William F. Maloney, 41–70. Washington, DC: World Bank.

Mares, David, and Nelson Altamirano. 2007. "Venezuela's PDVSA and World Energy Markets." Unpublished paper, Baker Institute for Public Policy, Rice University, Houston.

Marshall, Monty, and Keith Jaggers. 2007. "Polity IV Project, Political Regime Characteristics 1800–2004." Available at http://www.systemicpeace.org/polity/polity4.htm (accessed March 1, 2008).

Matland, Richard E. 1998. "Women's Representation in National Legislatures: Developed and Developing Countries." *Legislative Studies Quarterly* 23 (1): 109–25.

Matsen, Egil, and Ragnar Torvik. 2005. "Optimal Dutch Disease." *Journal of Development Economics* 78 (2): 494–515.

Maugeri, Leonardo. 2006. *The Age of Oil: The Mythology, History, and Future of the World's Most Controversial Resource*. Westport, CT: Praeger.

McCartney, Laton. 2008. *The Teapot Dome Scandal*. New York: Random House.

McCullough, David. 2001. *John Adams*. New York: Simon and Schuster.

McFaul, Michael, and Kathryn Stoner-Weiss. 2008. "The Myth of the Authoritarian Model." *Foreign Affairs* 87 (1): 68–84.

McGuirk, Eoin. 2010. "The Illusory Leader: Natural Resources, Taxation, and Accountability." Unpublished paper, Trinity College, Dublin.

McPherson, Charles. 2003. "National Oil Companies: Evolution, Issues, Outlook." In *Fiscal Policy Formulation and Implementation in Oil-Producing Countries*, edited by Jeffrey Davis, Rolando Ossowski, and Annalisa Fedelino, 204–15. Washington, DC: International Monetary Fund.

Meadows, Donella H., Dennis L. Meadows, Jorgen Randers, and William W. Behrens III. 1972. *The Limits to Growth*. New York: Universe Books.

Melhum, Halvor, Karl Moene, and Ragnar Torvik. 2006. "Institutions and the Resource Curse." *Economic Journal* 116 (1): 1–20.

Metcalf, Gilbert, and Catherine Wolfram. 2010. "Cursed Resources? Political Conditions and Oil Market Volatility." Unpublished paper, Tufts University, Boston.

Michael, Robert T. 1985. "Consequences of the Rise in Female Labor Force Participation Rates: Questions and Probes." *Journal of Labor Economics* 3 (1): S117–46.

Midlarsky, Manus. 1998. "Democracy and Islam: Implications for Civilizational Conflict and the Democratic Peace." *International Studies Quarterly* 42:485–511.

Miguel, Edward, Shanker Satyanath, and Ernest Sergenti. 2004. "Economic Shocks and Civil Conflict: An Instrumental Variables Approach." *Journal of Political Economy* 112 (4): 725–54.

Mill, John Stuart. [1848] 1987. *Principles of Political Economy*. Fairfield, NJ: Augustus M. Kelley Publishers.

Minor, Michael S. 1994. "The Demise of Expropriation as an Instrument of LDC Policy, 1980–92." *Journal of International Business Studies* 25 (1): 177–88.

Moghadam, Valentine. 1999. "Gender and Globalization: Female Labor and Women's Movements." *Journal of World-Systems Research* 5 (2): 367–88.

Mommer, Bernard. 2002. *Global Oil and the Nation State*. New York: Oxford University Press.

Montaner, Carlos Alberto. 2008. "Why Did Venezuela Surrender to Chavez?" *Miami Herald*, January 8.

Moon, Seungsook. 2002. "Women and Democratization in the Republic of Korea." *Good Society* 11 (3): 36–42.

Moran, Theodore. 2007. *Harnessing Foreign Direct Investment: Policies for Developed and Developing Countries*. Washington, DC: Center for Global Development.

Moreno, Alejandro. 2007. "The 2006 Mexican Presidential Election: The Economy, Oil Revenues, and Ideology." *PS: Political Science and Politics* 40 (1): 15–19.

Morgan, Edmund S., and Helen M. Morgan. 1953. *The Stamp Act Crisis: Prologue to Revolution*. New York: Collier Books.

Morrison, Kevin. 2007. "Natural Resources, Aid, and Democratization: A Best-case Scenario." *Public Choice* 131 (3–4): 365–86.

———. 2009. "Oil, Nontax Revenue, and Regime Stability." *International Organization* 63:107–38.

Moss, Todd, and Lauren Young. 2009. "Saving Ghana from Its Oil: The Case for Direct Cash Distribution." Working Paper. Washington, DC: Center for Global Development.

Myers, Steven Lee, and Andrew E. Kramer. 2007. "From Ashes of Yukos, New Russian Oil Giant Emerges." *New York Times*, March 27.

Nam, Jeong-Lim. 2000. "Gender Politics in the Korean Transition to Democracy." *Korean Studies* 24:94–113.

Nazir, Sameena, and Leigh Tomppert. 2005. *Women's Rights in the Middle East and North Africa: Citizenship and Justice*. Lanham, MD: Rowman and Littlefield Publishers.

Neary, J. Peter, and Sweder van Wijnbergen. 1986. *Natural Resources and the Macroeconomy*. Cambridge, MA: MIT Press.

Nooruddin, Irfan. 2008. "The Political Economy of National Debt Burdens, 1970–2000." *International Interactions* 34 (2): 156–85.

North, Douglass C. 1955. "Location Theory and Regional Economic Growth." *Journal of Political Economy* 63 (2): 243–58.

———. 1990. *Institutions, Institutional Change, and Economic Performance*. Cambridge: Cambridge University Press, 1990.

Nurkse, Ragnar. 1958. "Trade Fluctuations and Buffer Policies of Low-Income Countries." *Kyklos* 11:141–54.

O'Ballance, Edgar. 2000. *Sudan, Civil War, and Terrorism, 1956–1999*. New York: St. Martin's Press.

O'Donnell, Guillermo, Philippe C. Schmitter, and Lawrence Whitehead. 1986. *Transitions from Authoritarian Rule: Prospects for Democracy*. Baltimore: Johns Hopkins University Press.

O'Loughlin, John, Michael D. Ward, Corey L. Lofdahl, Jordin S. Cohen, David S. Brown, David Reilly, Kristian Skrede Gleditsch, and Michael Shin. 1998. "The Diffusion of Democracy." *Annals of the Association of American Geographers* 88 (4): 545–74.

Oakes, Ann, and Elizabeth Almquist. "Women in National Legislatures." *Population Research and Policy Review* 12 (1): 71–81.

Okruhlik, Gwenn. 1999. "Rentier Wealth, Unruly Law, and the Rise of the Opposition." *Comparative Politics* 31 (3): 295–315.

Olken, Benjamin. 2009. "Corruption Perceptions vs. Corruption Reality." *Journal of Public Economics* 93 (7–8): 950–64.

Olson, Mancur. 1993. "Dictatorship, Democracy, and Development." *American Political Science Review* 87 (3): 567–76.

Omeje, Kenneth. 2006. "Petrobusiness and Security Threats in the Niger Delta, Nigeria." *Current Sociology* 54 (3): 477–99.

Osaghae, Eghosa. 1994. "The Ogoni Uprising: Oil Politics, Minority Agitation, and the Future of the Nigerian State." *African Affairs* 94:325–44.

Østby, Gudrun, Ragnhild Nordås, and Jan Ketil Rød. 2009. "Regional Inequalities and Civil Conflict in sub-Saharan Africa." *International Studies Quarterly* 53 (2): 301–24.

Özler, Sule. 2000. "Export Orientation and Female Share of Employment: Evidence from Turkey." *World Development* 28 (7): 1239–48.

Palley, Marian Lief. 1990. "Women's Status in South Korea: Tradition and Change." *Asian Survey* 30 (12): 1136–53.

Palley, Thomas. 2003. "Combating the Natural Resource Curse with Citizen Revenue Distribution Funds." Unpublished paper, Washington, DC.

Papyrakis, Elissaios, and Reyer Gerlagh. 2004. "The Resource Curse Hypothesis and Its Transmission Channels." *Journal of Comparative Economics* 32 (1): 181–93.

Park, Jihang. 1990. "Trailblazers in a Traditional World: Korea's First Women College Graduates, 1910–45." *Social Science History* 14 (4): 533–58.

Park, Kyung Ae. 1993. "Women and Development: The Case of South Korea." *Comparative Politics* 25 (2): 127–45.

Pax Christi Netherlands. 2001. *The Kidnap Industry in Colombia: Our Business?* Utrecht: Pax Christi Netherlands.

Pearce, Jenny. 2005. "Policy Failure and Petroleum Predation: The Economics of Civil War Debate Viewed 'from the War-Zone.'" *Government and Opposition* 40 (2): 152–80.

Peluso, Nancy, and Michael Watts. 2001. *Violent Environments*. Ithaca, NY: Cornell University Press.

Penrose, Edith. 1976. *The Large International Firm in Developing Countries*. Westport, CT: Greenwood Press.

Piotrowski, Suzanne, ed. 2010. *Transparency and Secrecy*. Lanham, MD: Lexington Books.

Posner, Daniel N., and Daniel Young. 2007. "The Institutionalization of Political Power in Africa." *Journal of Democracy* 18 (3): 126–40.

Prebisch, Raul. 1950. *The Economic Development of Latin America and Its Principal Problems.* Lake Success, NY: United Nations.

Przeworski, Adam. 2007. "Is the Science of Comparative Politics Possible?" In *The Oxford Handbook of Comparative Politics,* edited by Carles Boix and Susan Stokes, 147–71. New York: Oxford University Press.

Przeworski, Adam, Michael E. Alvarez, José Antonio Cheibub, and Fernando Limongi. 2000. *Democracy and Development: Political Institutions and Well-being in the World, 1950–1990.* New York: Cambridge University Press.

Quinn, John James. 2002. *The Road Oft Traveled: Development Policies and Majority State Ownership of Industry in Africa.* Westport, CT: Praeger.

Radon, Jenik. 2007. "How to Negotiate Your Oil Agreement." In *Escaping the Resource Curse,* edited by Macartan Humphreys, Jeffrey Sachs, and Joseph E. Stiglitz, 89–113. New York: Columbia University Press.

Ramey, Garey, and Valerie Ramey. 1995. "Cross-country Evidence on the Link between Volatility and Growth." *American Economic Review* 85 (5): 1138–51.

Ramsay, Kristopher. 2009. "Natural Disasters, the Price of Oil, and Democracy." Unpublished paper, Princeton University, Princeton, NJ.

Razafindrakoto, Mireille, and Francois Roubaud. 2010. "Are International Databases on Corruption Reliable? A Comparison of Expert Opinion Surveys and Household Surveys in sub-Saharan Africa." *World Development* 38 (8): 1057–69.

Regnier, Eva. 2007. "Oil and Energy Price Volatility." *Energy Economics* 29 (3): 405–27.

Reinikka, Ritva, and Jakob Svensson. 2004. "Local Capture: Evidence from a Central Government Transfer Program in Uganda." *Quarterly Journal of Economics* 119 (2): 679–705.

Revenue Watch Institute. 2010. "2010 Revenue Watch Index." New York: Revenue Watch Institute.

Reynolds, Andrew. 1999. "Women in the Legislatures and Executives of the World." *World Politics* 51 (4): 547–72.

Risen, James, and Eric Lichtblau. "Hoard of Cash Lets Qaddafi Extend Fight against Rebels." *New York Times,* March 9, 2011, 1.

Roberts, Adam. 2006. *The Wonga Coup.* London: Profile Books.

Robinson, Geoffrey. 1998. "Rawan Is as Rawan Does: The Origins of Disorder in New Order Aceh." *Indonesia* 66:127–56.

Robinson, James A., and Ragnar Torvik. 2005. "White Elephants." *Journal of Public Economics* 89:197–210.

Robinson, James A., Ragnar Torvik, and Thierry Verdier. 2006. "Political Foundations of the Resource Curse." *Journal of Development Economics* 79 (2): 447–68.

Rosenblum, Peter, and Susan Maples. 2009. "Contracts Confidential: Ending Secret Deals in the Extractive Industries." New York: Revenue Watch Institute.

Rosendorf, B. Peter, and James R. Vreeland. 2006. "Democracy and Data Dissemination: The Effect of Political Regime on Transparency." Unpublished paper, Yale University, New Haven, CT.

Ross, Michael L. 1999. "The Political Economy of the Resource Curse." *World Politics* 51 (2): 297–322.

———. 2001a. "Does Oil Hinder Democracy?" *World Politics* 53 (3): 325–61.

———. 2001b. *Timber Booms and Institutional Breakdown in Southeast Asia*. New York: Cambridge University Press.

———. 2003. "Oil, Drugs and Diamonds: The Varying Roles of Natural Resources in Civil War." In *The Political Economy of Armed Conflict*, edited by Karen Ballentine and Jake Sherman, 47–72. Boulder, CO: Lynne Rienner.

———. 2004a. "Does Taxation Lead to Representation?" *British Journal of Political Science* 34:229–49.

———. 2004b. "What Do We Know about Natural Resources and Civil War?" *Journal of Peace Research* 41 (3): 337–56.

———. 2004c. "How Do Natural Resources Influence Civil War? Evidence from 13 Cases." *International Organization* 58:35–67.

———. 2005a. "Booty Futures." Unpublished paper, University of California at Los Angeles.

———. 2005b. "Resources and Rebellion in Aceh, Indonesia." In *Understanding Civil War: Evidence and Analysis*, edited by Paul Collier and Nicholas Sambanis, 35–58. Washington, DC: World Bank.

———. 2006a. "A Closer Look at Oil, Diamonds, and Civil War." *Annual Review of Political Science* 9:265–300.

———. 2006b. "Is Democracy Good for the Poor?" *American Journal of Political Science* 50 (4): 860–74.

———. 2007. "How Mineral-Rich States Can Reduce Inequality." In *Escaping the Resource Curse*, edited by Macartan Humphreys, Jeffrey Sachs, and Joseph E. Stiglitz, 237–55. New York: Columbia University Press.

———. 2008. "Oil, Islam, and Women." *American Political Science Review* 102 (1): 107–23.

———. 2010. "Latin America's Missing Oil Wars." Unpublished paper, University of California at Los Angeles.

Rosser, Andrew. 2007. "Escaping the Resource Curse: The Case of Indonesia." *Journal of Contemporary Asia* 37 (1): 38–58.

Rutland, Peter. 2006. "Oil and Politics in Russia." Unpublished paper, Wesleyan University, Middletown, CT.

Sachs, Jeffrey, and Pia Malaney. 2002. "The Economic and Social Burden of Malaria." *Nature* 415:680–85.

Sachs, Jeffrey D., and Andrew M. Warner. 1995. "Natural Resource Abundance and Economic Growth." Development Discussion Paper 517a. Cambridge, MA: Harvard Institute for International Development.

———. 1997. "Fundamental Sources of Long-run Growth." *American Economic Review* 87 (2): 184–88.

Sala-i-Martin, Xavier, and Arvind Subramanian. 2003. "Addressing the Natural Resource Curse: An Illustration from Nigeria." IMF Working Paper. Washington, DC: International Monetary Fund.

Salamé Ghassan. 1994. *Democracy without Democrats? The Renewal of Politics in the Muslim World*. London: I. B. Tauris Publishers.

Sambanis, Nicholas. 2001. "Do Ethnic and Non-Ethnic Civil Wars Have the Same Causes?" *Journal of Conflict Resolution* 45 (3): 259–82.

———. 2004. "What Is Civil War? Conceptual and Empirical Complexities of an Operational Definition." *Journal of Conflict Resolution* 48 (6): 814–58.

Sandbu, Martin E. 2006. "Natural Wealth Accounts: A Proposal for Alleviating the Natural Resource Curse." *World Development* 34 (7): 1153–70.

Sapiro, Virginia. 1983. *The Political Integration of Women*. Urbana: University of Illinois Press.

Sarbahi, Anoop. 2005. "Major States, Neighbors, and Civil Wars: A Dyadic Analysis of Third-party Intervention in Intra-State Wars." Unpublished paper, University of California at Los Angeles.

Schroeder, Jana. 2002. "Oil, Politics, and Scandal in Mexico." *World Press Review*, February 21.

Schultz, Heiner. 2006. "Political Institutions and Foreign Direct Investment in Developing Countries: Does the Sector Matter?" Unpublished paper, University of Pennsylvania, Philadelphia.

Schumpeter, Joseph A. [1918] 1954. "The Crisis of the Tax State." *International Economic Papers* 4:5–38.

Scott, James C. 1976. *The Moral Economy of the Peasant*. New Haven, CT: Yale University Press.

Shafer, D. Michael. 1983. "Capturing the Mineral Multinationals: Advantage or Disadvantage?" *International Organization* 37 (1): 93–119.

———. 1994. *Winners and Losers: How Sectors Shape the Developmental Prospects of States*. Ithaca, NY: Cornell University Press.

Shapiro, Ian. 2005. *The Flight from Reality in the Human Sciences*. Princeton, NJ: Princeton University Press.

Shaxson, Nicholas. 2005. "New Approaches to Volatility: Dealing with the 'Resource Curse' in Sub-Saharan Africa." *International Affairs* 81 (2): 311–24.

Singer, Hans W. 1950. "The Distribution of Gains between Investing and Borrowing Countries." *American Economic Review* 40:473–85.

Sjamsuddin, Nazaruddin. 1984. "Issues and Politics of Regionalism in Indonesia: Evaluating the Acehnese Experience." In *Armed Separatism in Southeast Asia*, edited by Joo-Jock Lim and S. Vani, 111–28. Singapore: Institute of Southeast Asian Studies.

Skocpol, Theda. 1982. "Rentier State and Shi'a Islam in the Iranian Revolution." *Theory and Society* 11:265–83.

Smith, Adam. [1776] 1991. *An Inquiry into the Nature and Causes of the Wealth of Nations*. New York: Prometheus Books.

Smith, Benjamin. 2007. *Hard Times in the Land of Plenty*. Ithaca, NY: Cornell University Press.

Smith, James. 2009. "World Oil: Market or Mayhem?" *Journal of Economic Perspectives* 23 (3): 145–64.

Snyder, Richard. 1992. "Explaining Transitions from Neopatrimonial Dictatorships." *Comparative Politics* 24 (4): 379–400.

Spengler, Joseph J. 1960. *Natural Resources and Growth*. Washington, DC: Resources for the Future.

Stern, Jonathan P. 1980. *Soviet Natural Gas Developments to 1990*. Lexington, MA: Lexington Books.

Stevens, Paul. 2008. "National Oil Companies and International Oil Companies in the Middle East: Under the Shadow of Government and the Resource Nationalism Cycle." *Journal of World Energy Law and Business* 1 (1): 5–30.

Stevens, Paul, and Evelyn Dietsche. 2008. "Resource Curse: An Analysis of Causes, Experiences, and Possible Ways Forward." *Energy Policy* 36 (1): 56–65.

Stiglitz, Joseph E. 2007. "What Is the Role of the State?" In *Escaping the Resource Curse*, edited by Macartan Humphreys, Jeffrey Sachs, and Joseph E. Stiglitz, 23–52. New York: Columbia University Press.

Suni, Paavo. 2007. "Oil Prices and the Russian Economy: Some Simulation Studies with Nigem." Helsinki: ETLA, Research Institute of the Finnish Economy.

Talvi, Ernesto, and Carlos A. Végh. 2005. "Tax Base Variability and Procyclical Fiscal Policy in Developing Countries." *Journal of Development Economics* 78 (1): 156–90.

Tarbell, Ida. 1911. *The Tariff in Our Times*. New York: Macmillan Company.

Tavares, José, and Romain Wacziarg. 2001. "How Democracy Affects Growth." *European Economic Review* 45:1341–78.

Tetreault, Mary Ann. 1985. *Revolution in the World Petroleum Market*. Westport, CT: Quorum Books.

Thies, Cameron G. 2010. "Of Rulers, Rebels, and Revenue: State Capacity, Civil War Onset, and Primary Commodities." *Journal of Peace Research* 47 (3): 321–32.

Thomas, Duncan, Dante Contreras, and Elizabeth Frankenberg. 2002. "Distribution of Power within the Household and Child Health." Unpublished paper, University of California at Los Angeles.

Tornell, Aaron, and Philip R. Lane. 1999. "The Voracity Effect." *American Economic Review* 89 (1): 22–46.

Transparency International. 2008. "Promoting Revenue Transparency: 2008 Report on Revenue Transparency of Oil and Gas Companies." Berlin: Transparency International.

Treisman, Daniel. 2007. *The Architecture of Government: Rethinking Political Decentralization*. New York: Cambridge University Press.

———. 2010. "Is Russia Cursed by Oil?" *Journal of International Affairs* 63 (2): 85–102.

Tripp, Aili Mari, and Alice Kang. 2008. "The Global Impact of Quotas: On the Fast Track to Increased Female Legislative Representation." *Comparative Political Studies* 41 (3): 338–61.

Tsui, Kevin K. 2011. "More Oil, Less Democracy? Evidence from Worldwide Crude Oil Discoveries." *Economic Journal* 121 (551): 89–115.

Tufte, Edward R. 1978. *Political Control of the Economy*. Princeton, NJ: Princeton University Press.

Ulfelder, Jay. 2007. "Natural Resource Wealth and the Survival of Autocracies." *Comparative Political Studies* 40 (8): 995–1018.

United Nations. 1991. *The World's Women: Trends and Statistics, 1970–1990*. New York: United Nations.

United Nations Conference on Trade and Development. 2009. "World Investment Report." New York: United Nations Conference on Trade and Development.

United Nations Development Program. 2002. *Arab Human Development Report*. New York: United Nations Development Program.

US Geological Survey. n.d. *Minerals Yearbook*. Washington, DC: US Department of the Interior.

van der Ploeg, Frederick, and Steven Phoelhekke. 2009. "Volatility and the Natural Resource Curse." Oxcarre Research Papers. Oxford: Oxford: Department of Economics, Oxford University.

Vandewalle, Dirk. 1998. *Libya since Independence: Oil and State-Building*. Ithaca, NY: Cornell University Press.

Vernon, Raymond. 1971. *Sovereignty at Bay: The Spread of U.S. Enterprises*. New York: Basic Books.

Victor, David, David Hults, and Mark Thurber. 2011. *Oil and Governance: State-Owned Enterprises and the World Energy Supply*. New York: Cambridge University Press.

Viner, Jacob. 1952. *International Trade and Economic Development*. Glencoe, IL: Free Press.

Vines, Alex, Markus Weimer, and Indira Campos. 2009. *Angola and Asian Oil Strategies*. London: Chatham House.

Walter, Barbara. 2002. *Committing to Peace: The Successful Settlement of Civil Wars*. Princeton, NJ: Princeton University Press.

Watkins, Melville H. 1963. "A Staple Theory of Economic Growth." *Canadian Journal of Economics and Political Science* 29 (2): 142–58.

Watts, Michael. 1997. "Black Gold, White Heat." In *Geographies of Resistance*, edited by Steve Pile and Michael Keith, 33–67. New York: Routledge.

———. 2007. "Anatomy of an Oil Insurgency: Violence and Militants in the Niger Delta, Nigeria." In *Extractive Economies and Conflicts in the Global South: Multi-Regional Perspectives on Rentier Politics*, edited by Kenneth Omeje, 51–74. London: Ashgate.

Wehrey, Frederic, Jerrod Green, Brian Nichiporuk, Alireza Nader, Lydia Hansell, Rasool Nafisi, and S. R. Bohandy. *The Rise of the Pasdaran: Assessing the Domestic Roles of Iran's Islamic Revolutionary Guards Corps*. Santa Monica: RAND.

Weinstein, Jeremy M. 2007. *Inside Rebellion: The Politics of Insurgent Violence*. New York: Cambridge University Press.

Wenar, Leif. 2008. "Property Rights and the Resource Curse." *Philosophy and Public Affairs* 36 (1): 2–32.

Werger, Charlotte. 2009. "The Effect of Oil and Diamonds on Democracy: Is There Really a Resource Curse?" OxCarre Research Papers. Oxford: Department of Economics, Oxford University.

White, Gregory. 2001. *A Comparative Political Economy of Tunisia and Morocco: On the Outside Looking In*. Albany: State University of New York Press.

Wick, Katharina, and Erwin Bulte. 2009. "The Curse of Natural Resources." *Annual Review of Resource Economics* 1:139–56.

Williams, Peggy. 2006. "Deep Water Delivers." *Oil and Gas Investor* (May): 2–12.

Williams, T. Harry. 1969. *Huey Long*. New York: Knopf.

Wintrobe, Ronald. 2007. "Dictatorship: Analytical Approaches." In *The Oxford Handbook of Comparative Politics*, edited by Carles Boix and Susan Stokes, 363–94. New York: Oxford University Press.

Wolfers, Justin. 2009. "Are Voters Rational? Evidence from Gubernatorial Elections." Working paper, Wharton School of Business, Philadelphia.

Wong, Lillian. 2008. *The Impact of Asian National Oil Companies in Nigeria, or "Things Fall Apart."* London: Chatham House.

World Bank. 2001. *Engendering Development*. New York: Oxford University Press.

———. 2004. *Gender and Development in the Middle East and North Africa*. Washington, DC: World Bank.

———. 2005. "The Status and Progress of Women in the Middle East and North Africa." Washington, DC: World Bank Middle East and North Africa Social and Economic Development Group.

———. n.d. "World Development Indicators." Available at http://data.world bank.org/.

Wright, Gavin, and Jesse Czelusta. 2004. "The Myth of the Resource Curse." *Challenge* 47 (2): 6–38.

Wuerth, Oriana. 2005. "The Reform of the Moudawana: The Role of Women's Civil Society Organizations in Changing the Personal Status Code in Morocco." *Hawwa* 3 (3): 309–33.

Yates, Douglas A. 1996. *The Rentier State in Africa: Oil Rent Dependency and Neocolonialism in the Republic of Gabon*. Trenton, NJ: Africa World Press.

Yergin, Daniel. 1991. *The Prize: The Epic Quest for Oil, Money, and Power*. New York: Simon and Schuster.

Yoon, Bang-Soon L. 2003. "Gender Politics in South Korea: Putting Women on the Political Map." In *Confrontation and Innovation on the Korean Peninsula*, edited by Korea Economic Institute. Washington, DC: Korea Economic Institute.

York, Robert, and Zaijin Zhan. 2009. "Fiscal Vulnerability and Sustainability in Oil-Producing sub-Saharan African Countries." IMF Working Paper. Washington, DC: International Monetary Fund.

Youssef, Nadia. 1971. "Social Structure and the Female Labor Force: The Case of Women Workers in Muslim Middle Eastern Countries." *Demography* 8 (4): 427–39.

Index

Abu Dhabi National Oil Company (ADNOC). *See* United Arab Emirates
Aceh Freedom Movement (GAM). *See* Indonesia
Acemoglu, Daron, 65, 96n66, 224n3, 231n17
Achen, Christopher, 23, 69n16, 96
Alesina, Alberto, 66n8, 150n18, 215n, 217
Alexeev, Michael, 190n, 214n, 215n
Algeria, 7, 20t, 36t, 48, 55, 63, 232t, 233t, 249; economic growth in, 191n, 192t, 198, 200t, 203, 207, 221, 226; female empowerment in, 12, 25, 124–25, 127, 129–31; government size in, 29, 30t, 32t; and Sonatrach, 43; war in, 1–2, 41, 156t, 201
Ames, Barry, 66n8
Anderson, Lisa, 63n
Angola, 15–16, 21t, 36, 55,192, 198, 200, 226, 231, 236, 244; civil war in, 1, 12, 145, 156t, 164n40, 165t, 177, 201; and Cabinda enclave, 165; secrecy of oil revenues in, 57, 59n62, 81, 246; and Sonangol, 60; female empowerment in, 4
Arab Human Development Report, 111
Aramco. *See* Saudi Arabia
Arellano, Manuel, 138n
Arezki, Rabah, 18n22
Argentina, 20t, 55, 74, 86, 198–200, 239–40
Armenia, 29
Ascher, William, 243n41
Aslaksen, Silje, 96n66, 100–101
Aspinall, Edward, 168n47
Aten, Bettina, 28, 95
Auty, Richard, 189n2, 196, 207
Azerbaijan, 5, 22, 28–29, 55, 200, 202, 228, 231, 246, 249; and Ilham Aliyev, 89; and SOCAR, 60

backward linkages, 45
Bahl, Roy, 239n34
Bahrain, 20t, 54, 63, 104, 124–26, 191–92, 198, 200, 211, 232–34
Bangladesh, 112, 233; and conflict in Chittagong Hills, 165
Barrett, David, 96
Bartels, Larry, 69n16

barter contracts, 13, 236–37, 242, 245, 249
Basedau, Matthias, 153n24
Bates, Robert, 243n40
Beblawi, Hazem, 63n
Beck, Nathaniel, 179
Belize, 10, 187n74
Besley, Timothy, 161n32, 210, 215n
Bevan, David, 28, 194n5
Beverly Hillbillies fallacy, 13, 95, 212, 214
Birdsall, Nancy, 238n28
Blattman, Christopher, 145n3
Blaydes, Lisa, 66n8
Block, Steven, 66n8
Boardman, Anthony, 240n37
Bodin, Jean, 224
Boix, Carles, 2n3, 65, 95n65, 213n42, 225n4, 226n8
Bolton, Patrick, 150n18
Bond, Stephen, 138n
booty futures, 174–78, 230
Bornhorst, Fabian, 31n, 32
Brady, Henry, 24n
Brautigam, Deborah, 225n6
Brazil, 10, 20t, 55, 59, 86, 239, 242; and Petrobras, 42
Bretton Woods system, 7, 11, 52, 228
Brewster, Karin, 112n3, 202n
Britain. *See* United Kingdom
British Petroleum (BP), 3–4, 7, 10, 17, 22, 42–43, 51, 55, 193, 195, 241
Brollo, Fernanda, 239n34
Brosio, Giorgio, 239n34, 240n36
Brunei, 21t, 168, 187nn74–75, 191–92, 198, 201, 231
Brunnschweiler, Christa, 190n
Buchanan, James, 35n11, 150n18
Bueno de Mesquita, Bruce, 68n14
Bulte, Erwin, 190n, 210n38
bundling, 236–37
Burma, 4, 80, 251; and the Karen rebellion, 147
Burns, Nancy, 112

Cairnes, John Elliot, 47
Cameroon, 59, 80–81
Campante, Filipe, 215n, 217